THE SAVAGE FRONTIER

An 1827 edition of *The Vicissitudes of a Soldier's Life* inspired in D. S. Richards an enduring fascination with military history. Born in 1922, during the war years he served in the RAF as a navigator, taking part in night operations over Germany.

He now lives in south-east London, close to the home of the Royal Artillery and the Military Academy at Woolwich, and retirement has freed him to expand his interest. He has amassed a large collection of books and militaria ranging from medieval times to Second World War. His previous book, *The Peninsula Veterans* (1975), is a history of the long and bloody campaign in the Iberian Peninsula.

THE SAVAGE
FRONTIER

A History of the Anglo-Afghan Wars

D. S. Richards

PAN BOOKS

for Nancy, Sally and Treloar

First published 1990 by Macmillan London Ltd

This edition published 2003 by Pan Books
an imprint of Pan Macmillan Ltd
Pan Macmillan, 20 New Wharf Road, London N1 9RR
Basingstoke and Oxford
Associated companies throughout the world
www.panmacmillan.com

ISBN 0 330 42052 6

1 3 5 7 9 8 6 4 2

A CIP catalogue record for this book is available from
the British Library.

Printed and bound in Great Britain by
Mackays of Chatham plc, Chatham, Kent

Contents

Preface

The present conflict in Afghanistan turned a spotlight on a region which has engaged the attention of politicians and the military from the early part of the nineteenth century until the Partition of India terminated Britain's special responsibilities in 1947. Yet for years the North-West Frontier with its popular images of wild mountain scenery and epic adventure has been a source of inspiration to authors, painters and historians, and in more recent times has served as a suitable location for film scripts and television programmes.

In the early and mid-Victorian era, officers with ambition eagerly sought active service, for by winning battle honours promotion was more readily achieved. Acts of conspicuous bravery were sure to be noted and if by showing an indifference to danger they succeeded in steadying the men, then they were merely behaving in the manner expected of an 'officer and a gentleman'. The same cannot explain similar behaviour by the rank-and-file soldier, who fought when and where he was ordered; rather, although the granting of commissions in the field was not uncommon, he fought because of a pride in his regiment and a confidence in his officers born of years of campaigning together.

I have tried through the experiences of those British officers and men, whose memoirs provide such a rich source of material, to highlight a small part of Britain's involvement in ensuring the security of one of the world's most rugged and savage frontiers. For a more comprehensive account there are many works available to the student of military history, only a few of which are listed in the Bibliography.

My closing chapter on the Soviet invasion of Afghanistan would have been the poorer but for the publishing firm of Cassell allowing me to quote from Mike Martin's book, *Afghanistan – Inside a Rebel Stronghold*, recommended reading for those wishing to learn more of the mujahiddin. My thanks also to the following publishers: Century Hutchinson, for permission to quote from Peregrine Hodson's *Under a Sickle Moon*; George Weidenfeld & Nicolson for allowing me to quote from Nigel Ryan's *A Hitch or Two in Afghanistan*; Michael Joseph for quotes from John Masters's *Bugles and a Tiger*; Arms and Armour Press for observations taken from John Prendergast's interesting account of service life on the Frontier, *Prender's Progress*; and Faber & Faber for extracts from *Old Soldier Sahib*, by Frank Richards. I am indebted to Colonel H. R. C. Pettigrew for comments relating to the Fakir of Ipi campaign and for allowing me to use observations from his book, *Frontier Scouts*. The extract taken from *Four Score Years and Ten* by General Sir Bindon Blood is reproduced by kind permission of Unwin Hyman Ltd.

I owe much to the staff of the London Library and the India Office Library for reference facilities and not least to my brother, Walter, for his assistance in reading and correcting the manuscript in its preliminary draft.

Dramatis Personae

First Afghan War 1838–1842

Alexander Burnes	British Resident at Kabul
Josiah Harlan	Aide-de-camp to Dost Muhammad
Major-General Sir Joseph Thackwell	3rd Light Dragoons
Captain Henry Havelock	13th Queen's Regiment
Lieutenant George Lawrence	2nd Regiment Light Cavalry
Major William Hough	48th Bengal Native Infantry
Ensign Neville Chamberlain	16th Regiment Native Infantry
Surgeon James Atkinson	Superintending Surgeon Army of the Indus
Lieutenant Henry Marion Durand	Royal Engineers
Captain George Broadfoot	Royal Engineers
Lieutenant Vincent Eyre	Bengal Artillery
Florentia, Lady Sale	Wife of General Sir Robert Sale
Captain Johnson	Shah Shuja's Contingent
Dr William Brydon	Shah Shuja's Contingent
Captain Charles Mackenzie	48th Madras Native Infantry
Lieutenant J. Greenwood	31st Queen's Regiment

Ambela Campaign 1863

General Sir Charles Napier	Governor of Scinde
Brigadier-General Sir Neville Chamberlain	Commander Ambela Expedition
Colonel John Ayde	Royal Artillery
Lieutenant-Colonel J. Luther Vaughan	5th Punjab Infantry
Major F. S. Roberts	Bengal Horse Artillery

Second Afghan War 1878–1880

Brigadier-General Sir Neville Chamberlain	British Mission to Kabul
Captain J. A. S. Colquhoun	Royal Artillery
Major-General Sir F. S. Roberts	Commander Kabul Field Force
Major Sir Louis Cavagneri	British Resident in Kabul
Major Reginald Mitford	14th Bengal Lancers
Howard Hensman	Special correspondent *Daily News*
General Sir Donald Stewart	Commander-in-Chief

Subsequent Developments 1880–1914

Lieutenant Winston Churchill	4th Queen's Own Hussars
Lieutenant Elliott-Lockhart	Corps of Guides
Major-General Sir Bindon Blood	Royal Engineers
Colonel H. D. Hutchinson	Special correspondent *The Times*
Lionel James	Reuters Agency correspondent
Corporal Frank Richards	Royal Welch Fusiliers
Colonel G. N. Molesworth	Somerset Light Infantry

Chitral Campaign 1895

Surgeon-Major George Robertson — British Agent at Gilgit

Captain Charles Vere Townshend — Central India Horse

Lieutenant W.G. Beynon — 3rd Gurkha Rifles

Lionel James — Reuters Agency correspondent

Captain George Younghusband — Queen's Own Corps of Guides

Major-General Sir Bindon Blood — Royal Engineers

Third Afghan War 1919

Colonel G. N. Molesworth — Somerset Light Infantry

Fakir of Ipi Campaign 1937

Lieutenant John Masters — 4th Gurkha Regiment

Lieutenant John Prendergast — Royal Sussex Regiment

Lieutenant Hugh Pettigrew — South Waziristan Scouts

Republic of Afghanistan and Soviet Invasion

Mike Martin — Freelance journalist

Peregrine Hodson — Correspondent *Sunday Times*

Nigel Ryan — Central Television

Prologue

The scimitar wind, which blew a flurry of snow across the tumbled mass of basalt, sliced through the tattered clothing of the solitary horseman.

The horrific events of the past seven days had sapped his strength and with an anxious glance at his mount's drooping head, the rider speculated whether the exhausted animal had sufficient energy to carry him to the walls of the fort. Sunk in reverie, he was not immediately aware of the mounted group picking its way over a debris of broken stone, but then his heart leaped at the sight of a scarlet coat and for a brief moment he assumed that a troop of irregular cavalry had ridden out to meet him.

Disillusionment was swift and brutal. One of the group of five turned in his saddle and with a shout spurred furiously towards him, an arm raised in a threatening gesture.

The sweep of the long Afghan knife was parried by the horseman's light infantry sword but such was the violence of the blow that the blade, already weakened from previous use, broke from its hilt. In a despairing act, the Scot flung the guard at the tribesman's head and bent down to gather his pony's bridle. The Afghan, perhaps thinking that his adversary was reaching for a pistol, turned and galloped after his companions who, with typical Afghan unpredictability, had seemingly lost interest in the affair.

Weakened from knife and sword cuts but conscious of

his continuing good fortune, Dr William Brydon, one of five fugitives and the only European still at liberty of an army which with its camp followers had numbered some 16,000 resumed his stumbling progress towards the safety of Jalalabad.

Chapter 1

An English Puppet

To the early Victorians, Afghanistan was regarded as the natural barrier to India, for only by means of a few savage passes could an invading army force its way to the banks of the Indus.

To the west of the kingdom of Kabul a bleak vista of mountain and desert, comparable in size to India herself and known as the Iranian Plateau, lay between Persia and Afghanistan. To the north, a formidable 600-mile-long barrier of ice-covered rock – the Hindu Kush – separated that kingdom from Turkestan, whilst to the south of the country the frontier was so obscure that it was difficult to establish where Afghanistan's tangled mass of mountains ended and the hills and ravines of Baluchistan began.

Only in the east with the great Indus River was there an established boundary between Central Asia and the Indian sub-continent but for the trade caravans bearing the fruits of Kabul to the plains of Hindustan, there was no alternative to the hazardous route through a mass of mountains inaccessible at all seasons except by certain narrow defiles or passes. Of these, the three most important were the Malakand in the north, the near-eighty-mile-long Bolan Pass in the south via the ancient cities of Herat and Kandahar, and the shorter route afforded by the Khyber Pass.

Jealously guarded by Afridi tribesmen, its thirty miles of twisting escarpments varied in width from a few yards to the span of a valley dotted with the distinctive round mud huts of the Afridi communities. 'If a single traveller endeavours to

3

make his way through,' warned a high-ranking government official in 1809, 'the noise of his horse's feet sounds up the long narrow valleys, and soon brings the Khyberees in troops from the hills and ravines.' This winding wilderness of rock and scrub, together with its predatory tribes, was to engage the resources of the Indian government and the attention of a British Parliament for the next seventy years.

The people of Afghanistan, a country of 250,000 square miles, and those living on the North-West Frontier – some 40,000 square miles bordering upon Afghanistan and ending at the Peshawar Valley – were all Afghans. Many were Pathans of Aryan stock whose tribes, varying in strength from thousands to hundreds of thousands, differed considerably in appearance. Some had fair complexions, aquiline noses and light-green eyes, whilst others were short in stature with broad faces and a dark-brown skin. Most were poor, grubbing out a living as farmers or nomad shepherds or soldiers in a feudal chieftain's army. All were averse to any form of discipline and lived according to their own law – Pakhtunwali – whose principal teachings in order of importance are Revenge and Hospitality.

In 1826, after a lengthy period of internecine warfare, Dost Muhammad came to the throne. An astute and determined man, he was to play a central role in the events of the next few years but now, as he surveyed his splintered kingdom, he was conscious of a more immediate threat. The Russians were beginning to show an interest in the Caspian and Aral Seas in Central Asia and were preparing an expedition against Khiva, a few hundred miles beyond his northern frontier.

For almost a century, Russia had been expanding her territories in the east and south at a rate which to political observers seemed inexorable. Their steady advance towards the frontiers of India had disturbed the peace of mind of English politicians since the latter half of the eighteenth century and much thought had been given concerning the best means of arresting the growth of Russian influence in Central Asia. From a narrow commercial viewpoint it seemed an excellent idea to introduce trade at rates which could be guaranteed to undercut Russian goods with ease, a policy which might be achieved by exploring a route more direct than any available to the Russians, thus greatly reducing the otherwise considerable cost in transport. At this point, a word of explanation concerning the East India Company and its unusual position of maintaining a native army might be of interest to the reader not so familiar with this period of British India's history. From small beginnings in 1600, when a charter was granted by Elizabeth I to the 'Company and Merchants of London trading with the East Indies', the Honourable East India Company grew to become the agent of the British Government for the military and civil administration of India.

When the Indian principalities began to disintegrate in the eighteenth century, the Company was obliged to raise native regiments officered by Britons to defend its valuable spice trade. In 1757 Clive's victory at Plassey effectively extended the Company's power and influence throughout Bengal. Its spice and pepper trade was expanded to include silks, calicoes, tea, and hand-painted fabrics then in much demand in London. As the Company's commercial power increased, so too did its military responsibilities. Each presidency – Bengal, Madras, Bombay – had its own army, which was separately maintained.

After the Sepoy Mutiny in 1857 the British Government, by an Act of Parliament, abolished the Company and ruled India direct from the Office of Governor-General (or Viceroy as it later became known).

In 1830, a gift of five English drays to a maharajah with a penchant for 'beautiful women, fine horses, and strong drink' afforded the East India Company an opportunity to chart the riverbed of the Indus and survey its banks as far as the Sikh capital of Lahore. The officer chosen for the task was a twenty-five-year-old Scot, Alexander Burnes, who had served in India from the age of sixteen and had earlier distinguished himself on a trade mission to Kabul.

Having delivered the horses to an appreciative Ranjit Singh, Lieutenant Burnes left for Ludhiana, where he met Shah Shuja-ul-Mulk, an Afghan exile who still entertained hopes of regaining the throne he had lost to Mahmud some twenty years earlier. Following the defeat of his forces in the

field, Shuja had first taken refuge with Ranjit Singh before
being granted asylum at Ludhiana in 1816. The British had
given him a house and a small pension, but little else. Now,
with an apparent threat to India's northern borders from an
expansionist Russia, Shuja hoped that his ambition might be
advanced with a measure of success. Should the British support his claim to the throne of Kabul, he confided to the Scot,
he would be prepared to grant them freedom of movement
through his territory to Central Asia.

Burnes was not greatly impressed and confessed to his
diary: 'I do not believe the Shah possesses sufficient energy
to seat himself on the throne of Kabul and if he did regain
it, he has not the tact to discharge the duties of so difficult a
situation.'

On his return from the Punjab, Burnes reported to Lord
William Bentinck at Simla and was successful in persuading
the Governor-General to underwrite his expenses for further
travels into Afghanistan and Central Asia. It was a venture
which was to bring the Scot wide acclaim and the sobriquet of
'Bokhara' Burnes after an account of his travels was published
in 1832.

In January Burnes set out with his small party wearing
native dress, with his head shaved and his beard dyed black.
He and his companions travelled without the comforts of a
tent, chair, table or bed. 'I now eat my meals with my hands,'
he wrote to his sister in Montrose, 'and greasy digits they
are. . . . I frequently sleep under a tree, but if a villager
will take compassion upon me I enter his house.'

Four months from the commencement of his journey Burnes
set foot in Kabul to a hospitable welcome as the guest of
Jubbur Khan, a brother of the Dost. Writing of the Afghans,
Burnes had this to say: 'they have no prejudices against a
Christian, and none against our nation. When they ask me
if I eat pork, I of course shudder and say it is only outcasts
who commit such outrages. God forgive me! for I am very
fond of bacon, and my mouth waters as I write the word. I
wish I had some of it for breakfast, to which I am now about
to sit down.'

If Burnes had a fault, it was his outrageous behaviour as

a womaniser, but his linguistic skills and easy-going manner won him many friends and, despite paying close attention to the Afghan ladies (who, he wrote, 'made ample amends when indoors for all their sombre exhibitions in public'), he was received courteously by Dost Muhammad.

Described by an English officer as having prominent Jewish features which any artist would recognise as bearing a close resemblance to the popular image of an Abraham, Isaac or Jacob, the Afghan King's vigorous conversation and humour made a favourable impression upon Burnes. So much so that he was moved to write of the Amir's 'accomplished address and manners' and his lively interest in European affairs. This was the man worthy of British support, thought Burnes, not the wretched Shah Shuja-ul-Mulk.

From Kabul, Burnes and his party made their way across the mountains of the Hindu Kush to the Oxus, a bleak and inhospitable region, which for six months of the year is swept by a winter wind that 'slices over the glacier slopes like an arctic razor and brings even the flight of birds to a stop'.

The fruit gardens on the riverbanks of the ancient city of Bokhara came as a welcome relief from the harsh desert landscape, but Burnes found the city, surrounded by a high wall, to be a fever-bed of sickness and plague. The Scot discovered the mosques and palaces 'pleasing to the eye and the great bazaars echoing to the sound of every tongue in Asia'. There were also European slaves to be seen, many of whom, he suspected, were Russian soldiers captured in border infringements.

Although Burnes and his companions were not molested, they were obliged to don black caps and wear ropes around their waists, this being the mandatory garb for foreigners. They were fortunate, too, in not encountering the murderous Nasrullah, Amir of Bokhara, whose proclivity it was to throw strangers into the city's infamous bug pit – a deep well infested with reptiles, in which the luckless victim was left to die among decomposing corpses, food and drink being lowered at intervals to prolong his agony.

Burnes returned to Bombay in January 1833 having been away for a year and his colourful account to the Indian government marked him out as a prime candidate for leading any mission to cultivate Anglo-Afghan relations. In the report, Burnes emphasised the improbability of a Russian advance through the mountainous barrier which separated Afghanistan from the plains of Turkestan. It would be much easier, he wrote, for them to advance on Kashmir where there were supplies in abundance. Once there, it would be a simple task to establish a base in an area such as Chitral, from which to mount an invasion of the Indian plains. He reported on the difficulties of the route he had followed from Bokhara to Merv and from there to Herat as being a wilderness so sandy that it was doubtful whether the elephants necessary to pull artillery would survive the journey. Concerning the marked increase in Russian diplomatic activity in the area, Burnes had noted the passage of couriers between St Petersburg and Bokhara, but was of the opinion that their efforts were directed towards the ransoming of Russian slaves. He found nothing to suggest that the Central Asian states were nervous of foreign aggression, but Russian intrigue in Persia had not ceased and was directed towards the encouragement of Muhammad Shah's military ambitions by supporting his bid to annex the Afghan city of Herat.

This thorough and detailed analysis singled Burnes out as the obvious choice for an intelligence-gathering operation, and in November 1836 he was nominated by the new Governor-General, Lord Auckland, to lead a commercial mission to Kabul. His brief was to monitor the progress of events in Afghanistan with particular emphasis on the effectiveness of Russian attempts to influence Afghan foreign policy.

Alexander Burnes reached Kabul in September 1837 bearing, as a gift to the Amir, a brace of pistols and a brass telescope. He also carried presents for the Amir's harem – an inexcusable breach of etiquette in one familiar with Oriental customs. Josiah Harlan, an American adventurer who as the Dost's aide-de-camp was a member of the court, records that the Amir was far from pleased and afterwards exclaimed: 'Behold! I have feasted and honoured this Feringee to the extent of six thousand rupees and have now a lot of pins and needles and sundry petty toys to show for my folly.'

Despite the affront to his dignity, the Amir betrayed no sign of his displeasure in Burnes' presence. At a midnight conference with the British envoy, the commercial aspect of his mission was quickly dealt with and Dost Muhammad turned the conversation to a subject close to his heart. Would the British give sympathetic consideration to his request that Peshawar be restored to his kingdom? This province, once the richest in Afghanistan, had been captured by Ranjit Singh some four years earlier when Dost Muhammad had rashly weakened the garrison when mobilising troops to defeat Shah Shuja's bid to regain the throne. Burnes, however, had not the authority to give such an assurance and he knew that Lord Auckland would have little sympathy with Dost Muhammad's plea. Such a move, he explained, would undoubtedly incur the wrath of Ranjit Singh and, although British India and the Punjab shared a common border, the Governor-General would not be prepared to interfere in the affairs of an independent nation.

It was an embarrassing moment for the envoy. Having thus failed to satisfy the Amir's desire to recover Peshawar for the Afghan nation, Burnes could only advise him that the correct course would be 'to appease the feelings of the powerful monarch whom he had offended'. British India, continued Burnes, simply could not afford to alienate the Sikhs, her most powerful allies on the North-West Frontier.

Burnes did his best to placate his host with assurances of goodwill and for the next three months his advocacy of Dost Muhammad as a useful and reliable ally continued, but Sir William Hay Macnaughten, Chief Secretary to the government of India, would have none of it. Priority must be given to the interests of Ranjit Singh and Burnes was instructed to warn the Amir not to enter into negotiations with any other state over the question of Peshawar.

It was then that an unforeseen situation arose with the arrival in Kabul of a Russian agent prepared to offer Dost Muhammad most of what the British had denied him. 'We are in a mess here,' wrote Burnes to a colleague. 'The Emperor of Russia has sent an envoy to Caubul to offer Dost Mahomed Khan money to fight Runjeet Singh!'

Towards the end of March, Dost Muhammad made one last appeal for the Governor-General to 'remedy the grievances of the Afghans and to give them a little encouragement and power', but, realising that he could expect nothing that might discomfit his enemy, Dost Muhammad turned to the Russian diplomat as his best hope for an ally against Ranjit Singh.

There was now little left for the dejected Scot but to abandon his mission after a stay of seven months and return to India with a gift of three horses from the Amir, and the questionable assurance from a court official that, should the British seek to remove Dost Muhammad from the throne in favour of Shuja-ul-Mulk, he would be willing to assist at a price. It was a suggestion that, however immoral, was viewed in Simla as the key to a situation in which Russia or a Russian-backed Persia might attempt to establish control in Afghanistan. A ruler on the throne of Kabul friendly to British interests would restore the balance of power in Britain's favour and remove a thorn from the side of Ranjit Singh. In Shah Shuja, because of his past acquaintance with Ranjit Singh, government advisers saw their ideal nominee.

Before the issue was finally resolved, Burnes was asked for his opinion and it was clear from his reply that the Scot's respect for Dost Muhammad had not diminished in any way. 'If half you must do for others were done for him, and offers made which he could see conduced to his interests,' he replied, 'he would abandon Russia and Persia tomorrow.' But if the installation of Shah Shuja was conducive to government interests then it was essential that the British take a major role, 'for the Afghans are a superstitious people and believe Shah Shoojah to have no fortune – but our name will invest him with it'.

The eventual plan for the removal of Dost Muhammad was largely the work of Sir William Hay Macnaughten, a man described by one modern historian as 'having the look of a pensive Groucho Marx'. But, whatever the impression created by his black moustache, thick eyebrows and thin-rimmed spectacles, his plan was embraced with enthusiasm by Lord Auckland and thus the first step in a decidedly risky undertaking was given the seal of official approval.

The key to success lay with the Sikhs, since they had much to gain from a change of rule in Kabul. In May 1838, Macnaughten journeyed to Lahore where he found Ranjit Singh in favour of the plan but unwilling to commit his own troops to anything but a supporting role. This Macnaughten accepted (influenced, it was said, by the potency of the local fiery spirits), which meant not only British financial backing but also the commitment of Company troops. Ranjit Singh, who knew full well how bitterly the tribes would resent the presence of foreign troops on their soil, was content to let the British play the major role.

Five months later the way was prepared in a manifesto issued in Simla which declared: 'The welfare of our possessions in the East requires that we should have on our western frontier an ally who is interested in resisting aggression, and establishing tranquillity, in the place of chiefs ranging themselves in subservience to a hostile power and seeking to promote schemes of conquest and aggrandisement.' Auckland then ignored the probable effect on the Afghans of having a ruler imposed on them by going on to state: 'His Majesty Shah Shuja will enter Afghanistan surrounded by his own troops and will be protected by a British army against foreign intervention and factious opposition.' In an attempt to allay fears of a permanent occupation of the country, Auckland was careful to make it known that, as soon as Shah Shuja's position was secure and the independence and integrity of Afghanistan established, the British force would be withdrawn. Thus the scene was set for the first military campaign of the new Queen's reign and the greatest catastrophe in the history of the British Army.

On 10 December 1838, the Army of the Indus, totalling some 10,000 British and Indian troops and 6000 irregulars of Shah Shuja's army, equipped from British magazines and led by British officers, began their separate journeys with a sharp touch of frost in the air.

The slow-moving and lengthy columns of infantry together with the cavalry, artillery and baggage train, not to mention the ubiquitous camp followers, made a colourful spectacle as they passed through Sind. British and Indian troops were smartly clad in thick red tunics, white cross belts and pouches, haversacks, and tall black shakos, whilst the gleaming brass helmets, white buckskin breeches, high jackboots and blue uniforms of the Bengal Artillery were evocative of feats of arms and the pomp of war.

The possibility that grazing for the horses would be poor or non-existent had not been overlooked and many of the camels were carrying fodder instead of provisions, thus adding considerably to their numbers; since each beast occupied some ten feet of road, the accompanying train of camp followers, pack animals and bullock carts, stretched for miles.

The route chosen was westward through the Bolan Pass to Quetta, rather than the shorter way through the Khyber. It had the advantage of the rivers Sutlej and Indus for the first 450 miles, permitting the use of flat-bottomed barges, and it also had the merit of showing the flag to the three Amirs of a disunited Sind, who were expected to contribute twenty-five lakhs of rupees towards the enormous cost of the expedition.

Under the overall command of Sir John Keane, two columns, one a Bengal contingent led by Major-General Sir Willoughby Cotton and Keane's own column travelling by sea from Bombay to Karachi, faced a 1200-mile trek through Baluchistan by way of Kandahar. To add to the discomfort of a thick serge jacket, each soldier wore a tight-fitting leather stock around his neck and bore the weight of a firelock, bayonet and sixty rounds of ball ammunition. A haversack containing a change of clothing, his accoutrements and a greatcoat were additional to the burden of a climate guaranteed to tax his physical powers to the limit.

The officers fared somewhat better and, because no luxury had been overlooked by the gentlemen of the Bengal Division, its numbers were swollen by as much as four times its fighting strength. Of the 30,000 camels accompanying the column, at least sixty carried the personal effects of just one brigadier who, it was rumoured, numbered forty servants among the complement of his household. As one observer commented: 'Many young officers would as soon have thought of leaving behind their swords and double barrelled pistols as march without their perfumes, Windsor soap, and eau-de-cologne.' He could have added that two camels carried nothing but cigars for the officers' mess, and that the 16th Lancers from Bengal were at pains to include a pack of foxhounds.

As to the leadership, whilst it was true that most junior officers were keen and courageous, the two generals were notable for their mediocrity: General Sir Willoughby Cotton who, despite thirty years of army service, dismissed the thought of sending out reconnaissance patrols, and General Sir John Keane, an ill-mannered veteran of the Napoleonic War of whom it was afterwards said that what little the troops knew of him 'did not fill them with any eager desire to place themselves under his command'. The real leader of the expedition was a civilian, Chief Secretary Sir William Hay Macnaughten, who, in his capacity as envoy, carried responsibility for the success or failure of the mission. It was perhaps unfortunate that, although fluent in Asiatic languages, he was completely ignorant of the country and its predatory tribes.

Since the Sikhs were sending a contingent through the Khyber, the Governor-General was reluctant to ask for further concessions and consequently the army's route to Kabul was long and difficult across arid plains and the scorching salt-impregnated deserts of Upper Sind, where there was not a single tree and scarcely a bush or a blade of grass. Little enough forage had been allocated to the needs of the cavalry and transport animals, and a disapproving General Thackwell, who commanded the cavalry of both the Bengal and Bombay contingents, noted in his diary: 'But forty maunds of grain has been collected instead of nine hundred. . . . There is no grass and the food for the camels is bad.'

With little variation in the scenery it was not surprising that the earlier sense of eager anticipation quickly gave way to acute boredom. 'All through the desert, the same kind of road and no soil – no vegetation except prickly thorn and tufts of long grass scantily diffused . . .' recorded the General. 'There was nothing to distinguish one day from another in the mind of each individual,' wrote Captain Henry Havelock, 'but the evasion and disappearance of his own or his comrade's camels,

and the efforts necessary to replace them.' This desertion of
hired labour with the attendant loss of camp equipage did not
seem to have adversely affected the degree of comfort enjoyed
by the officers in the field. Havelock, having ridden on with
a party of cavalry officers, was delighted to find spread out
for a picnic lunch 'an ample collation, cold beef, cold mutton,
cold game, bread, butter, and various other tempting and
substantial viands, wine of several kinds, beer, brandy and
cigars'.

An enforced diet of tamarisk and the scarcity of water
had a marked effect on the cavalry horses, however, and
each passing day saw a steady erosion in their numbers. The
camel losses, together with the stores they carried, were
particularly galling. Each beast carried a day's food for 160
sepoys, and with this loss the supply situation became critical. Yet another hazard confronted the long-suffering troops.
The most rudimentary arrangement for sanitation or hygiene
being notably absent, they could almost certainly expect a visit
from those ubiquitous scourges of Victorian armies, dysentery
and cholera.

Ten days of arduous toil along tracks strewn with jagged
stones and in the teeth of a howling gale brought the army
out of the Bolan Pass and into the plain of Shal and the town
of Quetta towards the end of March. The change of scenery
was a tonic to the weary troops of the Bengal Division. 'Oh!,
how grateful to the eye and ear . . .' Lieutenant George
Lawrence enthused. 'The horses no longer grinding and crunch-
ing through stones and shingle as they marched, but stepping
lightly and noiselessly on the grassy plain smooth as velvet.'
Quetta raised rather less enthusiasm: 'a most miserable mud
town' was the opinion of Major William Hough.

There had been difficulties in bringing up supplies from
the rear and the arrival of thousands of hungry troops in
the few narrow streets of mud houses and bazaars soon
exhausted the available grain stocks. Cotton was obliged to
put his men on half rations – an allowance barely sufficient
to save them from starvation. The unfortunate camp followers were left to fend for themselves. 'They did not murmur,'
observed Havelock, 'but the countenances of these famishing

men expressed suffering and dreadful apprehension. . . .' How they were expected to combat the exertions of a march and the labour of their allotted tasks troubled the conscience of only Havelock and a few like-minded individuals. General Thackwell's chief concern was for his beloved cavalry horses: 'our short rations of one seer, and sometimes not any corn, are fast destroying this fine cavalry. Fifty horses of the three regiments were cast and shot at Quetta and seventeen horses have died today of sheer weakness.'

On 31 March, Sir Willoughby Cotton was joined by Sir John Keane, whose Bombay Division together with Shah Shuja's contingent had suffered the unpleasant experience of picking a way through the nauseous detritus and decomposing carcasses left by the earlier passage of the Bengal Division.

Seven days later, the Army of the Indus marched out of Quetta and soon the Plain of Kandahar lay spread out before the troops, whose morale began to improve at the sight of fields of rich golden wheat. 'There are plenty of orchards and gardens in the vicinity,' wrote Major Hough, 'which contain apples, pears, quinces, nectarines, peaches, figs, plums, apricots, cherries. . . . The people have no knowledge of horticulture or gardening,' he added. 'Having sown the seed . . . they leave the rest to nature.'

On 2 April 1839, the city of Kandahar was taken without a fight and Shah Shuja, accompanied by Macnaughten, entered to a cool reception from the citizens and was enthroned as ruler of Afghanistan. It was perhaps significant that, given an eastern fondness for pageantry, the people of Kandahar viewed the whole affair with the greatest indifference. Their lack of passionate zeal did not disturb Havelock's peace of mind; he comforted himself with the thought that 'the population if not in ecstasies of enthusiasm . . . were at least tranquil, and well disposed to be outwardly civil to the army of Feringees. . . .'

A different view was taken by the commander of the Bombay Division. 'I really do believe,' wrote Major-General Sir William Nott, 'that the people of Afghanistan will not give up their country without fighting for it. . . .' That was a sentiment endorsed by young Neville Chamberlain in a letter to his mother: 'You cannot now leave camp a mile without going in a body and well armed, or else run the chance of being killed.'

It was a state of affairs that did not augur well for the future of the Army of the Indus.

Chapter 2

The Gathering Storm

That the Army of the Indus had so far met with only a token resistance was due in no small measure to Dost Muhammad's assumption that it would take the shorter route through the Khyber Pass. Acting upon this belief he had deployed his best troops, led by his favourite son Akbar Khan, to block the Khyber and was astonished when Keane left Nott in Kandahar at the end of June for a long gruelling march towards Ghazni, 200 hundred miles to the north-east.

The walled town was reached on 20 July. 'The fort of Ghuznee burst on our view,' wrote Major Hough.

> It looked formidable with its fortifications rising up, as it were, on the side of a hill. . . . The columns were advancing slowly, but steadily, on the wide plain, and no noise was heard, save that of the movement of the guns, the distant sound of the horses' feet and the steady tramp of the infantry; whilst there being a slight breeze, the distant clouds of dust indicated to those afar off, the approach of an army in battle array.

Ghazni was one of the strongest fortress towns in Central Asia, possessing walls seventy feet high surrounded by a wide moat, and garrisoned by soldiers of the Afghan Army under the command of Dost Muhammad's twenty-one-year-old son, Hyder Khan. Against walls of such height and thickness, mining or escalading were clearly impossible. The four great guns which had been brought from India with so much effort had been left with Nott at Kandahar, and to breach the walls

17

prior to storming would require nothing less than a siege train.

Burnes, on an earlier reconnaissance, had indicated that the fortress would not be defended, but the round shot and musketry which greeted Keane's arrival left the British General in some doubt as to the likelihood of taking the place by a *coup de main*. In the event, he was fortunate in obtaining vital information from a disenchanted nephew of the Dost who was predisposed to favour the cause of Shah Shuja. Abdul Rashid had been obliged to flee the fort and was more than willing to disclose the fact that, whilst most of the gates were bricked up, there was one – the Kabul Gate – which had been only lightly barred to allow the passage of troops.

Just before dawn on 23 July, in the teeth of a howling sandstorm which drowned the noise of their approach, a party of Sappers led by Captain Peat and Lieutenant Durand scrambled across a ditch and ran along a narrow winding road carrying seventy five-pound bags of powder. Despite being seen and fired upon whilst still 150 yards short of the gate, Durand and his party somehow managed to pile the sacks against the massive timbers and lay the long cotton hose of powder. At first, the portfire failed to ignite and the Lieutenant was tempted to flash the train of powder with his pistol, but at the second attempt it caught and Henry Durand barely had time to hurl himself into the ditch before the stacked gunpowder erupted in a tremendous cloud of smoke and dust to bring down part of the gate house and hurl the timbers of the gate in all directions.

With a resounding cheer, the forlorn hope led by Colonel Dennie of the 13th Foot dashed over the smoking rubble to the courtyard beyond. There was a moment of confusion when Captain Peat, who had been thrown to the ground and stunned by the explosion, told Brigadier Robert Sale that the passage was blocked and could not be forced, but the storming party with 'Fighting Bob' Sale at its head surged forward with outstretched bayonets stabbing and kicking a way through the heap of dead and dying Afghans. The main force was following close behind and the whole cheering mass of Queen's and Company troops poured through the breach to the open square where the defenders rushed to engage them in a savage bout of hand-to-hand fighting.

Sir John Keane, watching anxiously from an adjacent hillock, requested Captain Havelock 'to ride down to the gate and bring him news of the assault'. One of the first sights to meet Havelock's gaze was that of Brigadier Sale struggling on the ground with a powerful Afghan and calling loudly for someone to 'do him the favour to pass his sword through the body of the infidel'. A Captain Kershaw duly obliged and, after ensuring that the Brigadier had suffered nothing more serious than a minor facial wound, Havelock rode back and reported the complete success of the enterprise. 'The sepoys,' he wrote, 'gathering in groups around each Afghan, shot and hunted them down like mad dogs.' 'Very few of the defenders escaped,' commented Thackwell, 'owing to the cavalry being judiciously stationed round the town very early in the morning.'

As the light faded, the conflict, if anything, increased in ferocity. The fall of the citadel had brought little respite to the attacking force for the Afghans turned each house into a fort, 'blocking up the doors and firing from the roofs and windows . . . fighting till they died . . .'. The violence was not confined to the fighting troops for, according to William Hough, 'The centre square exhibited a scene of blood and confusion; horses, many wounded, were running about in all directions, fighting with each other, kicking and biting, and running quite furious at anyone they saw.'

By nightfall, however, all resistance had been overcome and Hyder Khan had surrendered himself to two British officers. The great fortress of Ghazni was in Keane's possession for the relatively small cost of 200 killed and wounded. 'Happily the gun-shot wounds, the most dangerous, were few,' reported Surgeon James Atkinson. 'All the sword cuts, which were numerous, and many of them very deep, united in the most satisfactory manner, which we decidedly attributed to the men having been without rum for the previous six weeks. . . .'

The plunder taken in the city was considerable and proved a severe temptation to the troops. 'For a time all discipline was lost,' Ensign Chamberlain confessed, 'the soldiers breaking into the houses to look for plunder, and in this way many were killed, by going down the streets of the lower end of the town, far away from their comrades.'

From his vantage point in the hills where he waited to fall upon Keane's defeated forces, the Dost's eldest son, Afzul Khan, stared in disbelief. In the dawn light which bathed the minarets of the city, the Union Jack was fluttering on its flag-pole above the citadel. He was not alone in his astonishment, for his father, having brought his entire army of 13,000 along the Ghazni road west of Kabul, failed to bring them to battle. Holding aloft a copy of the Koran, Dost Muhammad begged his followers 'not to desert the true faith or transfer their allegiance to a ruler who had filled the land with infidels'. Not a soul responded. Macnaughten's generous bribes to the chiefs had been so effective that, for the time being at least, his gold had bought a total withdrawal of support from the Amir. Enraged by the hasty departure of his followers, which had left a row of abandoned cannon across the road to Kabul, Dost Muhammad fled the field accompanied by his son, Akbar Khan, and a handful of loyal retainers.

On 7 August 1839, after thirty years of exile, Shah Shuja on a handsome white charger, rode into the city wearing a jewelled coronet of velvet and a robe ornamented with a pro-fusion of precious stones. On either side, resplendent in blue and gold diplomatic uniforms, rode Sir William Macnaughten and Alexander Burnes, followed by Sir John Keane with his staff and brigade commanders. Their brave show made a lasting impression upon Josiah Harlan, who witnessed their arrival. 'The polished shakos, scarlet uniforms and pipe clay of the infantry, the brass helmets and tiger skin rolls of the Bengal Horse Artillery', wrote the Pennsylvanian, 'all helped to create an imagery of power and precision.'

There were few welcoming smiles for Shah Shuja from the citizens of Kabul and, indeed, a noticeable absence of salaams. Henry Durand, in a letter to a friend, wrote: 'Shah Shooja enters his capital today, and certainly has the satisfaction of ruling over the most unprincipled, treacherous race that can well be imagined.' General Keane, in an interview with Durand before they both returned to India with the Bombay Division, forecast with uncanny accuracy the trouble to come.

'I cannot but congratulate you on quitting the country,' he told the young Lieutenant, 'for mark my words, it will not be long before there is here some signal catastrophe.'

If there were others who questioned the wisdom of staying, their voices were drowned in the noise of celebration. In Simla there was much excitement. Lord Auckland marked the installation of his puppet with a dazzling series of balls and galas, whilst in London the satisfactory conclusion of this the first military campaign of the new Queen's reign was looked upon as a notable achievement. Honours quickly followed the congratulations. An earldom was created for Auckland, Macnaughten and Keane received baronetcies, whilst Burnes and Sale were made knights of the realm. The death of Ranjit Singh at Lahore passed almost unnoticed. With the sixty-year-old Shah Shuja restored to the throne and a court friendly to the British in Kabul, Josiah Harlan was left without employment and he turned leisurely homeward, reaching Philadelphia in August 1841.

The troops who were to garrison the city moved into the Bala Hissar, an ancient citadel which overlooked Kabul from the brow of a hill. It was cold and uncomfortable and not a popular move with the troops. Kabul, although not a pearl of Asia, was as Lieutenant James Rattray described it, 'well built and handsome. The houses overhang the narrow streets; their windows have no glass but consist of lattice work wooden shutters, which push up and down and are often richly carved and otherwise ornamented'. Fruit, from a profusion of orchards, was displayed in shop windows open to the sun, whilst the Great Bazaar under a vaulted roof offered all manner of merchandise for sale, including costly shawls and China porcelain imported from Bokhara. Away from the mansions of the more prosperous Afghans with their enclosed courtyards and fountains sprawled a broken succession of clay-built dwellings whose flat roofs, strengthened only by chopped straw, were – in the opinion of James Atkinson – 'badly calculated for a climate in which so much snow falls . . .'. He found the gardens delightful though, and the air – in certain areas – had that 'crystal quality to be expected of mountain areas a mile above sea level'.

The autumn and winter of 1839 passed without notable incident. Parties of junior officers visited the mosques and explored the countryside around Kabul, unmolested by the tribesmen. Indeed, an ice-covered lake a few miles from the city proved a major attraction for British officers and Afghans alike. Skates were fashioned from iron smelted and hardened by the Afghan smiths in the city, and those skilled in the sport 'wheeled and turned to cut all manner of figures upon the ice'. The Rev. Gleig, Chaplain to the Forces, was told that the Afghans stared in amazement. 'Now we see that you are not like the infidel Hindoos that follow you,' a tribesman exclaimed to an officer of the 13th Foot: 'you are men born and bred like ourselves, where the seasons vary. . . . we wish that you had come among us as friends and not as enemies.'

Christmas Day was celebrated by the officers of the Kabul garrison in the time-honoured fashion. 'We had a very merry party,' wrote eighteen-year-old Neville Chamberlain to his mother,

> though we had nothing to drink but brandy and gin. . . . When Sir Alexander Burnes' health was drunk he got up and said: 'This day two years ago I was eating my Christmas dinner in this very room, but instead of being the guest of a British regiment I was entertaining a Russian agent.' . . . He is liked by everyone, as there is no political humbug in him like in most persons in that employ. . . .

In the early spring, at the insistence of Shah Shuja, who required the Bala Hissar for his seraglio, the citadel was vacated in favour of a cantonment outside the city walls and the troops settled down to a routine familiar to every military station in British India. There were impromptu horse races, sports contests, concerts given by the regimental bands, amateur theatricals and cricket matches which were watched in astonishment by the Afghan spectators. Streets of tents were erected, bungalows built, and gardens were created using vegetable and flower seeds brought from India. A dozen or so officers sent for their wives and families, whilst others without such responsibilities formed liaisons with the attractive ladies of Kabul, despite the jealousy such activities aroused among their menfolk. Foremost among those practising the amorous art was Sir Alexander Burnes.

As the months passed and prices soared, driven up by the free-spending army of occupation, the tribesmen grew increasingly restless. This unsettled state of affairs and the fact that the new Amir did not enjoy the support of his subjects, caused Macnaughten some uneasy moments. British gold had bought only a temporary peace from the tribal chiefs, but that was not all. Garrison strength in other parts of Afghanistan, even in such strategically important towns as Ghazni and Jalalabad, was woefully inadequate. In order to maintain communications and keep supply lines open, Macnaughten had been obliged to bring the hereditary free-booter tribes into the pay of the government, particularly the Pathan Ghilzais, who commanded the western approach to the Khyber. There was also the ever-present threat from Dost Muhammad, who was still at large despite numerous attempts to capture him. Events soon began to conspire against the envoy.

The summer of 1840 saw the Russians successfully negotiate a treaty with the Khan of Khiva, and reports confirmed a persistent rumour that Dost Muhammad was in Bokhara recruiting an Uzbek army for the recovery of his throne. By September, Macnaughten was at his wits' end. 'Never', he exclaimed, 'was I so much harassed in body and mind. . . . The Afghans are gunpowder and the Dost is a lighted match.'

A month later, Dost Muhammad was within forty miles of Kabul in the hills of Kohistan, a region overflowing with disaffected tribesmen eager to drive the infidel invader from their country. To prevent them from reaching Kabul, Sale was despatched on a forced march to the north with a strong contingent of cavalry supported by several batteries of horse artillery.

The opposing forces met on 6 November in a narrow valley among the precipitous Nijrao hills. A charge by Sale's Indian cavalry failed ignominiously when the sowars reined in leaving their British officers to cut their way out as best they could. It was now the turn of the Afghan cavalry to clear the field, but to the rumbling thunder of hoofs beating upon rock-hard ground was added the splintering crack of Sale's artillery. Grapeshot scythed through the mass of charging horsemen and threatened to annihilate a sizeable portion of the Afghan cavalry. In the face of such overwhelming superiority of firepower, Dost Muhammad was obliged to retire. His army had come close to Kabul but, without artillery, the Dost realised that he was unlikely to regain his kingdom by force of arms so long as the British remained.

An extraordinary sequel to the battle occurred the following evening as Sir William Macnaughten was returning from a ride in the country accompanied by George Lawrence. An Afghan suddenly sprang from the shadows of the city gate and, seizing the bridle of Macnaughten's mount, cried, 'The Amir! The Amir!' Before the envoy could recover the reins, a second horseman, elegantly dressed, pulled up beside him to grasp his hand in the Afghan gesture of submission. Dost Muhammad had acknowledged the fact of his defeat and was content to accept Macnaughten's offer of honourable exile in India, knowing that his son, Akbar Khan, would continue with the struggle in his absence.

Although the threat to peace posed by the Dost's army no longer existed, its removal did nothing to restore order or tranquillity to Kabul and the surrounding district. Shah Shuja possessed no natural talent for governing and he displayed a grasping rapacity in the collection of his revenues. Under his administration of corrupt officials a system of penal taxation was introduced which, when coupled with high food prices, reduced many of the poorer Afghans to a state close to beggardom. 'I doubt', commented Alexander Burnes, 'if ever a king had a worse set.'

Resentment spread as rapidly as the cholera, almost all of it directed against the occupying army. Fear of British strength of arms, which had first overwhelmed the tribes, gradually gave way to feelings of hatred, and plots began to hatch among the leaders. As yet, the disaffection was largely beneath the surface and the only visible storm cloud on Macnaughten's horizon seemed a distant 5000 miles away in England, where a general election in the summer of 1841 had brought a change of government from Whig to Tory, led by Sir Robert Peel.

This new regime, determined to fulfil their pledge to cut public expenditure, was known to regard the current Afghanistan policy as nothing more than an expensive military adventure and a drain upon the revenue of British India. Even without the cost of sustaining Shah Shuja upon the throne of Kabul, the East India Company's finances were in deficit by more than a million pounds a year. Clearly, cuts would have to be made and, acting upon instructions from Lord Ellenborough, the new Minister for Indian Affairs, preparations were put in hand for the break-up of the Army of the Indus. Auckland was also urged to reduce by more than half the £8000 annual subsidy paid to the Ghilzais, who held the passes between Kabul and Jalalabad.

On 10 October, the Bombay Division left Kabul en route for Quetta. Their difficulties began almost at once. Wrote General Thackwell:

> A severe frost in the morning; marched to Koord Kabul, ten miles. The road an ascent for the first three and a half miles, with small rocks and loose stones, to the Koord Kabul river. . . . This stream is crossed twenty six times and the road is rocky and indifferent. If well defended it would be next to impossible to force this defile, as the sides are very precipitous, and in one place approach to within forty yards.

One of the brigades, which included Sir Robert Sale's own regiment, the 13th Foot, encountered the full fury of the Ghilzais and was obliged to fight every yard of the way through the Khurd–Kabul Pass to the very walls of Jalalabad. 'We have certainly gained no laurels,' confessed Ensign Chamberlain. 'Our loss has been great – one hundred and fifty besides officers! We have lost ammunition, baggage, and treasure, and in fact, it has been a regular failure and I hope . . . we may not meet such again.'

All through 1841 storm clouds continued to gather in Kabul. Officers out shooting game were stoned by angry villagers, and soldiers were attacked in the streets. Alexander Burnes, virtually ignored by Macnaughten, continued his philandering and listened to rumours of conspiracy with amusement, regarding them as 'tempests in a tea pot'. 'His views', wrote Captain George Broadfoot, an intimate friend of Burnes, 'were except in details, those of Macnaughten, and he was nearly as blind to what was passing round him.'

Despite repeated warnings from his Afghan friends that, as the man universally believed to have guided the Kaffirs into the country, his name headed a list of those against whom anti-British feeling was directed, he refused to vacate the isolated Residency building. It was a decision which was to have fatal consequences for the occupants and draw upon the head of the perverse Scot accusations of selfish complacency. 'No man', reflected Lieutenant Vincent Eyre of the Bengal Artillery, 'in a highly responsible situation ... ought ever to indulge in a state of blind security, or to neglect salutary warnings, however small.'

In the early hours of 2 November, Burnes' chuprassi met the Wazir riding in haste towards the Residency. 'I go to warn Sekunder Burnes,' called Osman Khan breathlessly. 'I am come from those who seek his life.' His warning fared no better than any of the others and his plea that the three Britons in the Residency should accompany him to the Bala Hissar only succeeded in drawing from Burnes the exasperated retort: 'Do you come here, Wazir Sahib, to teach me my duty?' When the Wazir mounted and rode off, an angry gathering was already close to the Residency at the opposite end of the street.

A sepoy picket guarded the Residency grounds, which lay two miles outside the cantonments, but their numbers were wholly inadequate to resist the howling mob which suddenly invaded the courtyard. Even at this stage Burnes refused to acknowledge the seriousness of the situation. So little consequence did he place upon the disturbance that he expressly forbade the sepoy guard to open fire, choosing instead to check the riot with a few well-chosen words from the gallery which ran along the upper part of the house. He might as well have attempted to address a pack of wolves. The mob, swollen to several hundred, surged forward angrily as he harangued them and a few of the bolder spirits began to scale the Residency walls.

Slugs from a dozen jezails splintered the timber railing as Burnes was joined on the balcony by his brother Charles and one Captain William Broadfoot. In a fierce exchange of shots, Broadfoot was the first to fall after accounting for six of the attackers with his double-barrelled pistol. 'In him', wrote Eyre, 'was lost to the state not only one of its bravest . . . but a man who for honesty of purpose and soundness of judgement, I am boldly aver, could not be surpassed.'

The Burnes brothers could do nothing to check the progress of an enraged mob and, with the stables burning furiously, they decided to escape through the garden. Hastily they donned Afghan robes and followed an unknown Kashmiri who had offered to conduct them safely to the Amir's palace. The subterfuge almost succeeded. But, when the group were just a few yards from the house, their guide halted. 'See, friends,' he cried, 'here is Sekunder Burnes!' A howl of rage was the last sound the brothers heard before a dozen long knives sliced them to pieces. Later that day, an Afghan who had spent many convivial evenings with Burnes buried their remains.

The killing of the three Britons did little to diminish the crowd's blood-lust and it became the turn of the bazaar's Hindu traders to experience mob fury. In an orgy of looting, merchants were hacked down, shops gutted and houses burned. Not even the clatter of hoofs and the beat of drums, which signalled the approach of a contingent of Shah Shuja's guard, could disperse the crowd and the picket was soon brought to a halt in the narrow streets by sniping from the rooftops. Even at this late stage order might have been restored by the Company's troops, and as Florentia, Lady Sale noted with a degree of cynicism hardly misplaced in the circumstances: 'It appears very strange that troops were not immediately sent into the city. But the state of supineness and fancied security of those in power is the result of deference to the opinions of Lord Auckland, whose sovereign will and pleasure it is that tranquillity do reign in Afghanistan, that the lawless Afghans

are as peaceful as London citizens and . . . most dutifully do
we appear to shut our eyes to our possible fate.' 'Thus the 2nd
November slowly waned away, and at last closed in apathy
and confusion,' wrote George Lawrence. 'Sorely cast down in
mind and greatly fatigued in body, I went to rest, with many
a sad foreboding for the coming day.'

General Sir Willoughby Cotton had returned to India for
reasons of health and his successor, Major-General William
Elphinstone, who had been chosen by Auckland as a figure-
head unlikely to question Macnaughten's decisions, was aged
and crippled with rheumatic gout. With his old-world courtesy
and gentle manner, he was not the man for a crisis, and decisive action to remedy the situation fast developing in Kabul
was noticeably absent. Wrote the General to the envoy after
learning of Burnes' murder: 'We must see what the morning
brings and then think what can be done. . . .'

When the morning came, all that the troops were able to
do, given that most of Kabul had gone over to the rebels, was
to cover an almost total withdrawal to the cantonment area,
leaving Shah Shuja isolated in the Bala Hissar with a small
body of troops under Brigadier Shelton. News of the murders
and the apparent failure of the British to exact revenge
spread quickly through the surrounding district. Attacks
upon isolated groups of soldiers multiplied and, as the days
passed, the 6000 troops penned inside the cantonments found
themselves to all intents and purposes in a state of siege.

The ground occupied by the troops was a rectangular
patch no larger than 1000 by 600 yards surrounded by a
rampart and a narrow ditch. 'With a strange contempt for
all military science,' reported Lawrence, 'the cantonment was
placed in low swampy ground, overlooked and commanded by
a low range of hills, and several small forts. . . .' At one end
was a second enclosure almost half as large again, known
as the Mission Compound. Here, in an irregular jumble of
houses, was accommodated the envoy, his guard and the
various officials connected with the mission. On the eastern
side flowed the Kabul River and between the river and the
cantonment was a wide canal. So ill suited to the purpose

of defence was this area that Elphinstone on his arrival in April had offered to purchase a portion in order to demolish buildings likely to afford an attacker cover within two hundred yards of the perimeter. His generous offer was refused.

Due to some inexplicable oversight the garrison's grain and medical store had been placed in an old stone fort nearly a quarter-mile beyond the low earthen rampart which enclosed the cantonment area. It soon came under attack and each attempt at reinforcing the defenders was beaten back with considerable loss to Elphinstone's troops. A final operation under the cover of darkness ended in near farce when the relief party came upon the fort's defenders coming to meet them, having abandoned the store house with everything it contained.

The next morning the garrison was treated to the sight of thousands of Afghans taking away everything that could be carried including the troops' jars of rum. The activity around the fort reminded Captain Johnson of nothing so much as 'something similar to a large ants' nest'. Fortunately the loss did not constitute a crisis since there was sufficient food in the cantonment for three days and the commissariat had been successful in obtaining a small supply of wheat and fodder from the village of Bemaru, whose inhabitants had remained friendly.

The outlook for the future, however, was such as to give Macnaughten cause for concern. Sale's brigade was five days' march from Kabul at Gandamak, but the Ghilzais had gathered like a swarm of hornets between Sale and his route back to the cantonments. It would take Nott at Kandahar five weeks to reach Kabul, always assuming that the passes were not blocked by snow, or that his sepoys could function as a cohesive force in the sub-arctic temperatures.

On 19 November it was agreed that any hope of the army being able to winter in Kabul was futile. In a letter to the General, Sir William advised Elphinstone to consider the garrison's future proceedings as a matter of urgency. He was, however, vehemently against any thought of immediate retreat, pointing out that it was the garrison's duty to hold on as long as possible. A retreat towards India,

Macnaughten wrote, would not only prove disastrous, but would be dishonourable. Valuable government property would be sacrificed and Shah Shuja, whose authority it was the army's duty to uphold, would be abandoned. This argument failed to make an impression upon Elphinstone, who was incapable of decisive action, and he continued to be badgered by Macnaughten to the extent that he was obliged to complain to George Broadfoot 'that he felt he had been reduced from a General to the Lord Lieutenant's head constable'.

Concern for the vulnerability of their position was ever a topic of conversation but a suggestion from a junior officer that the cantonment be abandoned in favour of the Bala Hissar was rejected by his superior officers on the grounds that the garrison would have to fight its way there. 'For one mile and a half,' commented Lady Sale derisively. 'If we could not accomplish that, how were we to get through a week's march to Jalalabad?'

Macnaughten, and even such junior officers as Lieutenant Vincent Eyre, had hoped that the arrival of the black-bearded, one-armed Brigadier John Shelton, from the Bala Hissar, might have induced some stiffening in morale, but to no avail. The Brigadier, who in Lawrence's opinion was 'a great croaker and anxious to return to India', had no suggestions and indeed appeared to have lost all interest in the proceedings of a council of war, which had been called to discuss the garrison's perilous position.

Before the end of November, the tactical situation had deteriorated to such an extent that Macnaughten felt obliged to point out that, if the garrison was to remain in cantonments, it was imperative that the Afghan artillery be driven from the Bemaru Heights. Stung into action by the envoy's forthright accusation that 'if you will not advance and take these two guns by this evening, you must be prepared for any disgrace that may befall us,' Shelton marched out with a strong force of infantry and four squadrons of cavalry.

Those left behind watched anxiously from the cantonments as the column wound its way up the hill, but before Shelton's troops could reach the summit the Afghan cavalry were upon them. The 44th Foot, who were in the van of the column, were immediately thrown into confusion. Lady Sale, sheltering behind a brick chimney to escape the bullets which continually flew past, had a good view of the engagement from her rooftop vantage point. 'The Afghan cavalry charged furiously down the hill upon our troops,' she entered in her diary. 'No squares were formed to receive them. All was regular confusion. My very heart felt as if it had leapt to my teeth when I saw the Afghans ride clean through them. The onset was fearful. They looked like a great cluster of bees, but we beat them and drove them up again.'

The 44th weathered the storm and reformed, covered by the two guns which Eyre was now working to good effect. The heights were taken in a rush and the enemy cannon overturned and spiked before Shelton's troops returned to the cantonments claiming a fine victory. Three days later, the Bemaru Heights were reoccupied and the garrison's harassment began all over again.

On 23 November an attempt to take Bemaru village, now sheltering a large enemy force, was made when, in the small hours, 800 of the garrison sallied forth from the west gate and deployed across the plain, led by two squadrons of cavalry but accompanied by only a single gun drawn by Sergeant Mulhall and his team. In the darkness it was far from easy to manoeuvre the six-pounder up an incline of loose rocks, but eventually the gun was positioned and a sharp fire directed against the Afghans in the village. There was little response from the enemy who could be seen leaving the village in droves, but to the chagrin of the impatient infantry Mulhall's good work was not followed up by an assault on the village. Brigadier John Shelton did not approve of night attacks.

Daybreak saw Shelton's little force drawn up in squares on a narrow ridge with the cavalry behind them, 'presenting a solid mass against the aim of perhaps the best marksmen in the world', commented Vincent Eyre. The solitary gun of Sergeant Mulhall fired into the massed Afghans with telling effect for almost three hours until the vent of the gun became too hot for serving. The enemy, reinforced from the city, then moved forward in a dense mass against which the wildly inaccurate muskets of Shelton's troops seemingly had no effect. Shelton, who had been struck five times by spent bullets, started to go back to the second square with the intention of bringing more men to the front. His few paces to the rear were unfortunately misinterpreted by the leading file, who by now had lost all confidence in their weapons, and their sudden surge down the hill precipitated a rout. The remnants of the broken battalions turned in a headlong rush for the shelter of the cantonments. General Elphinstone, in a vain attempt to rally the panic-stricken soldiers, limped out of the gate, but in minutes he was back behind the perimeter wall, almost swept there by the onrush of humanity. 'Useless, sir, useless!' he complained to Macnaughten. 'They're no better than a flock of sheep on the run. I did manage to get a handful together. But Lord, sir, when I said to them "Eyes right!" they all looked the other way.'

The action had lasted from dawn until shortly after midday and Brigadier Shelton does not seem to have been entirely without blame for the débâcle. Vincent Eyre thought the day's misfortunes were due in no small measure to his tactical blunders, and his decision to take only one piece of artillery.

Later that afternoon, when hostilities had been suspended in favour of negotiations, Lawrence and his friends, curious to see what manner of troops had won the day over their own, scanned the ranks of the insurgents closely. 'To our deep humiliation,' recorded Lawrence, 'we found that instead of being stalwart and devoted clansmen . . . the troops who had chased the British banner from the field chiefly consisted of tradesmen and artizans of Kabul. . . .'

Within a week, Dost Muhammad's son, Akbar Khan, arrived from Turkestan to provide the leadership that the Afghans, like the British, so badly needed. His arrival was welcomed by Macnaughten for, with the Dost held hostage in India, it was to be expected that Akbar would hold the Ghazis in check. Lady Sale certainly hoped so. 'If once in his power we might be safe, but these Ghazees are fanatics and would cut us into mincemeat.'

By the end of November, the garrison was close to

starvation, with the horses gnawing voraciously at tent pegs and the bark of trees. 'Camels and Tattoos [ponies] are dying fast,' Lady Sale recorded in her diary, 'and the air is most unpleasantly scented at times.' Morale had sunk to rock bottom and almost any rumour, no matter how ill founded, was given credence even among those better able to refute it. 'It is more than shocking, it is shameful to hear the way that our officers go on croaking before the men,' wrote that indomitable lady. 'It is sufficient to dispirit them, and prevent their fighting for us.' Lieutenant Vincent Eyre, although equally concerned, put it more delicately: 'Our force resembled a ship in danger of wrecking, for want of an able pilot.'

Rumours of a relief force had been the main topic of conversation for several days before a messenger reported that Brigadier Sale had marched from Gandamak. Not in the direction of Kabul, but on to Jalalabad. Lady Sale, when she heard the news, did not believe it. Her diary entry for 16 November records:

A report has come in from the Bala Hissar that Sale has gone on the way to Jalalabad, which Brigadier Shelton told me he believed on the principle of 'being out of a scrape, keep so'. Most people believe the reports to be a ruse of the enemy, to shut out hope of relief coming to us. We, however, doubt Sale's ever having received the order to return.

In this, Lady Sale was mistaken. Her husband had received an order from General Elphinstone but had chosen to ignore it.

Any hope of relief from that quarter could now be discounted, leaving the garrison with an unenviable choice: abandon the cantonments without the assurance of a safe conduct from the Afghans, or remain and perish.

Chapter 3

The Storm Bursts

Sir William Macnaughten now applied his considerable skill to the task of extricating by political means an army which had demonstrated its inability to save itself by force of arms.

On 11 December, with supplies sufficient for only two days, the envoy met a deputation of Afghan chiefs on the banks of the Kabul River. At first, the talks went well, with the British agreeing never again to set foot in Afghanistan unless called for by the Afghan government, and Akbar Khan in return promising to furnish the necessary provisions and an escort of tribesmen as far as Ludhiana.

The withdrawal was to begin on 15 December but the difficulties in obtaining supplies and transport for the women and the sick proved too great an obstacle. A late payment of a lakh of rupees to Akbar from the military chest had produced neither camels nor food, and the mood of the garrison was close to despair. 'To prove our good faith and our belief in the chiefs, we are today placed entirely in their power,' complained Lady Sale. 'They know we are starving; that our horses and cattle have pretty well eaten up the twigs and bark of trees. . . . Nothing is satisfied except the pariah dogs who are gorged with eating dead camels and horses.'

In fact, the situation was not quite so desperate as Lady Sale apparently believed, for quantities of produce were occasionally brought in for sale by the villagers, but these were often intercepted by the crowds of thieves and cut-throats swarming outside the cantonments. 'The ghazis', recalled Captain Johnson, 'were without exception the most

bare faced, impertinent rascals under the sun. Armed with
swords, daggers, and matchlocks, they acknowledge no chief,
but act independently. . . . People from the town, bringing us
grain or bran, are often plundered and beaten. . . .'

The third week in December brought the first fall of snow,
sufficient to cover the ground to a depth of five inches. 'Thus
a new enemy entered upon the scene', wrote Vincent Eyre,
'which we were destined to find even more formidable than any
army of rebels.' The sepoys on guard duty at night suffered in
particular from the cold but, although there was fuel enough,
for some inexplicable reason fires were not allowed.

The failure of the Afghan leaders to honour their promise
of supplies forced an increasingly isolated Macnaughten into
a dangerous game of intrigue. In his talks with the rebels
he had learned that the return of Dost Muhammad was by
no means welcomed by all the chiefs. Remembering the iron
fist with which the Dost had ruled them, some had begun
to favour Shah Shuja. To Macnaughten, this apparent split
in their ranks presented him with a unique opportunity to
play off one faction against the other. 'If any portion of the
Afghans wish our troops to remain in the country,' he wrote
to an Afghan conspirator, 'I shall think myself at liberty to
break the engagement which I have made to go away, which
engagement was made believing it to be in accordance with
the wishes of the Afghan people.'

Unhappily for the envoy, a document he had signed
agreeing to the abduction of a leading chief, Aminullah
Khan, came into the possession of Akbar Khan and, at
a meeting on the river bank on the morning of the 23rd,
the deception was exposed. Macnaughten, annoyed at being
jostled by the crowd, complained that there were too many
Afghans crowding him. This brought the retort from Akbar
Khan, 'They are all in the secret.' Before Macnaughten could
recover from his astonishment, Muhammad Akbar was heard
to call out, 'Begeer! Begeer!', and, as his escort turned to fly,
the luckless envoy was knocked to the ground and brutally
killed.

Macnaughten's murder had taken place less than a quarter-
mile from the cantonments but, recorded Lieutenant Eyre,

'Not a soldier stirred from his post, no sortie was even thought of; treachery was allowed to triumph in open day.' Lady Sale noticed a great crowd around a body, which the Afghans were seen to strip. 'It was evidently that of a European,' she noted. 'But strange to say, no endeavour was made to recover it, which might easily have been done by sending out cavalry.'

This tragic turn of events paralysed the dithering Elphinstone, who refused to believe that anything had gone wrong. A plea for an immediate attack on the city fell upon deaf ears. All that he would consider was that the treaty, which had included a proviso that the officers surrender themselves as hostages for the safe return of Dost Muhammad, must first be formally approved by both sides.

'A more cheerless Christmas Day perhaps never dawned upon British soldiers in a strange land,' complained Lieutenant Eyre. On 25 December, an ultimatum was presented to the garrison by the Afghan leader. In return for a safe passage to Peshawar, the army was to leave behind the military treasure. Only six field pieces were to be taken and those hostages held by him were to be exchanged for all the married men and their families.

At a council of war held two days later, it was agreed that there was now no alternative to a general evacuation and, if improved terms could not be obtained by negotiation, the garrison must be prepared to fight its way through the winter snows. The news did little to lift the spirits of the men, and Florentia Sale was merely reflecting popular opinion when she confided to her diary: 'I fear but few of us will live to reach the provinces whether we go by treaty or not.'

As the year of 1841 drew to its close, there followed days of prevarication, with the Afghans postponing the day of withdrawal on the grounds that they had not yet accumulated sufficient supplies for the journey and that Akbar Khan was still arranging for an escort. Johnson's Afghan friends had warned him to place no trust in the promises of the chiefs, least of all in Akbar Khan, and now a prominent figure from within the Bala Hissar voiced his concern for the uncertain path events seemed to be taking. 'Was the army going to forsake him in his hour of need?' asked Shah Shuja. The army would not be drawn on the subject, although Lady Sale entered into her diary the opinion that 'The Afghans do not wish to put him to death, but only to deprive him of his sight.'

New Year's Day brought no word from Akbar concerning the troops' withdrawal, and the anxiety of the garrison was only temporarily arrested by a message from Brigadier Sale three days later. In the note, brought by a friendly Afghan, he did his best to reassure his wife by stating that the Kandahar column was nearing Kabul. In this, however, he was mistaken. It had not even started.

Finally, on the morning of 6 January 1842, despairing of the escort promised by the Afghan leader, 690 Europeans, 3800 Indian troops including cavalry, 36 British women and children and 12,000 camp followers with their families, withdrew from the cantonments having first sent into the city those too ill to make the journey. 'How dreary a prospect we have before us,' Captain Johnson remarked to a brother officer. 'Ninety miles! And the greater part of this distance through snow upwards of a foot deep, and the thermometer at night below zero.'

Each officer carried away whatever possessions he could manage. William Brydon reserved his favourite chestnut for his own use and mounted his servants and boxes of clothing on his other five ponies. Eyre was perhaps reflecting upon Captain Johnson's remark when he wrote: 'Dreary indeed was the scene over which with drooping spirits and dismal forebodings we had to bend our unwilling steps. Deep snow covered every inch of mountain and plain with one unspotted sheet of dazzling white, and so intensely bitter was the cold, as to penetrate and defy the defences of the warmest clothing.'

When the garrison was seen to be evacuating the cantonment area, scores of heavily armed tribesmen swept down from Bemaru to loot the deserted compound. It was dark before the main body of troops had debouched upon the plain and in the confused fighting the rearguard lost fifty of its number, and the starved, frozen and terrified camp followers surged forward to throw the whole line of march into confusion. Shah Shuja's 6th Infantry abandoned their colours and, taking advantage of the chaos, deserted en masse, preferring imprisonment in Kabul to the uncertainty of continuing with the main column.

The pace of the column was slow and when the troops halted that afternoon, having marched six miles through snow a foot deep, no shelter was available nor were any supplies issued. The rearguard, which came in after dark, was left to scrape away the snow for a resting place. Behind them the night sky reflected the leaping flames of the cantonment they had recently vacated.

Preparatory to leaving her quarters, Lady Sale had discovered a copy of Campbell's *Poems*, which she had opened by chance at 'Hohenlinden'. The last verse was to occupy her thoughts constantly in the days to come.

> Few, few shall part where many meet,
> The snow shall be their winding sheet;
> And every turf beneath their feet
> Shall be a soldier's sepulchre.

In the biting cold that night, it was perhaps surprising that only a dozen men died from exposure, but, when at first light the column moved off, many more discovered that their feet were beginning to blacken from the effects of frostbite – 'like charred logs of wood', recalled Brydon. 'The very air we breathed', wrote Lieutenant Eyre, 'froze in its passage out of the mouth and nostrils forming a coating of small icicles on our moustaches and beards.' Florentia Sale, as she sat for hours on her horse in these freezing temperatures, was grateful to accept a tumbler of sherry, which 'at any other time would have made me very unladylike', she confessed, 'but now merely warmed me and appeared to have no more strength in it than water'.

To preserve any degree of discipline among a 'mingled mob of soldiers, camp followers, and baggage cattle', as Eyre described the scene, was virtually impossible and many of the sepoys, paralysed with the cold, cast their muskets aside before joining the hordes of civilians in their headlong flight towards Hindustan. Some, lacking the will to persevere with the march, sat frozen and apathetic by the side of the road waiting for death to overtake them. The sight of one tiny tot was to haunt Captain Charles Mackenzie all his life. 'It was a beautiful little girl about two years old, just strong enough to sit upright with its little legs doubled under it, its great black eyes dilated to twice their usual size, fixed on the armed men, the passing cavalry and all the strange sights that met its gaze.' Mackenzie thought of taking up 'this poor little native of a foreign climate . . .' – but to what purpose? The little Indian girl was, he reflected sadly, 'one of the many innocents already slaughtered on the road'.

The next morning the march was resumed with the rear of the column subjected to constant harassment from Afghan horsemen who dashed in and out of the line of march, cutting down stragglers and driving off baggage animals with impunity. Even the Afghan children, Mackenzie noted, 'were seen stabbing with their knives wounded grenadiers, one of whom, the day before, could have put a dozen of those children's fathers to flight with his bayonet'.

Daylight had brought with it no promise of food or fuel from Akbar Khan. Except for those who, like Dr Brydon, had adopted the Afghan custom of carrying a bag of parched grain and raisins at their saddle-bow, few had anything to eat. The column had left Kabul with rations sufficient for five days, enough it was thought to reach Jalalabad providing there were no delays. The attacks on the rearguard, however, were such that Elphinstone had little option but to call a halt and send back what troops and guns he could spare.

It was impossible to clear the road ahead of the multitude of camp followers and, in the chilling cold which paralysed the mind and numbed the limbs, morale dropped to its lowest ebb. Wrote Lieutenant George Lawrence: 'The silence of the men betrayed their despair and torpor, not a voice being heard. . . .' On that day, 7 January, the distance covered on the march was just two miles, less than the day before.

The next morning there was worse to come, as the straggling column drew near to the dreaded Khurd–Kabul Pass, so deep that a wintry sun never reached the icy stream which rushed down its centre. The rocky heights were lined with ferocious Ghilzais and, as the jumbled mass of troops, baggage carts, animals and camp followers entered its five-mile length, they came under a withering fire from the tribesmen's long-barrelled jezails. Akbar Khan, fearful of reprisals from an avenging British army, could be heard remonstrating with the fanatical 'Warriors of God', but seemed powerless to control them. 'They had erected small stone breastworks behind which they lay,' recorded Captain Mackenzie, 'dealing out death with perfect impunity to themselves.'

The pass echoed to the sharp crack and whine of Afghan bullets and, as the casualties mounted, all resemblance to an orderly retreat vanished. The panic-stricken soldiers simply broke and ran. By a fortunate chance, Vincent Eyre's wife was among the first to clear the pass when her horse took fright and bolted. Lady Sale did not escape the hail of bullets but she was unabashed at her near brush with death. 'I had fortunately, only one ball in my arm. Three others passed through my poshteen . . . without doing me any injury.'

Another who counted himself fortunate to survive was William Brydon. In crossing the icy bank of the stream which ran through the pass, his saddle turned, throwing him into the water: 'the enemy's fire was particularly sharp,' recalled the thirty-one-year-old Scot. 'I managed to get close under a rock to right the saddle, and both I and my horse escaped untouched.'

When eventually the column cleared the ambush, some 500 British and Indian soldiers together with five times that number of camp followers had perished among the rocks.

As the survivors settled down to their third night in the open, Lady Sale was awakened by a commotion outside her tent. A number of half-frozen sepoys, having burned the greater part of their clothing for the sake of a few minutes' respite from the numbing cold, were endeavouring to force their way into the tent and even beneath the poshteens spread over the women occupants. It was an impossible task, for the thirty women and children were jammed so tight that few could even turn in their sleep. During the night, recorded Lady Sale in her diary, 'Many poor wretches died around the tent.'

The following morning, 9 January, dawned even colder with the promise of another day of misery for the many hundreds who were without food or adequate clothing. 'The snow', wrote Lieutenant Eyre, 'was the only bed for all, and of many, ere morning, it proved the winding sheet.' Many others suffered the agonies of snow blindness. 'My eyes', complained Captain Johnson, 'had become so inflamed from the reflection of the snow that I was nearly blind, and the pain intense.'

Shortly before noon, a British officer held hostage by Akbar Khan brought a proposal to Elphinstone's headquarters to the effect that all married men with families should place themselves under his protection. The General, Akbar pointed out, must have seen from yesterday's events that it was the only way to save the families from certain death at the hands of the Ghilzais. General Elphinstone was reluctant to provide further valuable hostages but he really had little choice in the matter. Few of the women had eaten more than a crust of bread since leaving the cantonment three days before, and one or two were in an advanced state of pregnancy. Among the group taken to a fort some two miles distant where Akbar had set up a temporary residence, were numbered Lady Sale, Lieutenant Eyre and his wife Emily, and several wounded officers, including Captain Mackenzie and Lieutenant Lawrence.

Later that afternoon General Elphinstone ordered the troops to stand to when a party of Afghan horsemen were seen to be massing for an assault. The expected attack did not materialise, which was perhaps fortunate, for the 44th Foot could muster only 200 muskets, and the sepoy regiments 120.

At the Tunghi Taraki Gorge on 10 January, the Ghilzais were again waiting in ambush. This defile, although barely fifty yards long, was so narrow that the leading troops were obliged to negotiate a passage in single file or at best in pairs, and a rain of boulders greeted the 44th and some fifty sowars of the 5th Cavalry. When the main body entered the gorge, a withering fire from the tribesmen occupying the heights quickly turned the narrow defile into a death trap from which few escaped. Major Ewart, commanding the 54th Native Infantry, had both arms broken by jezail slugs and was butchered before he could rejoin the column. Lieutenant Henry Melville, in defending the regimental colours, received five severe wounds yet managed to crawl through the snow to where the 44th were working the one remaining Horse Artillery gun. He was left there at the side of the road and escaped death only by giving a purse of rupees to an Afghan who had known him in cantonments. Melville later joined the hostages at Tezeen after having his wounds dressed personally by Akbar Khan.

There was no reprieve for the sepoys, who having thrown away their muskets sought shelter among the rocks, for the Afghans, seeing no necessity for the expenditure of valuable ammunition, swarmed down the slopes and set to work with their long Khyber knives. The last small remnant of the native infantry regiments bringing up the rear was soon scattered and annihilated.

Late that afternoon when the forward elements staggered into the village of Tezeen, only 240 Europeans and 3000 of the original 12,000 camp followers remained, together with a mere handful of sepoys, of the columns which had left Kabul.

Although no Afghans were to be seen, there could be no rest for the exhausted survivors of Elphinstone's command. Twenty miles to the east there stood a formidable obstacle in the two-mile-long Jagdalak Pass, whose narrow precipitous slabs of basalt provided the perfect site for an ambush by hundreds of Afghan marksmen. The one chance of avoiding this deadly trap lay in slipping through the pass under cover of darkness before the enemy received sufficient warning. It was a ruse which might have succeeded but for the mass of followers.

The night was clear but frosty and the little column made good progress until it neared Barik-ab, when a few random shots were heard. The noise panicked the camp followers who swarmed to the front of the column, obstructing the passage of the 44th and generally creating confusion and delay. When the sky lightened, the column was still ten miles from its objective and there could now be no escape from the tribesmen already massing on the heights.

As the morning progressed, the rearguard under Brigadier Shelton became increasingly involved in skirmishes with Ghilzais, who outnumbered them by seven to one. By mid-afternoon, the survivors, after fighting their way through two feet of snow, had reached the village of Jagdalak, where a halt was called behind the shelter of a crumbling stone wall.

The Army of the Indus was now reduced to 150 men of the 44th, 16 dismounted artillerymen and 25 troopers of the 5th Light Cavalry.

At 5.00 p.m. after the soldiers had assuaged their pangs of hunger (but not their thirst) by swallowing a scanty meal of raw camel's flesh and wild liquorice, Akbar Khan summoned Elphinstone, Shelton and Johnson to his camp with an offer to negotiate with the chiefs. The tribesmen, he told them, were willing to call off their attacks, and the long-awaited food supplies were being made ready. This latter promise proved to be as empty as the others, however, for as Captain Johnson noted later, 'we had the extreme mortification to learn that not one particle of food or water had been tasted by the troops from their arrival to their departure from Jagdulluk.'

The next day talks began in earnest, but it soon became apparent that Akbar Khan had little control over the Ghilzai chiefs, who screamed their hatred of the infidel and demanded that every Feringhee be put to death.

Towards sunset, sporadic firing could be heard from the direction of the Jagdalak Pass and a report was brought to Akbar that the European troops, impatient of delay, were moving off through the pass followed by a swarm of Ghilzais. Elphinstone protested that honour demanded that he should be allowed to return to his men. Salaaming facetiously, Akbar Khan replied that the sahibs were hostages for the safe return of his father at Ludhiana and regrettably it was not permitted that they should be allowed to leave his camp. As they drank refreshing beakers of hot tea in front of a brushwood fire, Elphinstone and the other two officers could only ponder on the caprice of fate which had saved them from destruction at the expense of captivity.

For the officers and men braving the fire from the Afghan marksmen on the heights, there was little choice but to continue their retreat towards Jalalabad. The drystone wall afforded little cover and throughout the day casualties mounted. A determined assault by the Afghans was repulsed by the men of the 44th, who used their bayonets freely, but by nightfall it became obvious to Brigadier Thomas Anquetil that unless his men could pass undetected through the defile they were lost.

At first, with the deep shadows cast by the wall of rock throwing a friendly cloak over the movements of the small band, all went well. Then, at the top of the defile where the track narrowed to little more than a goat path, they found the way ahead blocked by two barriers of prickly 'holly-oak'. This obstruction took some time to remove and gave the Ghilzais the opportunity to collect in force.

A punishing fire from every side threw the milling mass of redcoats into a panic, and they fought among themselves in a frantic attempt to escape yet another death trap. A few of the officers, infected with the general malaise, spurred their horses through the scrimmage of infantry, who, enraged at being ridden over, discharged their muskets at them. When, an hour later, the survivors broke free from the tangle of branches, Brigadier Anquetil was dead and, one by one as their beasts tired, those officers who had escaped the massacre were overtaken by Afghans and ruthlessly cut to pieces.

On 13 January, a little group of no more than twenty made their final stand huddled together on an icy hill near the village of Gandamak. The officers had only their swords and pistols, Sergeant Mulhall and a dozen or so men of the 44th still possessed muskets with perhaps three or four cartridges in their pouches. Each and every one determined to sell his life as dearly as possible.

In a savage hand-to-hand encounter the one-legged Captain William Dodgin of the 44th cut down five Afghans with his sword before being mortally wounded by a ball fired at close range. His men, having expended their last rounds of ammunition, fought on with bayonet and clubbed musket.

Forty years later, the site was still littered with bones bleached white by the sun. 'These remains of a noble regiment', recorded Captain George Younghusband, then writing of another expedition, 'were re-interred so that the hillock no longer shows white as if covered by chalk.'

Only four prisoners were taken by the Afghans: three gunners and Captain Thomas Souter of the 44th, who had wrapped thirty-six square feet of embroidered silk around himself under his poshteen. The tribesmen, mistaking the regimental colours for a rich garment, thought that he was a person of high rank and worth a substantial ransom.

A few hours earlier, Dr William Brydon had found himself at Gandamak, having burst through the barrier of thorns. In company with five others he had taken a route over the hills towards Jalalabad. Now, on the afternoon of the 13th, after several confrontations with hostile villagers, he rode on alone slumped across the neck of a dying pony, to meet the astonished gaze of sentries searching from the ramparts for a sign of Elphinstone's army. An escort of cavalry was sent to bring him in, wounded, exhausted and believing himself to be the sole survivor of the original 16,000.

Colonel Dennie, the garrison commander, with uncanny foresight had earlier declared to a sceptical audience: 'You'll see. Not a soul will escape from Kabul except one man; and he will come to tell us that the rest are destroyed.' His voice, as Brydon was brought in, now sounded like the response to an oracle as he exclaimed, 'Did I not say so? Here comes the messenger.'

Havelock, who was watching Brydon from the wall of the fort, observed that 'he was covered with slight cuts and contusions, and dreadfully exhausted. His first few hasty sentences extinguished all hope in the hearts of the listeners regarding the fortune of the Cabul force. It was evident that it was annihilated.'

Chapter 4

Prisoners of the Amir

The withdrawal of the British force from Kabul had left Shah Shuja with, at best, an uncertain future, safe from an assassin only so long as he remained behind the protective walls of the Bala Hissar, where many of the Afghan elders felt that Akbar Khan was becoming too powerful.

Although it was widely recognised among the chiefs that Shuja-ul-Mulk was the one person most able to mitigate the vengeance that the British were sure to exact, such were the vicissitudes of Afghan politics that the Shah was required to prove his adherence to the faith by promising to lead an army against Sale at Jalalabad. This he was reluctant to do and it came as no surprise when early in April 1842 he was murdered whilst reviewing his troops.

Meanwhile, in India a new Governor-General had replaced Auckland with a firm commitment to a total withdrawal from Afghanistan. First, however, it was important that British prestige in Asia be restored and, although his policy was now in shreds, one of the last duties of Lord Auckland was to despatch a relief column through the Khyber to Jalalabad.

Led by the cautious but astute General George Pollock, the Army of Retribution, as it was somewhat grandly known, did not commit the folly or marching directly into the Pass; instead, by sending out strong patrols to flush the tribesmen from the heights, Pollock secured his flanks against attack and drove the disconcerted Afridis out of the Khyber.

The column reached Jalalabad on 16 April, to discover that Sale and the garrison, far from being in a state of demoralised starvation, had already defeated the Afghans in a battle outside the city and driven in a flock of 500 sheep and goats. Their morale was high and General Pollock was received by the regimental band of the 13th Queen's facetiously playing an old Jacobite lament, 'Eh, But Ye've Been Lang a'Coming'.

There remained the business of freeing the hostages. Public concern at their fate and a desire for revenge obliged Ellenborough to modify his plans for evacuation by giving General Nott at Kandahar the choice of retiring upon the Indus by way of Kabul. It was the loophole for which the two generals had been waiting and each embraced these new instructions with enthusiasm. An agreement was reached that Nott would divide his force, one part retiring through Baluchistan to Sind, whilst the General himself with the greater part advanced on Kabul, with General Pollock marching north in support.

Pollock left Jalalabad on 20 August and with him went Brigadier Sale, elated at the prospect of rescuing his wife and daughter. 'Hurrah!, this is good news,' he signalled to Pollock. 'All here are prepared to meet your wishes to march as light as possible. . . . I am so excited that I can scarce write!'

By adopting the Afghan practice of occupying the heights on either side of his line of march, General Pollock easily swept away the small bands of tribesmen obstructing his advance and he reached the site of the 44th's last stand at Jagdalak on 8 September. The scene made a lasting impression upon Lieutenant John Greenwood, who described it in all its grisly detail.

> The top of the hill was thickly strewed with the bodies of the slain. Some were mere skeletons, whilst others were in better preservation. Their hair was still on their heads, and their features were perfect, although discoloured. . . . a vulture which had been banqueting on them hopped carelessly away to a little distance, lazily flapping his huge wings. . . . As the foul bird gazed listlessly at me, I almost fancied him the genius of destruction gloating over his prey.

The ground over which his men were passing was littered with the bones, and sometimes the frost-preserved bodies, of Elphinstone's ill-fated column, which served to inflame the temper of the troops, who turned to face the increasingly savage attacks of the Ghazis with an eagerness which had been noticeably absent among the broken remnants of the Kabul garrison. Bitter hand-to-hand combats raged the length of the Tezin and Jagdalak Passes until the tribesmen's losses forced them to break off the action.

'There is a ferocity about the Afghans', wrote Greenwood,

which they seem to imbibe with their mother's milk. A soldier . . . saw a Kyberee boy apparently about six years of age with a large knife, which his puny arm had scarcely sufficient strength to wield, engaged in an attempt to hack off the head of a dead sergeant. The young urchin was so completely absorbed in his savage task, that he heeded not the approach of a soldier of the dead man's regiment – who coolly took him up on his bayonet and threw him over the cliff.

This was Akbar Khan's last serious attempt to dispute Pollock's advance. Having lost his artillery and suffered more than a thousand dead, he withdrew northwards, leaving the road to Kabul open to the blue-coated cavalrymen and the redcoats of Pollock's infantry.

When the troops entered the Khurd–Kabul Pass, they became ever more incensed at the sight of the skeletal remains, many still retaining the tattered rags of familiar regimental uniforms. 'I shall never forget the sight I saw here,' confessed Lieutenant Greenwood. 'The poor fellows who had fallen in Elphinstone's retreat, lay together in heaps. Their bodies absolutely choked up the narrow pass, and our men were marching amid a mass of human corruption.'

On 15 September, the British entered Kabul for the second time and made camp on the site of a racecourse laid out by Elphinstone's men in the peaceful days before the uprising. Two days later, Nott arrived with his force from Kandahar. 'The sight of Kabul', wrote Lieutenant George MacMunn, who commanded a Kashmiri mountain battery, 'was a magnificent one . . . streets of tents as far as the eye could see and masses of men in scarlet coats and black shakos paraded and marched in every direction. Brass helmets flashed in the sun, guns peered from every corner of vantage.'

The British were back and with the Union Jack streaming above the ramparts of the Bala Hissar, the Afghan chiefs were understandably fearful of what their enemy would do. In fact retribution on a large scale was not the order of the day. Acting within his jurisdiction and as punishment for the Afghans having exhibited Macnaughten's mutilated corpse there, Nott simply destroyed the Char Chowk bazaar and a punitive column was sent into Kohistan under the command of Brigadier Sale to raze the towns of Istalif and Charikar. There remained for him now just one task to be brought to a successful conclusion: the rescue of Lady Sale and the other hostages.

With the exception of General Elphinstone, the five dozen hostages – men, women and children – were in good health. At first they had been driven along in the wake of the retreating Army of the Indus, an experience which had a profound effect upon all of them. 'It would be impossible for me to describe the feelings with which we pursued our way through the dreadful scenes that awaited us,' wrote Lady Sale.

> The road covered with awfully mangled bodies, all naked: fifty-eight Europeans were counted . . . the natives innumerable. Numbers of camp followers were still alive, frost bitten and starving, some perfectly out of their senses and idiotic. . . . The sight was dreadful, the smell of blood sickening, and the corpses lay so thick it was impossible to look from them, as it required care to guide my horse so as not to tread upon the bodies.

An hour's ride brought the prisoners to a small fort perched on the edge of a precipitous bank of shale where, recorded Vincent Eyre, 'We entered the gate with a mistrust by no means diminished by the ferocious looks of the garrison.' The accommodation into which they were herded – three dark windowless rooms – possessed a wood fire, and despite being half blinded and stifled by the smoke the prisoners considered it luxury indeed compared to the anguish they had suffered in the snow.

On 14 January, the hostages were moved to a village in the Laghman Valley some thirty miles north of Jalalabad. The four-day journey began with the fearful evidence of the previous night's struggle, and the spectacle of small groups of frost-bitten and starving camp followers emerging from fissures in the rockface where they had sought protection from the biting wind. The fate of these poor wretches was a matter for concern to many of the hostages: 'death in its most horrid and protracted form stared them in the face,' wrote Eyre, 'and the agonies of despair were depicted in every countenance.'

An experience very much more pleasing to the eye happened when the party took a northerly direction to climb into regions above the snow line where the cold was intense. Numerous waterfalls, checked in their downward plunge by the frost, now hung suspended in glittering cataracts of ice. 'Under less depressing circumstances,' reflected Eyre, 'it would have called forth exclamations of wonder and admiration.' Eyre also passed within a mile of a plain white building which he was told was the tomb of Lamech, the father of Noah, and a popular place of pilgrimage with the Afghans.

In the early hours of the 17th they arrived at Budiabad, a sizeable mud fort, the property of a relative of Akbar Khan. The English prisoners, men, women and children, were put into five cramped and squalid rooms, none of which possessed any sanitary facilities. 'Although compelled to occupy the same room at night,' wrote Mackenzie, 'the most perfect propriety was observed, the men of the party clearing out early in the morning, and leaving the ladies alone. . . .'

The coarse food irregularly served by their captors, 'boiled rice, mutton boiled to rags and thick cakes of unleavened dough', as Lieutenant Eyre described it, interfered greatly with the prisoners' digestive systems. But of only slightly less consequence than heartburn was the vermin which infested everyone's clothing. 'There are very few of us that are not covered with crawlers,' complained Lady Sale, 'and although my daughter and I have as yet escaped, we are in fear and trembling.' Vincent Eyre thought the ladies remarkably sanguine and was amused to learn that they went so far as to distinguish between lice and fleas by referring to the former as infantry and the latter as light cavalry. The one luxury to which Lady Sale admitted was being able to wash. 'It was rather a painful process, as the cold and glare of the sun on the snow had three times peeled my face, from which the skin came off in strips.'

The hostages were confined for the better part of three months and during that time were allowed to exchange messages with the garrison in Jalalabad, subject only to a primitive form of censorship. The women even received a quantity of chintz and cloth as a gift from Akbar Khan, although Florentia Sale thought it likely that he was being generous at little cost to himself, 'it being part of the plunder of our camp'. Captain George Lawrence, who was entrusted with the unenviable task of distributing food and clothing, found it quite impossible to give satisfaction. 'Mrs Eyre, having but one gown, begged a lady who had trunks full to lend her another. The answer was, she could not spare any!'

In February the bitter cold gave way to unusually mild weather and during the morning of the 19th the hostages were suddenly thrown into a state of panic by a violent rocking of the earth. The indomitable Lady Sale was on the flat roof of the building drying washing. 'For some time I balanced myself as well as I could till I felt the roof giving way. I fortunately succeeded in removing from my position before the roof of our room fell in with a dreadful crash. The roof of the stairs fell in as I descended them, but did me no injury. . . .' She continues her narrative: 'When the earthquake first commenced in the hills in the upper part of the valley, its progress was clearly defined, coming down the valley and throwing up dust like the action of exploding a mine. . . .'

Lady Sale was fortunate to escape with nothing worse than minor cuts and bruises, for the earthquake which struck Budiabad at that time was the worst in the living memory of many of their captors. Thirty miles away at Jalalabad, the shock-wave was such that it demolished in a moment the new defence works it had taken the garrison three months to erect. The mud fort at Budiabad suffered less damage than any in the valley but a cycle of smaller quakes persuaded most of

the prisoners to bivouac in the open. 'All last night', wrote
Lady Sale on 24 February, 'there was a tremulous motion as
of a ship struck by a heavy sea accompanied by the sound of
water breaking against a vessel. At other times we have the
undulatory motion of a snake in the water; and reports like
explosions of gunpowder: but the most uncommon sensation
has been that of a heavy ball as if rolling over our roof, with
a sound of distant thunder.'

Early in April the hostages were once again on the
march, this time to a fort more distant from Jalalabad
and from any attempt which might be made to rescue
them. In the course of the move most of the prisoners
were robbed of their possessions, Lady Sale losing a chest
of drawers. 'My chest of drawers, they took possession of
with great glee,' wrote that lady with justifiable indignation.
'I left some rubbish in them and some small bottles. I hope the
Afghans will try their contents and find them efficacious; one
bottle contained nitric acid, and the other a strong solution of
lunar caustic.'

The rigours of the journey decided the fate of General
Elphinstone, whose poor physical condition – he was suffering from a wound in his side which refused to heal – was no
preparation for almost four months of captivity. On 23 April
he realised that his end was near. 'Moore,' he whispered to
his batman. 'I wish to wash; bring me that blue shirt which
Captain Troup gave me.' His wish was carried out and his shirt
changed. 'Lift up my head, Moore,' the old man requested; 'it
is the last time I shall trouble you.' The batman, in tears, did
as he was bidden and General Elphinstone breathed his last,
worn out by feelings of remorse and the violent dysentery
which racked his body. 'To the very last moment of his being,'
wrote Eyre,

he exhibited a measure of Christian benevolence, patience, and
high-souled fortitude, which gained him the affectionate regard
and admiring esteem of all who witnessed his prolonged sufferings
and his dying struggles, and who regarded him the victim less of
his own faults than of the errors of others, and the unfathomable
designs of a mysterious Providence.

At Tezeen, the hostages were found permanent quarters and they began to enjoy a degree of comfort hitherto denied them. From the contents of letters carried from India by native messengers, they learned of the column led by Major-General George Pollock. They also received an addition to their number, which, wrote Lawrence, occasioned much laughter from Muhammad Akbar when he learned of the birth, saying, 'the more of us the better for him'.

On 23 May the prisoners were moved again, this time westward towards Bamian. In sharp contrast to the retreat of four and a half months earlier, spring flowers were everywhere in bloom and the scent of wild rose filled the air. This pleasant scenario was short-lived, for as they neared the Khurd–Kabul Pass Vincent Eyre and his fellow hostages again encountered the many hundreds of decomposing corpses which marked the path taken by the ill-fated Army of the Indus. 'The defile', recorded that Lieutenant, 'being now absolutely impassable from the stench of dead bodies, we took the direct road towards Cabul, having Alexander the Great's pillar in view nearly the whole way . . . one of the most ancient relics of antiquity in the East and conspicuously situated on the crest of a mountain range which bounds the plain of Cabul on the south east. . . .'

From his elevated platform some 2000 feet above the plain, Eyre marvelled at the panorama spread out beneath him. One hundred miles away, the snow-capped mountains of the Hindu Kush range bounded the horizon. Far below, the Logur River meandered as a thread of silver across the cultivated valley, whilst just discernible was the Bala Hissar, from whose battlements the young Lieutenant occasionally heard the boom of cannon, 'betokening the prolongation of the strife between hostile tribes and ambitious chiefs'.

Smarting from his reversals at the hands of Sale and Pollock, Akbar Khan retired with the officer prisoners to a fort in the Siah Sung hills, arriving there on 25 May. Here, at Aman Koh, two miles from Kabul, the hostages took to wearing native dress in order to avoid attracting attention, for despite enjoying a better relationship with their captors the group had every reason for being cautious. The rich price Europeans brought in the slave markets of Turkestan

was an ever-present temptation to even the most amiable of
their guards. It was possibly just such a notion that occurred
to Lady Sale when she confided to her diary: 'What will now
be our fate seems very uncertain: but I still think he will not
cut our throats; not out of love for us, but because . . . they
could at least obtain a handsome sum as our ransom.'

To freshen their jaded palate and perhaps remind them that
rescue was close at hand, the prisoners received some bottles
of sherry and brandy in June, forwarded from Jalalabad. 'But',
wrote George Lawrence, 'we had been so long without these
stimulants that few of us cared for them.'

By late July the tribesmen had been thrown into such
disarray by the Army of Retribution that many Afghan chiefs,
noting the relentless advance of Pollock and Nott on Kabul,
began to express pro-British sentiments even to the point of
supplying muskets to the hostage officers and allowing them
to levy taxes on a passing caravan of merchants.

Their eventual release, heralded by an officer of Sale's
brigade cantering towards them, came as something of an
anti-climax, the little group having begun to make its own
way towards Kabul on the very day that Nott marched into the
city. The Army of Retribution's timely arrival had ensured the
freedom of '20 officers – half of them wounded, 54 other ranks,
2 civilian clerks, 22 children, 10 ladies, and two soldiers'
wives'. They were all that remained of the Army of the Indus.

Lady Sale no doubt expressed the feelings of them all with
the entry she made that day in her diary: 'It is impossible
to express our feelings on Sale's approach. . . . Happiness, so
long delayed as to be almost unexpected, was actually painful
and accompanied by a choking sensation that could not find
relief in tears.' Her husband was likewise affected, for when
Mackenzie congratulated the Brigadier on the safe return of
his wife and daughter, 'The gallant old man turned towards us
and tried to answer, but his feelings were too strong; he made
a hideous series of grimaces, dug his spurs into his horse and
galloped off as hard as he could.'

Although another son of Shah Shuja was on the throne –
Shah Fath Jang having elected to leave with Pollock's army
– Akbar Khan still hoped to reach an understanding with

the British. Lord Ellenborough, in the pursuit of his policy of non-interference in Afghan politics, would have none of it. On 1 October 1842 he drafted a proclamation at Simla. In part it read:

> Disasters unparalleled in their extent unless by the errors in which they originated, and by the treachery by which they were completed have, in one short campaign, been avenged. . . . The British arms now in possession of Afghanistan will now be withdrawn to the Sutlej. The Governor-General will leave it to the Afghans themselves to create a government amidst the anarchy which is the consequence of their crimes.

Twelve days later, having destroyed most of the city with the exception of the Bala Hissar, Pollock's army marched through the gates of Kabul en route for Peshawar, with Nott bringing up the rear on his handsome chestnut.

The journal which Neville Chamberlain sent to his mother paints a melancholy picture of the cantonments lately occupied by Elphinstone's army:

> We marched one mile past the cantonments and encamped. They were a perfect waste, and where so much money had been spent not a house or barrack or tree left. Everything like its unhappy tenants, destroyed and gone for ever; only here and there a trace of some gallant soldier might be distinguished in a small mound of earth. . . . What scenes of woe and misery were here enacted, and this desolate place is a type of our miserable policy.
>
> The destruction of our political influence is not more complete than of our cantonments. Twenty thousand men and fifteen crores of rupees have been swallowed up all in vain.

Inevitably Pollock's rearguard was harassed in the passes by Ghilzais anxious to speed the departure of the infidels, but no serious opposition was encountered, and on 23 December the army reached Ferozepur. There, Lord Ellenborough and the Commander-in-Chief were waiting to greet the two returning generals beneath a triumphal arch, facetiously described by Lieutenant Greenwood as 'a scaffolding of bamboos resembling a gigantic gallows and covered with strips of yellow, blue, and red rags, meant to represent the gorgeous hues of the east when the orb of day makes its appearance'. He continued: 'Under this arch . . . the whole army marched, and peals of merriment as they did so burst from the soldiers, it was such an absolute caricature of anything triumphal.'

The festivities lasted for a week and were brought to a fitting conclusion in a grand review during which 40,000 men and 100 guns were paraded, after which the various regiments were dispersed to their peacetime stations. There was in fact little enough to celebrate. The British were back at the starting line from which they had launched the invasion of 1839 and had succeeded only in making themselves an object of hatred in Afghanistan, instead of the Russians, who were still advancing in Central Asia. The Indian Army had lost some 15,000 officers and men, to say nothing of the many thousand native traders and camp followers. Fifty thousand camels had perished, whilst the cost to the Treasury amounted to almost £20,000,000. It was true that Russia had relinquished her claim to Khiva and had given Britain a number of satisfactory assurances, but nothing had been gained which could not have been accomplished by diplomatic means, without the necessity for a costly expedition.

In sharp contrast to the euphoria which had marked the enthronement of Shah Shuja, the return of the Army of Retribution to India brought few rewards. Only the Sales, when they returned in late December, were greeted as heroes. Pollock and Nott were virtually ignored. Florentia Sale, after the death of her husband three years later at Mudki, was granted a special pension by the Queen. It is perhaps fitting to record that when Florentia died at Cape Town on 6 July 1853, a simple granite obelisk was erected to mark her tomb, inscribed:

Underneath this stone reposes all that could die of Lady Sale.

The disaster of Kabul had exposed the myth of British invincibility to the Asian world and few politicians now believed that any useful purpose was served by seeking to subjugate the people of Afghanistan.

In January 1843, Dost Muhammad returned from exile to take his seat on the throne for the second time, with the approval of everyone concerned. During his twenty-year reign he more than justified Alexander Burnes' opinion of him as a competent and trustworthy ruler. Dost Muhammad's son, Muhammad Akbar, although frequently in dispute with his father, was made Wazir. He died in 1847 at the early age of twenty-nine, but his memory was kept alive by generations of simple tribesmen in song and poem as a great hero who had defeated the British, sparing only one man from the Kabul garrison to tell the tale.

Chapter 5

The Fanatics

Between Afghanistan and the lower reaches of India lie the flat and largely desert regions of Sind, and to the west the hills and mountains of Baluchistan. Because of their geographical position astride the trade routes from Karachi to Kandahar, these areas were of considerable importance to the East India Company. For the past eleven years since 1830 the Company had enjoyed the right to use the waters of the Indus and its tributaries for purposes of trade, and a treaty with the three Amirs of Sind in 1838 had ensured the safe passage of the Army of the Indus a year later. Now, despite the presence of Colonel Outram, the British Resident at Hyderabad who effectively controlled the foreign policy of Sind, Lord Ellenborough was sceptical of the Amirs' good intentions. The hostile attitude directed against the troops, following the disasters in Afghanistan, and the tyrannous regime of the Amirs convinced Ellenborough, himself irascible and domineering, of the necessity for 'introducing to a brigand infested land, the firm but just administration of the East India Company'.

The man to whom he turned was a hero of the Peninsular War and one of a famous family of brothers. Sixty-year-old General Sir Charles Napier, despite his age and eccentric appearance, possessed an unbounded degree of energy and commanded the unquestioning obedience of his soldiers, whose affectionate nickname for their General was 'Old Fagin', on account of his long unkempt hair, staring eyes and huge hooked nose.

The moral justification for military action against the Amirs did not trouble Napier. 'We have no right to seize Sind,' he wrote after packing for the journey at Poona, 'yet we shall do so, and a very advantageous, humane, and useful piece of rascality it will be.'

The opportunity he sought came in February 1843 when a ferocious attack was made by 8000 Baluchi mercenaries on the Residency, where Colonel Outram and his staff after a resistance of barely four hours' duration were fortunate to escape upriver in two armed steamers.

By the middle of February, Napier's small force of 2600 was marching south towards the capital of Lower Sind and to where the Baluchi army was drawn up at Mianai. Outnumbered by almost eight to one, Napier fought two battles, at Mianai and Hyderabad, and utterly routed the Amirs with their armies of 20,000 men, thus paving the way for the Company's formal annexation of Sind the following month.

Napier was appointed Governor and true to his principle of 'showing a country great kindness after a good thrashing', he set about the business of establishing law and order. 'Oh! if I can do one good thing to serve these poor people where so much blood has been shed in accursed war,' he exclaimed, 'I shall be happy.' He launched into the task of administration with such ferocious energy and honesty that within a short time the natives came to look upon him as a god. Napier's perception of the code of justice was often at variance with the country's established customs. On one occasion he was approached with a request for clemency on behalf of a tribal chief who had murdered a member of his harem simply because he was angry with her. 'Well,' replied Napier, 'I am angry with him and I mean to hang him.'

Napier's administration was of necessity a military one and, when marauding bands of Baluchi tribesmen began to plague the border villages of Sind, small garrisons of sepoys were stationed along the western boundaries to deter the raiders. These forts were, however, largely ineffective and a constant source of irritation to the sepoys from Oude for whom service across the Indus was considered an affront to their caste. So often did the border tribes attack that Napier was eventually forced to mount a punitive expedition across the frontier. It met with little success and the raids continued, reaching a peak in December 1846, when in the deepest penetration yet into British territory 1500 Bugtis carried off 15,000 head of cattle.

January saw the arrival upon the scene of a remarkable character in the personage of Captain John Jacob of the Sind Irregular Horse. The son of a West Country vicar, this thirty-five-year-old who bore a remarkable likeness to Ulysses S. Grant, abandoned completely the idea of forts manned by static troops and initiated instead a programme of co-ordinated cavalry patrols across the desert and into the northern foothills bordering the province. So successful were these patrols, using only two regiments, that Jacob, now the Political Commissioner for Upper Sind, was able to pacify an area the size of England and Wales, and he succeeded Napier as Governor less than two years later.

John Jacob's growing reputation was not wholly dependent upon an efficient policing of border villages. He was also associated with an enlightened programme of irrigation and cultivation, and by 1848 he could state with some justification: 'peace, plenty, and security everywhere prevail in a district where formerly all was terror and disorder.'

Having brought peace and prosperity in his capacity as Governor, Jacob began to open up the country in an energetic programme of road and bridge building. His considerable talents did not go unrecognised and five years after first taking office he was rewarded with an appointment as Commissioner for the whole of Sind, and with promotion to the rank of brigadier-general. In 1857, exhausted in mind and body, he died at the relatively early age of forty-six.

The events which follow, although not strictly part of any narrative of the North-West Frontier, nevertheless serve to explain something of the circumstances in which the British took responsibility for the administration of the Frontier, and also to introduce men of stature who were to play leading roles in the years to come.

North-east of Sind and further along the broad expanse of the Indus lies a vast and barren tract of land known then as the Punjab. Following the death of Ranjit Singh in 1839 the Sikh court became embroiled in a desperate and bloody struggle for the succession to the throne. The Khalsa Army, who as a buffer between the Afghans and northern India had been well drilled by the Company's European officers, had exacted as much as they could from the Punjab Treasury. Now, with the coffers depleted, they turned their attention to the riches to be found on the British side of the border. In November 1845 they poured across the Sutlej at a point twelve miles from the British cantonment at Ferozepore and invaded British India with an army 40,000 strong, heavily supported by artillery. It was the beginning of the first Sikh War.

The challenge was quickly taken up by the Bengal Army, led by Sir Hugh Gough, who narrowly defeated the Sikhs in two bloody battles, Mudki and Ferozeshah, in which both General Sale and the now Major Broadfoot were to meet their end. Early in the following year, Sir Harry Smith won another costly battle at Aliwal and Gough caught the main Sikh force with its back to the Sutlej at Sobraon. Each engagement was a viciously fought affair with the brunt of the fighting falling upon the Queen's regiments and the two Gurkha battalions, but the victory at Sobraon proved decisive and Gough's army went on to occupy the Sikh capital of Lahore.

Resisting calls for annexation, although some Sikh territory was ceded to the East India Company, the new Governor-General, Sir Henry Hardinge, who had succeeded Ellenborough, allowed the Sikhs to retain their independence. There were, however, certain provisos. The Sikh Army was reduced and British garrisons were stationed at strategic points along the frontier, including Peshawar. The new frontier extended to the foothills of the mountain range west of the Indus, where the Pathan tribes still pursued an anarchic way of life undeterred by numerous attempts to impose law and order.

The British Resident at Lahore was Major Henry Lawrence, who some thought bore a strong resemblance to Abraham Lincoln, and to assist him in the task of building an efficient administration he recruited a band of helpers whom he later described as his 'young men'. Among them were his brothers John and George, and such future giants as Herbert Edwardes, John Nicholson, Harry Lumsden and William Hodson.

In order to administer these large areas of tribal territory, a highly mobile and disciplined auxiliary corps was required, skilled in guerrilla tactics and able to skirmish ahead of the slow-moving Company army. Such a body was formed in 1846, and it became known as the Pathan Queen's Own Corps of Guides. The credit for its existence must go to Henry Lawrence, but the responsibility for raising the Corps was that of the twenty-five-year-old Political Agent and Indian Army officer, Harry Lumsden. Part cavalry and part infantry, the Corps of Guides became one of the most prestigious regiments in the Indian Army and fierce was the competition among Pathans, Sikhs, Gurkhas, Moslems and high-caste Hindus to join its khaki-clad ranks.

There was soon to be work in plenty for the Guides and other regiments, for in April 1848 the Sikhs rebelled against Company rule and the second Sikh War began. Reports that the fortress town of Multan had risen, following the murder of two British officers, sent Lieutenant Herbert Edwardes and John Lawrence riding south-west with a handful of Frontier Pathans to investigate. John Nicholson rose from his sickbed in Peshawar and journeyed south to secure the crossing of the Indus at Attock. Despite this prompt action, without the support of the Company's native regiments there was little Lawrence's 'young men' could do to prevent the Sikhs from taking control, and even with the arrival of a division of Queen's and Company's troops to reinforce the Guides, Multan held out until January 1849.

Meanwhile, Gough had crossed the Chenab and on 13 January he met the Sikh Army at Chillianwallah. It was a typical Gough engagement in which the doughty old General spurned the use of artillery, considering it to be unsporting, and after a bloody encounter which lasted from midday until nightfall, the Sikhs, although undefeated, were forced to retreat in company with their Afghan allies.

Because of the appalling casualties suffered by his troops –

some 2500 – Gough was to be replaced by Sir Charles Napier, but before he could be relieved of command the old war-horse atoned for his previous tactical blunders by skilfully attacking a combined Sikh and Afghan force at Gujerat on 21 February, and despite their numerical inferiority his troops completely routed the enemy. The victory at Gujerat brought the second Sikh War to a successful conclusion and added a further 80,000 square miles to British India with the annexation of the Punjab on 30 March 1849.

Much criticism has been levelled at Britain's policy of annexation but it is interesting to note the comments of a Punjab historian, Syad Muhammad Latif. Writing in 1889, he had this to say:

> The country was desolate, and vice, cruelty, extravagance and profligacy overspread its surface. Strife became chronic, and anarchy reared its head everywhere. . . . But is it not now one of the most secure, and has it not become one of the most prosperous and flourishing of the countries of the globe under the fostering care of the English? Witness the gigantic railway projects. . . . Witness the vast public works. . . . Witness the grand schemes of irrigation. . . . Witness the blessings of religious tolerance and freedom enjoyed by the meanest subject . . . a state of things unparalleled in any other country under the sun. . . .

The western borders of the Company's territory now extended along the mountain ranges from Sind to the Hindu Kush – a boundary some 700 miles in length which, as the North-West Frontier, inspired the imagination of countless writers of popular adventure fiction.

The clans which roamed this savage frontier had never accepted the rule of law and there was nothing in the appearance or demeanour of their peoples to suggest that they ever would. Beneath a dirty, loosely wound turban, commented one observer, 'were fixed the eyes of a hawk, the beak of a vulture, and the mouth of a shark'. The Pathan's dress was simple in the extreme, consisting of a long white robe and a pair of cotton pyjamas held in place with a broad cummerbund. He usually wore a tunic festooned with amulets of various kinds and he invariably carried an assortment of knives, flintlock pistols and a razor-sharp tulwar tucked into the cummerbund. The tribesman's most prized possession, however, was a long-barrelled jezail always primed and ready to fire, and cradled over the crook of his arm.

The task of governing these primitive people now became the problem of British India and in particular that of Henry Lawrence and his brother John, who together administered the Company's affairs from Lahore. Their solution was to divide the terrain into six districts, each under a deputy commissioner familiar with the frontier from his army experience. The avowed intention of each administrator was to protect his villages from marauding tribesmen, see that trade prospered and endeavour to maintain law and order along the border. It was no job for the faint-hearted.

There were too many tribes to permit of military dominance and any policy of conciliation was certain to be exploited by the Pathans as a sign of weakness. To lend teeth to the administration an elite force was raised from Sikhs, Pathans, Punjabis and Gurkhas, based upon the successful Corps of Guides. The officers were chosen with care from the Company's regiments, many of whom became part of frontier lore such as Deighton Probyn, Coke, Daly and Sam Browne – the inventor of that well-known belt. This new force, known as the Punjab Irregulars and dressed in grey or rifle-green, was responsible only to the Punjab administration, although supported by regular troops of the Bengal Army.

The cantonment set up at Peshawar by the Corps' first commander, Sir Colin Campbell, was close to the border; conscious of the danger, Sir Colin was careful to restrict the troops to as small an area as was commensurate with their duties, the whole enclosed by a heavily guarded perimeter. Field-Marshal Lord Roberts, in recalling his days there as a junior officer, wrote:

> every house had to be guarded by a chokidar, or watchman, belonging to one of the robber tribes. The maintaining of this watchman was a sort of blackmail, without consenting to which no-one's horses or other property were safe. . . . No-one was

allowed to venture beyond the line of sentries when the sun had set, and even in broad daylight it was not safe to go any distance from the station.

The wisdom of this was effectively demonstrated on one occasion when a lieutenant of the 98th Queen's Regiment was mortally wounded as he strolled with a lady friend close to the guard post.

Outrages such as this were infrequent, but the tribe held responsible was heavily punished by the confiscation of a large part of its grain or livestock, a reluctance to pay the fine being met by the despatch of a punitive column, which drove off the tribesmen's cattle and destroyed their crops.

Occasionally the severity of the punishment meted out shocked Company officials, and a report sent in by a Colonel Bradshaw so enraged Sir Charles Napier that he replied:

It is with surprise and regret that I have seen . . . that villages have been destroyed. . . . I desire to know why a proceeding at variance with humanity and contrary to the usages of civilised warfare, came to be adopted. I disapprove of such cruelties, so unmilitary and so injurious to the discipline and honour of the Army. Should the troops be again called upon to act, you will be pleased to issue orders that war is to be made on men; not upon defenceless women and children, by destroying their habitations and leaving them to perish without shelter. . . .

The serving soldier may have considered Napier out of touch with the realities of frontier warfare; certainly, between the years 1849 and 1857 fifteen similar sorties were mounted all along the frontier, the largest of which – in 1853 against the Afridis – used four cavalry regiments, six battalions of infantry and a team of elephants pulling two batteries of nine-pounder field guns.

An altogether different matter from tribal policing was the question of how best to safeguard the administered districts against Russian or other foreign incursions. The defence of India, to be at all effective, depended upon possession of the passes, which meant deploying troops in eastern Afghanistan, but with the disaster of the first Afghan War still fresh in their minds, this idea – which became known as the 'Forward Policy' – found little support among the diplomats of the 1850s.

In the event the problem was resolved when the Amir of Afghanistan, faced with a Persian claim to Herat, signed a treaty in 1855 with the East India Company. Afghanistan would recognise the Company's tenure of the trans-Indus province, on the understanding that the Company would make no claim to Afghan territory. Each party would be 'the friend of its friends and the enemy of its enemies'. When Persia occupied Herat during the winter of 1856 without firing a shot, the British reacted promptly by sending an expeditionary force from India to the Persian Gulf, which forced the Shah to withdraw from the city.

In January 1857, heartened by Britain's stance against Afghanistan's traditional enemy, Dost Muhammad arrived in Peshawar to ratify formally the treaty of friendship and alliance drawn up the previous March. Recalling the occasion, Harry Lumsden's brother Peter wrote of the Dost:

> that he had the happiest remembrance of his association with the British, yet, he would if he had the power, sweep unbelievers from the face of the earth. 'But, Sahib,' he would say, 'as this cannot be, I must cling to the British to save me from the cursed Persians, and having made an alliance with the British Government, I will keep it faithfully to death.'

When in May of the following year the Sepoy Mutiny began in Meerut, the frontier tribes began to look to their weapons and urged Dost Muhammad to strike for the recovery of Peshawar. But, mindful of the respect shown to him by the British, the Amir chose not to break faith with the Company, leaving its army free to devote its undivided attention to the suppression of the Mutiny at a time when the fate of all northern India hung in the balance.

The aftermath of the Great Mutiny brought about many changes, most importantly the end of Company rule and the transfer of government to the Crown. The sepoy regiments were completely reconstructed and those Europeans serving in the Company's army were obliged to transfer to the Queen's regiments – a fundamental change that precipitated the so-called 'White Mutiny'. The ranks of the Bengal regiments were no longer drawn solely from the Moslems and Hindus of Oude and, as time passed, it became fashionable to brigade British and Gurkha battalions and Royal Artillery batteries, to serve alongside their Indian Army counterparts. The Punjab Irregular Force still exercised a degree of independence, however, and were quickly in action after the Mutiny, punishing the Wazir tribe in 1859 for the murder of a British officer, and the Mahsuds a year later for persistent raiding against peaceful traders.

The greatest trouble in the post-Mutiny period came not from the border tribes but from a sect living at the foothills of the Mahabun mountains north of Attock. These people were known to the Pathans as mujahiddin or Warriors of God. Their ranks had been swollen by mutineers fleeing Bengal and so troublesome did their raids along the Yusafzai frontier become that the Punjab government had to mount an expedition against them in 1858, which drove the sect from their stronghold at Sitana.

Three years later the Fanatics, as they were known to the British, were back in their old haunts and for the next two years resumed their plundering and kidnapping of peaceable native traders virtually unchecked. In October 1863 it became necessary to resort to military-style operations and an expedition numbering 6000 men with nineteen guns under the command of Sir Neville Chamberlain – now a brigadier-general – to destroy this troublesome sect. The General's orders were brief and to the point: 'Saf Karo', or, loosely translated, 'effectively rid the frontier of the chronic cause of the disturbance'.

These instructions were received somewhat reluctantly by Chamberlain, for at forty-three he was racked with malaria and suffering greatly from the effects of wounds sustained in the Indian Mutiny. When it became known that he was to lead the expedition, Chamberlain wrote to his brother Crawford expressing a fervent desire to return to the life of a country gentleman: 'I may escape, but it looks as if my last days in the frontier are to be spent in fatigue and exposure. I have no wish for active service, but want to turn my sword into a shepherd's crook. . . .' He was also experiencing difficulties with the mountain artillery and arrangements for transport. 'I have never before had such trouble or things in so unsatisfactory a state,' he complained to Crawford. 'Carriage, supplies, grain bags, all deficient. Some of our guns, and the five-and-a-half-inch mortars have to be sent back as useless. . . .'

In order to prevent the blue-robed Fanatics from dispersing into the hills, a plan was drawn up to drive the enemy south-east from their new settlement at Malka towards the Indus, where another British force was waiting. Much depended upon the neutrality of the Bunerwal tribe north of the Ambela Pass, who were believed to have little sympathy with the Fanatics, but, unfortunately for Chamberlain and the Ambela column, the tribal chiefs had been influenced by a visit from holy men, who warned the Bunerwals that the real purpose of the expedition was to lay waste and annex their territory.

Now that it seemed likely that an advance upon Malka would be opposed not only by the Bunerwal people but by the entire country, Chamberlain modified his original plan of campaign. Instead of swinging south to attack the Fanatics on their own ground, he decided to restrict operations to seizing and destroying the village occupied by the Sitana Sayyids, who were inciting the Bunerwals to defy British authority, power and prestige.

On 22 October the Ambela Pass was reached and to secure communications with the rear the Commissioner of Peshawar was requested to occupy the lower portion of the pass with his native foot levies. Meanwhile, Chamberlain considered that a halt near the crest of the nine-mile-long gorge was not without advantage. It would oblige the enemy to keep a large body of tribesmen together, with the attendant difficulties of feeding them, and force them to become the attacking party against a position eminently suitable for defence.

In order to guard the main camp, an outer screen of pickets was posted on the slopes protected by sangars, or breastworks of stone and rock. Their field of fire was somewhat restricted by the huge boulders littering the hillside, but any movement of tribesmen towards the picket positions would bring down an instant response from the mountain guns sited on the high ground above the trees.

It was not long before the guns were called into action. 'Fortified by prayer and promises of Paradise, with war drums beating and shrill pipes screeching', 15,000 tribesmen battled fiercely for possession of these vantage points. At times, the sharp bark of artillery and the rattle of small arms reverberated around the rockface to such an extent that it temporarily deafened attacker and defender alike.

The fighting raged day and night for three weeks in a slow-moving pall of black powder, which often reduced visibility to no more than a few feet. If a picket was overwhelmed or forced to withdraw, an immediate counter-attack was mounted to restore the position. In one such sortie, a breastwork at the eastern end of the pass was recaptured by the 5th Gurkhas who, in the words of a contemporary observer, 'followed the enemy some distance, ripping open and be-heading their victims with their kukries'.

A typical night attack by tribesmen is graphically described by Colonel John Ayde:

Suddenly comes a wild shout of Allah! Allah! The matchlocks flash and crack from the shadow of the trees; there is a glitter of whirling sword blades, and a mob of dusky figures rush across the open space and charge almost up to the bayonets. Then comes a flash and a roar, the grape and canister dash up the stones and gravel, and patter among the leaves at close range. The whole line lights up with the fitful flashes of a sharp file-fire, and as the smoke clears off the assailants are nowhere to be seen.

These spirited attacks left the British General in no doubt as to the mood of the tribes and he soon set about strengthening his position. The north side of the pass at a spot where it debouched into the plain was commanded by two steep pinnacles of tumbled rock, one aptly named the Eagle's Nest, the other the Crag. These two strongpoints were fortified with screw guns – so called because the muzzle and breech screwed together – from the Peshawar Mountain Battery and manned by sepoys with Colonel Luther Vaughan commanding the Eagle's Nest and Colonel Wild the Crag.

The Crag was the first to come under attack when at dawn on 26 October a great number of tribesmen rushed down the steep slopes sword in hand, determined to sweep away the infidel intruder. Despite suffering casualties from the enfilading fire of the mountain gun, which had been dragged up the rock slope, the Afghans, making skilful use of the cover afforded by a ridge running up to the position, succeeded in driving out the picket. Three companies of Gurkhas regained the position only after severe hand-to-hand fighting. Later, the Eagle's Nest came under attack, but there the picket, whose only protection was a low wall of loose stones, managed to drive off their assailants at the expense of forty casualties.

The next day a ceasefire was arranged to enable the Bunerwals to bury their dead, and Chamberlain seized the opportunity to persuade the tribal leaders that continued opposition was futile. The headmen were courteous but determined and they made it plain to Chamberlain that despite serious losses they would not give ground to infidels. 'The men of the Bunerwal tribe were brave and worthy foes,' wrote Colonel Ayde. 'The bolder spirits . . . had fully made up their minds to a hand to hand fight. . . .' In the days that followed, it seemed that every tribe between the Indus and Kabul rivers was of a similar mind to the Bunerwals.

On the night of 29/30 October, a group of Malka Fanatics reached the enclosure of the Crag picket without being seen, and launched a ferocious attack just as daylight broke. To Colonel Vaughan and Major Brownlow, the first intimation that something was wrong came as they waited for orders. 'A peculiar and sinister noise struck our ears,' wrote Luther Vaughan, 'followed by the rattle of stones and clouds of dust from the Crag picket. The dust was caused by a confused mass of animals, followers, and a few soldiers coming headlong down the craggy hillside.' The sepoy picket had been swept away before it could fire a shot and it took a determined counter-attack to restore the position. The Fanatics fought with their backs to the rockface and such was the ferocity of this hand-to-hand encounter, in which two Victoria Crosses were won, that the sortie only succeeded at the cost of fifty-four casualties.

On 19 November, Sir Neville Chamberlain signalled for urgent reinforcements but, before any reply was forthcoming, the Crag picket was attacked yet again. It was rapidly gaining a reputation as a place of slaughter and Chamberlain felt that, to hearten the men, he must lead the next assault to regain the position. This he did, and had almost reached the Crag to accompanying cheers from the 71st Highland Light Infantry when he was struck in the forearm by an Afghan bullet. He continued to direct the attack but so troublesome did the wound become that he was ultimately forced to relinquish command to Major-General John Garvock, who arrived with the much-needed reinforcements on 30 November.

About the same time that General Chamberlain received his wound, Lieutenant-Colonel Luther Vaughan was struck by a jezail ball. 'The sensation was as if someone had hit me a most violent blow across both thighs.' Fortunately for Vaughan, although it bled profusely, the wound proved not to be serious and the Colonel led his men for more than a mile in pursuit of the enemy before seeking attention from the surgeon.

The continuous fighting had taken a heavy toll of the Bunerwals, who had borne the brunt of the invasion and now found their limited supplies consumed by tribesmen from distant provinces. As the British prepared to advance on Malka they came forward to pledge their support in any action the British Commander might decide to take against their erstwhile ally, the Fanatics.

At daybreak on 15 December, two columns of infantry supported by a mountain battery took the offensive against a large concentration of tribesmen around the village of Lalu to the east of the Crag. Called upon by the shrill notes of the bugles, 5000 men rose from cover and rushed for the base of a steeply conical hill with loud cheers and extended bayonets.

'Pathans, Seiks, and Goorkas vying with the English

soldiers as to who should first reach the enemy . . .' recalled
Colonel Ayde,

> it took but a few seconds to cross the open ground, and then
> the steep ascent began; our men having to climb from rock to
> rock. . . . Foremost among the many could be distinguished the
> scarlet uniforms of the 101st Fusiliers which steadily breasted
> the mountain and captured the defences in succession at the
> point of the bayonet, the enemy's standards dropping as their
> outworks fell; whilst here and there the prostrate figures of our
> men scattered about the rocks, proved that the hill men were
> striking hard to the last. Nothing, however, could withstand the
> impetuosity of the assaults. . . . ere many minutes had elapsed,
> the conical peak from foot to summit was in the possession of
> British soldiers.

Another attack the following day drove the tribesmen
into the valley where, rather than risk finding their line of
retreat blocked, they began to melt away through the Buner
Pass. Leaving the village of Ambela in flames, the Royal
Fusiliers pursued the Fanatics to within sight of the pass
and then bivouacked for the night.

When daylight came, it was decided that, instead of
maintaining the pursuit, a better purpose would be served
by allowing the Bunerwals, led by British officers, to destroy
the settlement at Malka – 'a handsome valley', Ayde called
it, 'the dwellings recently built of pinewood . . .'.

During the morning of 22 December, Malka was duly
torched and, accompanied by an escort of Guides, a small
party of Bunerwals took part in the destruction of the
Fanatics' camp. Although no resistance was offered by the
villagers, they did not attempt to conceal their feelings. Major
Roberts, who was there in the capacity of an observer, wrote:
'they gathered in knots, scowling and pointing at us, evidently
discussing whether we should or should not be allowed to
return.'

The journey back was not without incident, for the winding
track was lined each side by Pathans spoiling for a fight.
One banner-waving Amazai rushed towards the punitive
party intent on drawing its fire. 'Fortunately for us,' Roberts

continued, 'he was stopped by some of those less inimically disposed; for if he had succeeded in inciting anyone to fire a single shot, the desire for blood would have quickly spread, and in all probability not one of our party would have escaped.'

On the 23rd, the camp in the Ambela Pass was broken up and by Christmas Day Frederick Roberts was reunited with his wife in Peshawar and the regiments were back in the Punjab. Originally planned as a three-week excursion into the hills, the Ambela operation had taken three months with a correspondingly high casualty list: 238 officers and men killed, and 670 wounded.

Considering that barely five years had elapsed since the Mutiny, the sepoys had served their British officers loyally. Many Pathans in the Guides had blood relations among the enemy, but that one soldier noticed his father among a group of rebel tribesmen did not prevent him from taking a pot-shot, the result of which is not recorded. That incident was exceptional, but verbal exchanges between kin were not uncommon and were often attended by humour. 'On the Gurroo mountain our pickets and sentries were constantly within speaking distance of the tribal outposts,' reported Luther Vaughan, 'and were constantly reproached by them for fighting against their kindred, and exhorted to desert and join them. But these appeals were invariably disregarded, and were met by counter-invitations to join our own ranks, and enjoy the benefits of British service.'

Much had yet to be learned of the special skills required in mountain fighting, but the Ambela campaign had, if nothing else, effectively demonstrated that, in taking a position at the point of a bayonet, British and Sikh troops had few equals, whilst the little men from Nepal had proved their worth in the dangerous business of stalking the enemy among the boulders and scree of the high mountain passes.

Chapter 6

The Forward Policy

It was as well that the new Indian Army of the 1860s had been reconstructed on a firm and efficient basis for a threat to British security in the Indian sub-continent had never been more acute. Before the Mutiny, a thousand miles of arid desert had separated Peshawar from Imperial Russia's nearest outpost in Central Asia. Seven years later and with the Crimean War little more than a memory, the armies of Alexander II were again on the march.

In 1864 a report prepared for the Imperial Court drew attention to the necessity for containing the volatile Moslem border tribes if Russia's own frontier was to remain inviolate. Prince Gorchakov, the Russian Foreign Secretary, did not disagree and gave his approval to a cautious advance, but 'caution' was not a word Russia's military leaders found easy to accept.

In June 1865 Tashkent was annexed and the new province of Turkestan created. Three years later, Samarkand went the same way and in the spring of 1869 General Konstantin Kaufmann forced the Amir of Bokhara into a treaty, thus extending Russian influence to the northern boundary of Afghanistan. In 1873 Khiva too fell to General Kaufmann, which so alarmed the Amir, Sher Ali, that an envoy was hastily despatched to Simla with a request for a definitive statement of Britain's intentions in the event of Russian aggression.

Lord Northbrook, a diplomat with a poor understanding of the Asian mind, merely passed to him the terms of an agreement reached by Gladstone's government with the Tsar, in which the Russians had conceded that Afghanistan was outside their sphere of influence. This reply did nothing to allay the Amir's anxiety and in an attempt to resolve his dilemma he decided to negotiate directly with the Russians. However, whilst Russian diplomats were in Kabul, a change of government took place in England. The electorate turned to Disraeli in February 1874 and Lord Salisbury as Secretary of State for India embraced a school of thought that formed no part of Northbrook's political philosophy.

The 'Forward Policy' was the new catchphrase of the Conservative administration and when Salisbury urged him to press Sher Ali into accepting British agents in Herat to monitor events in Central Asia, Northbrook could not agree and resigned. Edward Robert Bulwer-Lytton, the new Governor-General, was a distinguished poet and diplomat with a growing reputation. An enthusiastic supporter of Salisbury's forthright doctrine, he lost no time in advising Sher Ali that it was his intention to send a special envoy 'to discuss with your Highness matters of common interest to our two governments'. Lytton hoped to use this visit as a basis for establishing a friendly relationship with forty-year-old Sher Ali Khan, who had succeeded to the throne after years of civil war following the death of Dost Muhammad in 1863.

Great was Lytton's indignation, then, upon hearing that the Afghan ruler had already conferred with General Nicholai Stolietoff and was of the opinion that, if British agents were to be admitted to his court, Russia would demand the same privilege. Despite the misgivings of his advisers, Lytton reacted to the news by warning Sher Ali that a refusal to receive British officers would be regarded as an unfriendly act which might lead the British government to reconsider its treaty obligations to Afghanistan.

Whatever Sher Ali's reaction, upon one issue the Governor-General was determined. He had long held the view that the chain of mountains marking India's North-West Frontier was an unsatisfactory boundary. Now, mindful of this latest Russian threat to the Khyber and Bolan Passes, he suggested to Disraeli that far greater security could be achieved by stationing troops on the northern slopes of the Hindu Kush. Lytton did not go so far as to advocate the breakup of Afghanistan but sought rather to offset a possible Russian advantage by demanding the right to install political observers in the cities of Kabul and Herat.

Parliament duly gave its approval and on 14 August 1878 Sher Ali was informed that a British envoy was on his way to Kabul for friendly discussions concerning a matter of the greatest importance. Lytton's arrogant proposal was ignored by the Amir and when Sir Neville Chamberlain, leading the British Mission, reached Jamrud at the head of the Khyber on 21 September, he was bluntly told that the road ahead was blocked by Afghans and any attempt to proceed further would be opposed by force. That same evening, he sent a signal to the Governor-General: 'The first act has been played out; and I do not think that any impartial looker-on can consider any other course has been left open to us consistent with dignity than to openly break with the Amir.'

The Governor-General reacted in predictable fashion by writing to the Secretary of State claiming that refusing an audience to Chamberlain whilst welcoming the presence of a Russian diplomat 'has deprived the Amir of all claim upon our further forbearance'. The Government of India, he continued, proposed to take the following measures: first, the issue of a manifesto defining the cause of offence; second, the expulsion of the Afghans holding the Khyber Pass; and, thirdly, the mobilisation of a column to advance on Kandahar.

Somewhat apprehensively, Disraeli's Cabinet gave its approval and on 2 November Lord Lytton sent an ultimatum to the Amir demanding an apology and the acceptance of Chamberlain's Mission in Kabul. Otherwise British troops would cross into Afghanistan. However, Sher Ali, as Neville Chamberlain so colourfully expressed it, 'had no more intention of apologising than of turning Christian and applying for a Bishopric', and at dawn on the 21st three columns crossed the border into Afghanistan. The second Afghan War had begun.

The invasion of 1878, unlike the disastrous undertaking of thirty-nine years before, was to be made on three fronts, the objective being the pacification of the important Frontier areas and the destruction of the Amir's army rather than his removal from the throne. In the south, 12,000 well-equipped troops led by Major-General Sir Donald Stewart marched unopposed from their base at Quetta to Kandahar. In the north, a second column 10,000 strong under the command of the one-armed Major-General Sir Samuel Browne VC marched from Peshawar through the Khyber to Jalalabad, whilst a third was ordered into the Kurram Valley to form a central front.

The latter and smallest of the three columns comprised 6600 men with eighteen guns and was commanded by forty-six-year-old Frederick Sleigh Roberts VC, now a major-general and described by one historian as 'a diminutive, red-faced, bandy-legged gamecock with the bearing of a lightning rod'. His courage during the Indian Mutiny had earned for him the Victoria Cross and he was not unfamiliar with the ways of the Frontier since his father had commanded a brigade in the first Afghan War. Command in the field was a new experience for Roberts, but a desire for success together with outstanding leadership qualities were to single him out as being amongst the most talented generals of the Victorian age.

The three columns, totalling some 29,000 troops and 140 guns, greatly exceeded the numbers thought sufficient by Lord Lytton, whose faith in the new breech-loading rifle led him to believe that the expedition should have been limited to a single division. His argument in favour of saving the Treasury the considerable extra cost had been vehemently opposed by Sir Neville Chamberlain. The British force, Chamberlain pointed out, might easily meet with as many as 15,000 Afghan regular troops with artillery, in addition to tribal lashkars. Furthermore, the column's strength was almost certainly to be reduced by sickness and the necessity of guarding the ever-lengthening lines of communication. It was a point of view which gained little sympathy from such an advocate of British imperialism as Lord Lytton, and the Governor-General, although giving way on the issue, later felt moved to write: 'Our Commander-in-Chief and his whole Staff are a coagulation of mediocrities and inveterately obstinate stupidities, and they have weighed upon me and upon India like a horrible incubus throughout the war.'

This bickering between the generals and the cost-conscious administrators could only result in a compromise solution at the expense of the troops' welfare. Cuts in medical and commissariat services had the inevitable result of Stewart's Kandahar Field Force experiencing the illness and privations of their predecessors. Nevertheless, the column made steady progress throughout December and when it arrived in Kandahar on 8 January 1879 it discovered that the Afghan garrison had retired in favour of merchants who were fully cognisant of the profits to be made from feeding an army.

On the other two fronts the troops had not been as fortunate. Sir Samuel Browne's column had passed through the Khyber without loss but were then faced with the formidable task of taking the fort of Ali Masjid. There, a defiant Faiz Muhammad awaited events with 3000 regular infantry, 200 cavalry, several cannon and 600 tribesmen massed in the neighbouring hills. The fortress, built on a hill 5000 feet above the pass with strongpoints on either side, was subjected to an artillery bombardment which seemingly left the defenders untouched. Despite the dangers this presented, the bugles sounded the advance and the 81st Regiment, with the 14th Sikhs in support, moved forward in skirmishing order and the fighting began in earnest.

Browne, who had earlier sent one of his brigades on a wide turning movement designed to surprise the enemy's rear, now launched his infantry in a frontal assault. Throughout that frosty November day, British troops battled their way up the lower slopes but when darkness fell and brought to an end earlier hopes of success they were recalled. General Browne spent an uncomfortable night having heard nothing from his two flanking brigades, and with his infantry, cavalry and artillery scattered and confused at the foot of the Khyber.

Fortunately for Browne, just as dawn was beginning to silhouette the range of mountains, a Kashmiri merchant cautiously approached the pickets at the lower end of the pass. He had been confined in the fortress for the past few

days, he confessed, 'but risked a bullet to come over and tell
the Sahibs that there was nobody now inside the fortress'.
The Afghans, fearing encirclement, had silently abandoned
their defence works and retired upon Jalalabad.

The third column, led by Roberts, advanced rapidly from
the Indian side of the frontier and was soon in possession of
the whole of the Kurram Valley to the relief of its inhabitants,
who had been suffering from the attentions of plundering
tribesmen. This cheerless boulder-strewn wilderness was
unfamiliar territory to the British and they soon discovered
that, whilst the road was suitable for camels, it was totally
unsuited to the passage of guns and heavy transport.

It was not long before they also discovered that the way
ahead was blocked by Afghan troops firmly ensconced along
the summit of a ridge overlooking a narrow pass at Peiwar
Kotal, 9000 feet above sea level. The 5000-strong force was
commanded by Karim Khan, one of the Amir's more capable
generals, and a rain of shot from his six-pounder guns forced
Roberts' troops into an undignified flight from their bivouac
area.

A frontal attack was out of the question but an examination of the cedar-lined heights through a spy-glass revealed
a possible route along a valley which could turn the Afghan
flank. It was then that Roberts demonstrated a grasp of
Frontier warfare that showed he had little to learn from
his adversary. Leaving two battalions of infantry and two
squadrons of cavalry to distract attention from the real point
of attack, Roberts led a thousand men over the frost-hardened
ground on a night march designed to outflank and catch the
enemy by surprise.

Snow was falling and it was bitterly cold for the British and
Indian soldiers, who had been issued with two blankets and,
for the first time, wore puttees, or leg bandages. 'For either
mounted men or infantry soldiers they are a most useful,
warm, and neat looking dress,' observed Colonel Colquhoun,
'but the only objection is that they take a little time to put
on. Nearly everyone, officers and men, wore them through
the campaign.'

The path from the village to the Kotal was steep, and

baggage mules frequently lost their footing on the loose shale. The difficulties in following a winding track in the dark caused a mountain battery of the Royal Horse Artillery and the 2nd Punjab Infantry to take a wrong turning. Fortunately, they were located before they had strayed too far. As the rest of the column neared the enemy position, two rifle shots fired by disloyal Pathans who were reluctant to fight against their co-religionists almost betrayed its presence, but, astonishingly, although an Afghan guard heard the noise and alerted his commander, no action was taken by Karim Khan.

With the first grey streaks of dawn, the leading Gurkha battalion, closely followed by the 72nd Highlanders, reached the foot of the Spingawai Kotal. Skilfully they picked a way through an obstruction of loose boulders which littered the lower slope and made a concerted rush for the first sangar, where after a brief exchange of fire they soon had the defenders in full flight westward. There was no halting the Highlanders and, guided by the flashes from the tribesmen's jezails, the leading company took a second sangar and by 7.30 a.m., having carried the length of the Spingawai Kotal, Roberts was able to heliograph the camp 2500 feet below to commence the frontal attack. This assault, despite the difficulties of a thick pine forest, was equally successful and by midday Frederick Roberts was in a position to threaten the enemy's rear.

The Royal Horse Artillery had by now moved up to the Peiwar Kotal where they began to shell the Afghan camp, clearly visible in the valley below. The range was short and the shells, arriving with an ear-splitting crack in what was regarded by the Afghans as a safe area, turned alarm into panic. Soon the camp was shrouded in smoke. Tents were enveloped in flames, camels stampeded and the drivers, together with the camp guards, made off as fast as their legs could carry them. The 8th King's Regiment, which had worked its way along the ridge of the Peiwar Kotal, boasted a fair share of marksmen who put their skill to deadly effect by shooting down the Afghan gunners from a range of 800 yards. The Afghans, dismayed at the spectacle of their camp in flames, had no heart for a fight and, by the early afternoon, the key position together with eighteen enemy guns was in British hands.

'The sight which presented itself was a curious one,' reported Colonel Colquhoun. 'The Kotal was quite deserted by the enemy, who had evidently fled in a hurry, leaving their tents standing, food ready cooked, and everything that they had. The gunners had even left their silver-mounted brass helmets and forage caps.' Another and equally interesting find was a document, allegedly from Sher Ali, calling for jihad and promising Paradise to those who died and everlasting torment to all who shunned it. 'Wage a holy war on behalf of God and his Prophet, with your property and your lives,' ran the edict. 'Let the rich equip the poor. Let all die for the holy cause. A foreign nation, without cause or the slightest provocation, has made up its mind to invade our country and conquer it. . . .'

That night there were 20° of frost, but as he lay on the ground with his men an elated Roberts slept as soundly 'as I had ever done in the most luxurious of quarters and I think others did the same . . . no-one I could hear of suffered from that night's exposure.'

Next morning the column resumed its march and by 9 December a satisfactory route had been reconnoitred to the top of the Shutargardan Pass. All that stood between them and the road to Kabul was a rugged and dangerous descent on the other side of the pass. To have secured the entire Khost region, at the expense of only two officers and eighteen men killed and three officers and seventy-five men wounded, was no mean achievement, and it drew a congratulatory message from Queen Victoria and a KCB for General Roberts. It also earned him the unanimous thanks of both Houses of Parliament.

The way to Kabul was now open and when it became obvious to the Afghans that it could not be defended, Sher Ali appealed to the Russian Mission for military assistance. General Kaufmann had no intention of being drawn into a war with the British, however, and, pointing out that the passes through the Hindu Kush were blocked by snow, he urged the Amir to settle for the most favourable terms he could get.

A disappointed Sher Ali had one last card to play and on 13 December he left Kabul for Russian-occupied Turkestan with the departing members of the Russian Mission. His intention was to reach St Petersburg and there ask the Tsar to plead his case before the Congress of Berlin. Unfortunately for the Amir, his expectations were to prove unduly optimistic for, although Kaufmann invited him to Tashkent, he made it clear to Sher Ali that approval for a continuation of the journey to St Petersburg had not been received.

It was a bitter blow to the Amir's self-esteem which, more than anything else, emphasised the hopelessness of his cause. Giving way to despair, Sher Ali refused all food and medicine and died on 21 February 1879 from gangrene without ever setting foot in Russia.

Yakub Khan, who had assumed power as Regent, decided to sue for peace. Apprehensive at the progress made by the British through his country, he drafted a conciliatory letter to Major Sir Louis Cavagnari – a Franco-Irishman who was Browne's chief Political Officer – informing him of the death of Sher Ali and adding 'as my exalted father was an ancient friend of the British government, I have out of friendship sent you this intimation.'

Lytton, whose expressed opinion of Yakub Khan was 'a very slippery customer whom we shall be well rid of if he disappears', was nevertheless prepared to negotiate a peace. He had little choice. Haunted by the spectre of the 1839 campaign, Parliament was in disarray. The Liberal opposition led by Gladstone was clamouring for Disraeli's head. They held the view that, in approving the action taken by the Governor-General, the Prime Minister had only succeeded in alienating Britain's best ally against the Russian menace. The Church also voiced its unease and, from the pulpit of St Paul's Cathedral, the Dean reminded the congregation that 'those who sow the wind of aggressive ambition, must look to reap the whirlwind of disaster'.

On 26 May a treaty was drawn up at Gandamak close to the spot where the men of the 44th had made their last stand in the retreat of 1842. It was signed by Yakub Khan and by Cavagnari as the representative of Lord Lytton. Under the terms of the treaty Yakub Khan agreed to accept British guidance of Afghanistan's foreign affairs, the continuation of British control of the Kurram Valley, and the presence of accredited British officers in Kabul. In return, he was to be recognised as Amir and receive an annual subsidy of six lakhs of rupees and the promise of military support against foreign aggression. The Khyber and Kandahar columns were to withdraw just as soon as an outbreak of cholera in the Peshawar Valley ended and climatic conditions allowed.

The British Resident in Kabul was to be Major Cavagnari, an officer of some thirteen years' frontier experience, and it fell to the newly knighted Sir Frederick Sleigh Roberts to escort him part of the way to the Shutargardan Pass. That evening at dinner, Roberts was called upon to propose a toast to the health of Cavagnari and the others in the Mission. 'Somehow,' he wrote, 'I did not feel equal to the task; I was so thoroughly depressed, and my mind was filled with such gloomy forebodings as to the fate of these fine fellows, that I could not utter a word.'

On 16 July as they rode together, Cavagnari noticed a solitary magpie. Reminding Roberts of the old adage concerning that species, 'One for sorrow, two for joy', he asked Roberts not to mention it to Lady Cavagnari. When they parted with a handshake after meeting the Afghans sent to escort the Mission to Kabul, Roberts was conscious of a strong feeling that he would never see the envoy again.

Cavagnari entered Kabul on the 24th with his assistant William Jenkyns, accompanied by Surgeon Ambrose Kelly and a detachment of Guides commanded by Lieutenant Walter Hamilton VC. The Guides' reputation as a fighting force was unique among the Frontier regiments but Cavagnari's escort numbered no more than twenty-five troopers and fifty sepoys of the Corps of Guides, a woefully inadequate force for such a hazardous undertaking.

Chapter 7

'These Dogs Do Bite'

For Sir Louis Cavagnari and his companions, as they enjoyed the summer months of 1879, there was no hint of the outbreak of violence to come with its tragic consequences. Indeed, in his July signal to Simla, Cavagnari had commented upon the respectful and civil manner of his reception in Kabul:

> Embassy entered the city and received most brilliant reception. Four miles from city sirdars with some cavalry and two elephants met us.
>
> We proceeded on the elephants with a large escort of cavalry. Outside the city two batteries of artillery and nine regiments of infantry were drawn up in column . . . their bands playing the British National Anthem. Large crowd assembled and was orderly and respectful. Amir enquired after Viceroy's health and Queen and Royal Family. Amir's demeanour was most friendly.

The telegraph line had only been recently completed between Peshawar and Kabul and Cavagnari used it regularly to send reports to Lytton, almost all of which were uniformly dull and concerned with the mundane rather than useful political intelligence. 'Cholera has occurred during the last four days,' he telegraphed; and in another report, 'Violent earthquake last night.' In his only reference to the new Amir, the envoy signalled: 'Notwithstanding all people say against him, I personally believe Yakub Khan will turn out to be a very good ally, and that we shall be able to keep him to his engagements.'

Events were soon to prove him wrong, for the Resident's interference in native affairs and the freedom with which he had distributed money, drove the headmen to complain to Yakub Khan: 'No longer is the Amir King of Afghanistan. Cavagnari is King.' Not knowing quite what to do, Yakub, who bitterly resented the presence of Cavagnari's Mission, took council with his sirdars. 'Tomorrow the Herati regiments come for their pay,' they told him. 'Send them to Cavagnari!'

Thus the scene was set for the overthrow of the Resident with the arrival at the end of August of two regiments from Herat, who went into cantonments at Sherpur. Their boast of never having been beaten by infidels, and their swaggering gait in the streets, led a retired Afghan Guides officer at that time in Kabul to warn the Resident of impending trouble.

'Never fear,' replied Cavagnari in the Persian idiom. 'Keep up your heart, dogs that bark don't bite!'

'But these dogs do bite,' persisted the Ressaldar. 'Sahib, the Residency is in great danger.'

Cavagnari, however, refused to listen. In a characteristic reply, he dismissed the warning with the words: 'They can only kill the three or four of us here, and our deaths will be avenged.'

On 2 September he telegraphed Lytton at Peshawar. 'All well in the Kabul Embassy.' That signal was his last.

The next day the Herati regiments paraded at the Bala Hissar to receive three months' wage arrears, only to discover that, due to revenues not being collected, they were to be given only one month's pay. In the uproar which followed a voice was heard suggesting that the British were rich and that gold in plenty was to be found in the house of the Feringhees. As the tension mounted and an angry crowd milled about the Residency, Cavagnari appeared on the balcony. He tried to reason with them. They were soldiers of the Amir, he argued, and their pay was no concern of the British government. The escort of Guides drawn up on the square for drill had a calming effect upon the crowd and, although a shot was fired, it seemed that the threat of violence had receded. The Herati troops could be seen forming up in a loose semblance of order before marching off to their cantonment, but Cavagnari must have known that it would not be long before they would return bearing arms.

The Residency was ill suited to the purpose of defence. Its roof was overlooked by several taller houses nearby and only one of its buildings possessed a protective parapet. Hamilton did his best to organise a defence during this respite, but without reinforcements it was obvious that the Mission could not hold out for long. There remained just one faint hope of rescue and Cavagnari immediately despatched a sepoy to Yakub Khan with a request for assistance. He then took up a position on the roof armed with a breech-loading Martini–Henry rifle.

He was soon in action for within the hour 2000 Heratis had invaded the compound and a ragged but persistent barrage of musket shots began to raise puffs of dust and splinters from the Residency walls and roof. Cavagnari was the first casualty, struck in the head by a ball which ricocheted from a stone wall. Half blinded from the blood which poured from a deep gash across his scalp, he nevertheless mustered enough strength to stagger from his post and lead a bayonet charge against a group of tribesmen who had successfully scaled the wall. It was the envoy's last defiant act. In a state of collapse from his head wound, Cavagnari was helped back to a cot inside the building, and there he later died.

A second message was sent to Yakub Khan and this time the Amir responded by sending his young son and a mullah escorted by a troop of Afghan cavalry. The mullah's plea for the mob to disperse was greeted with jeers and a shower of stones. The Afghans were dragged from their horses, and a copy of the Koran was kicked out of the mullah's hand. Wisely, perhaps, the party decided that discretion was the better part of valour and promptly retreated.

By this time the main building was ablaze and Hamilton could do nothing to quench the flames. A quarter of his men were casualties and by midday only three Britons and thirty native Guides were fit enough to maintain an increasingly hopeless resistance. A last appeal was made to Yakub Khan. The Uzbek Tartar who carried Lieutenant Hamilton's note made no attempt to conceal himself but, although he reached the palace unscathed, it was only to learn that the Amir was powerless to help.

At the Residency, drifting clouds of smoke masked the approach of two field pieces which were brought into action by the rioting Heratis to shell the compound from point-blank range. The end was in sight and Hamilton called for a sortie against the guns. Led by the twenty-year-old subaltern, a dozen Guides joined by Surgeon Kelly and the Political Assistant Jenkyns dashed across the compound and threw open the gate.

The Afghans were caught by surprise and the storming party reached the guns without losing a man. Clubbing and hacking at the gunners with a fury born of desperation, they managed to turn one gun-carriage and begin the laborious haul back to the main gate. The victory was short-lived, for a renewed outbreak of musketry brought down Kelly and six sepoys. Hamilton, Jenkyns and the surviving six Guides were forced to abandon their prize and fall back on the Residency.

For Lieutenant Hamilton VC the setback was merely temporary and the Guides had barely time in which to catch their breath before he again urged upon them the necessity for spiking the guns. A jezail slug tore away most of Jenkyns' head before he had covered twenty feet, but the others stumbled through a pall of acrid smoke to reach the abandoned gun, only to be forced back again by sheer weight of numbers.

Inside the Residency, flames were threatening to consume the defenders and, when the burning timbers collapsed around them, Hamilton and the twenty sepoys – all that remained of Cavagnari's escort – retired into the building's brick bathhouse. They did not stay long. Under Hamilton's inspired leadership the men charged out yet again and, this time, three Guides managed to hitch their belts to the cumbersome gun-carriage. For a few seconds the Heratis stood as though paralysed at the audacity of the tiny assault force, then with a scream of rage the tribesmen rushed forward. Exhorting his men to redouble their efforts to get the gun moving, Hamilton advanced towards the oncoming mob, emptying his revolvers into them before being engulfed in a wave of fanatical swordsmen. The diversion created by his courageous act enabled the five survivors to rejoin their comrades in the Residency, but the battle was now in its closing stages. For eight hours, seven dozen Guides had fought gallantly against greatly superior odds as testified by the bodies of six hundred tribesmen.

When it became clear to the Heratis that all the Europeans were dead, the Moslems among the Guides were given a choice of returning to their homes. The offer was rejected with contempt by Jemadar Jewand Singh, who replied that they would come out but not to surrender. At his signal, the gallant dozen sallied forth, resolved to sell their lives as dearly as possible. Within five minutes they were all dead. Jemadar Jewand Singh was the last to fall, having accounted for eight of his opponents.

The courage of the Guides did not go unrecognised. Lieutenant Hamilton received the posthumous award of a second Victoria Cross, and the widows and orphans of the dead Guides were awarded double pensions. In the National Army Museum, Chelsea, there is a life-size plaster cast of Lieutenant Walter Richard Pollock Hamilton VC. The casting, presented to the Museum by the Royal Dublin Society, depicts Hamilton's last sortie against the Heratis whilst his men attempted to retrieve the gun-carriage. It is a truly inspiring work of art, commemorating also Sir Louis Cavagnari, his assistant William Jenkyns, Surgeon Ambrose Kelly and the seventy-five men of the Queen's Own Corps of Guides who died with them.

News of the tragedy reached India on 5 September and Roberts, then in Simla, made ready to lead an avenging army on Kabul with orders from the Governor-General to punish all concerned 'in a manner most likely to impress the populace'. Retribution rather than justice was to be the order of the day. Lord Lytton had considered putting Kabul to the torch but had abandoned the idea as impractical, 'the houses being largely built of non combustible materials'.

Roberts' newly formed Kabul Field Force, which was to avenge Cavagnari, consisted of four cavalry regiments, two infantry brigades and two mountain batteries of four guns each – in all, some 6500 men, and 'none too large for the work before it', he wrote. A grave shortage of pack animals and experienced transport officers prevented Roberts from moving with anything like the speed necessary to achieve surprise.

Indeed, before he could move at all, two court officials arrived with a message from their master. If the General so wished, he could spare his men the arduous sixty-mile march through hostile country and leave it to the Afghan authorities to disarm the regular troops and punish the offenders. The General, however, had no wish to delay the column. He had received reports indicating that Yakub Khan was even then inciting the frontier Ghilzais against him and he sent the envoys back with a reply that could leave the Amir in no doubt as to the mood of the Indian government: 'so long as the bodies of those officers and men remain unburied or uncared for in Kabul, I do not believe the English people will ever be satisfied. They will require the advance of a British force, and the adequate punishment of the crime. . . .' Roberts also hinted that two other columns, one from Kandahar and the other from the Khyber, had already marched for Kabul.

On 30 September, his forty-eighth birthday, Roberts raised the flag and, with an escort of cavalry, advanced towards the Shutargardan Pass. When the top of the mist-enshrouded gorge was reached, an unexpected and embarrassing situation confronted him. The Amir, accompanied by his son and Daoud Shar, the Afghan Commander-in-Chief, were waiting in the British camp at Kushi. At the camp, in a valley known to the Afghans as the Land of Delight, thirty-two-year-old Yakub Khan expressed his regret at Cavagnari's murder and bewailed his inability to prevent it. He begged Roberts to halt his march, explaining that he had left the ladies of the court in the Bala Hissar with only a small escort to guard them and that he no longer had any power, having been deposed by his own mutinous troops.

'What his true reasons for this step may have been we never knew,' wrote Major Mitford, '. . . certainly not the one he gave, for no Afghan ever told the truth intentionally!' Sir Frederick Roberts was certainly not impressed by the

Amir's plea – or by his almost chinless appearance. 'He was possessed moreover of a very shifty eye and I felt that his appearance tallied exactly with the double dealing that had been imputed to him.' Roberts suspected that Yakub's real motive was to delay his advance and to notify the Ghilzais of the column's strength and the tactics to be employed – a suspicion which seemed well founded when Scouts brought him the news that thirteen regiments of Afghan regular troops and a tribal lashkar were massing along a range of hills at Charasia, twelve miles south of Kabul. Since the British were outnumbered four to one, there was every need for haste and on 6 October Roberts adopted the plan he had employed with considerable success at Piewar Kotal.

The bulk of the Afghan force was deployed along a jagged ridge almost 1000 feet above the advancing British Infantry. This advantage was soon lost however, for the Seaforth Highlanders were adept at rock climbing and their fire discipline was a decisive factor in the running fight that followed. Reginald Mitford watched the advance of the 92nd, which, he reported, was a splendid sight.

> The dark green kilts went up the steep rocky hillside at a fine rate though one would occasionally drop and roll several feet down the slope, showing that the rattling fire kept up by the enemy was not all show. Both sides took advantage of every available atom of cover, but still the kilts pressed on and up, and it was altogether as pretty a piece of Light Infantry drill as could well be seen.

Roberts, watching anxiously through his glasses, was particularly taken by the action of one man 'pushing up the precipitous hillside considerably in advance of everyone else, and apparently utterly regardless of the shower of bullets falling about him'. Subsequent enquiry revealed him to be one Hector Macdonald, Colour-Sergeant of the 92nd, and a man destined to be commissioned in the field and eventually progress to the exalted rank of major-general.

The bugles sounded a general advance and, confronted with a bayonet charge by Highlanders, Gurkhas and Pathan hillmen from the Punjab Frontier Force, the enemy line

wavered and finally broke. By mid-afternoon the Afghan
Army had been routed, leaving behind twelve guns and
several hundred corpses. British losses amounted to twenty
killed and sixty-seven wounded, remarkably light considering
the difficult terrain. Gatling guns had been in action for the
first time but, since one of the two employed by Roberts
jammed after only ten rounds, their contribution to his
successful action was minimal.

Yakub Khan had followed the progress of the battle
with great interest, questioning everyone on his interpretation of what he had observed. Roberts, who had been
acutely embarrassed by the Amir's presence, could not resist
a moment of gloating over his victory: 'it was, without doubt,
a trying moment for him, and a terrible disappointment,' he
wrote. 'But he received the news with Asiatic calmness and
without the smallest sign of mortification, merely requesting
my Aide-de-Camp to assure me that, as my enemies were his
enemies, he rejoiced at my victory.'

On 12 October 1879, General Roberts made a formal
entry into Kabul accompanied by a thoroughly chastened
Yakub Khan, who had earlier announced his intention to
abdicate. 'His life had been most miserable,' he confessed to
Roberts, 'and he would rather become a grass cutter in the
English camp than the Ruler of Afghanistan.'

The passage of the Kabul Field Force through the streets
to the Bala Hissar was a compliment to the martial and work-
manlike appearance of the troops – from the scarlet tunics of
the Punjab Infantry to the bottle-green of the 5th Gurkhas.
The Gordons, resplendent in green plaid kilts and pipe-clayed
cross-belts, were followed by the Seaforth Highlanders in
trews, then came the plumed helmets, red turbans and red
and gold pennons of the 14th Bengal Lancers and the Punjab
cavalry. Kabul's population of 50,000 was suitably impressed.
'This has been a very eventful day, and now I am really King
of Cabul,' wrote Roberts to his wife. 'It's not a kingdom I covet
and I shall be right glad to get out of it, but the occasion seemed
worthy of a glass of champagne.'

Naturally, the centre of interest was the scene of the
3 September massacre. 'Our first view of the Residency',

reported Howard Hensman, special correspondent for the *Daily News*,

> was of the rear wall, still intact, but blackened on the top where the smoke from the burning ruins had swept across. At each angle where the side walls joined were seen the loopholes from which the fire of the little force on the roof had been directed against the overwhelming numbers attacking them. Every square foot round these loopholes was pitted with bullet marks, the balls having cut deeply into the hard mud plaster.

At the Bala Hissar the General visited the scene of the Embassy's defence, where he found the floors and walls of the Residency stained with the blood of the ill-fated Mission members and, among the ashes of a fire, a heap of human bones. 'I had a careful but unsuccessful search made for the bodies of our friends,' Roberts confirmed. 'It may be imagined how British soldiers' hearts burned within them at such a sight, and how difficult it was to suppress feelings of hatred and animosity towards the perpetrators of such a dastardly crime.'

Roberts' mission was to punish the guilty and no time was lost in putting this into effect. The Mayor of Kabul and a dozen of the mutinous Heratis were summarily hanged after a court of enquiry had established that they had paraded Cavagnari's head through the city streets, and notice of arrest was given for all those who had borne arms against the British since the beginning of September. Among those arrested were the Wazir and the Mustaufi, who were given to understand that they would remain in custody until an investigation established their innocence.

During the morning of the 16th, a series of explosions destroyed most of the Kabul arsenal. Thousands of cartridges and six tons of gunpowder stored in the building had ignited. The Afghans accused the occupying force of wanton destruction, whilst the British, who had suffered some twenty casualties in the blast, blamed Afghan insurgents. The true cause of the explosion was never determined. Hensman thought it likely to have been the result of a careless action:

an Engineer officer had been seen entering the building with a pipe clenched between his teeth. 'The Arsenal was little worthy of the name, the building being merely made up of a score or more of go-downs [sheds],' Hensman informed the readers of the *Daily News*. 'In these go-downs there was none of that care and precaution taken such as is insisted upon in English arsenals and magazines. The gun powder was chiefly stored in huge earthenware gurrahs . . . and in many instances these had been tilted over and loose powder scattered on the ground.'

Conscious of the problems to be faced in the occupation of a city, Frederick Roberts set up a board to investigate complaints against the behaviour of the troops. He expressly forbade fraternising with the ladies of Kabul. It would be 'likely to arouse the personal jealousy of the people of Cabul, who are of all races, most susceptible in all that regards their women'. It says much for the discipline of this second army of occupation that not one Afghan complained of mistreatment, despite the many outlets for the airing of such grievances.

With the imminent approach of winter, measures to protect the troops from the intense cold were becoming increasingly important, and the partly fortified Sherpur cantonment a mile north-east of the city was put into a fit state of repair to serve as winter quarters. It was close to the site originally chosen by Elphinstone and was reluctantly adopted by Roberts only because it offered the best facility for a hurried concentration of troops should the Afghans attack.

That eventuality was a distinct possibility for, even as the engineers strengthened the cantonment defences, a travelling mullah was preaching jihad to tribal gatherings all over Afghanistan. When the Mullah, Mushki-Alam, reached Kabul, Roberts, rather than invite trouble by arresting him, considered it prudent to telegraph Jalalabad for reinforcements. His message went out on 8 December – not a day too soon for, from the roof of the partly destroyed Bala Hissar, three Afghan lashkars could be seen throwing up thin curtains of snow in the Chardeh Valley as they converged on a range of hills to the west of the city. Roberts realised that, outnumbered as he was, his best chance lay in bringing each of the three columns to battle before they could combine forces against him.

During the next six days the British troops, including a recently arrived Corps of Guides, became embroiled in a series of running fights which were as savage as they were confusing. Two columns were employed by Roberts, each about a thousand strong. One, under Brigadier-General Macpherson, halted three miles north-west of the city at Kila Ashar. The other, led by Brigadier-General Baker, marched south towards Charasia on the 9th, but with orders to turn westward in the direction of Arghandah twenty miles away in the vicinity of Ghazni. A large concentration of Afghans was broken up by Macpherson but the opportunity of inflicting a damaging defeat was lost, largely through the incompetence of the cavalry commander, General Massy, who allowed the Afghans to disperse in various groups to swell the numbers gathering under the banner of Sirdar Muhammad Jan.

Now that the location of the main Afghan Army had been discovered, a joint plan was set in motion to ensnare it west of Kabul. Macpherson was instructed to leave early on the 11th for Arghandah, whilst Baker, who was by now twenty miles south-west of the city, was ordered to march with all possible speed for Arghandah. Thus, should the Afghan Army resume its advance on Kabul, Baker would be at its rear, Macpherson on its flank, and the remainder of Roberts' force – a sizeable 3000 – free to contest its advance. If Muhammad Jan should decide not to break camp, he would be caught between two columns attacking from opposite directions.

General Massy, who, it was said, was so slothful and incompetent that Roberts only employed him with the greatest misgivings, was ordered to move his cavalry and guns along the road to Arghandah in support of Macpherson, but to avoid giving battle unless Macpherson himself chose to engage the enemy. Massy, however, did not fully understand the part he was to play. Rather than march along the winding Kabul–Arghandah road, he decided to shorten the march by going across country to the Ghazni road.

He had not gone far into the Chardeh Valley before the sound of drums to his front betrayed the presence of large numbers of Afghans and, in breasting the crest of the rising ground, Massy was astonished to find the whole of Muhammad Jan's army spread out on the plain before him. In a matter of minutes, 10,000 tribesmen were rapidly closing upon his own tiny force of 300 troopers and four Horse Artillery guns. Massy at once opened fire with his six-pounders but to little effect, and he was forced to beat a hasty retreat.

Four miles away in the Sherpur cantonment, Roberts heard the sound of gunfire and realised that his plan to trap the Afghan Army had misfired. When he reached the open ground beyond Bhagwana a remarkable sight presented itself. An unbroken line of Afghans extending for some two miles was moving rapidly across the ground towards him.

It was Roberts who saved the day by covering his line of retreat with a cavalry charge. It enabled Massy to pull back the guns, but a charge by the Bengal Lancers over broken ground and against odds of more than forty to one could end only in gallant failure. In a savage bout of hand-to-hand fighting Roberts was unhorsed and only saved from serious injury by the intervention of a Moslem from the 1st Bengal Lancers.

For the British it was a day of disaster. One of the guns overturned in a twelve-foot ditch and had to be spiked. The troops just managed to reach the village of Bhagwana, where the villagers greeted them with a fusillade of shots from the house tops. Fortunately, the pursuing Afghans were misled into thinking that the village was defended by a strong detachment of British infantry, giving Roberts time to make an organised withdrawal.

Macpherson arrived an hour after the action had begun but in time to press upon the enemy's rear. Slowly the tide of battle changed and, as Macpherson's troops increased their pressure, the Afghans turned and fled. Meanwhile, victory had boosted the morale of the tribesmen and hundreds flocked to Muhammad Jan's banner, including many who until now had wavered in their allegiance to him. Roberts, who had hoped to prevent the Afghan forces from uniting, now decided to withdraw from all isolated positions and seek the shelter of the Sherpur cantonment to avoid heavy loss of life.

By 11 December, the Kabul Field Force was in a virtual
state of siege behind the walls of Sherpur, as Elphinstone's
Army of the Indus had been thirty-six years earlier. There was
no communication with the outside world, for the telegraph
line was down and the winter overcast prevented the use of
a heliograph. On that day Howard Hensman reported: 'The
enemy have beaten us at our own game – has outmanoeuvred
us – and instead of Muhammad Jan being a fugitive, he is
calmly occupying the peaks to the south of the Bala Hissar
Ridge, and his standards are flying in sight of Cabul and all
the country around.'

For a few days an uneasy calm pervaded Sherpur. General Roberts, knowing that Muhammad Jan's numerical
superiority over his own force was as much as eight to
one, waited anxiously for the arrival of the second brigade under Brigadier-General Charles Gough that he had
requested before the Afghans cut the wire. On 21 December
a heliograph informed him that the brigade expected to reach
him the next day but that Gough had been obliged to part
with most of his cavalry in order to keep the tribesmen at a
respectful distance in his rear.

But on the 22nd there was still no sign of the relief force.
In Kabul, crowds were celebrating the religious feast of
Moharran. The Moslems were in a highly emotional state and
any Hindu merchant suspected of having sold goods to the
British was ruthlessly hunted down and put to death.

On the last day of the festival, a flaring beacon lit in the
early hours by a mullah on the Asmai Heights was a signal
for a concerted attack against the defences of Sherpur by
the entire Afghan force. 'From beyond Bemaru and the eastern
trenches and walls', wrote the Special Correspondent of the
Daily News, 'came a roar of voices so loud and menacing
that it seemed as if an army 50,000 strong were charging
down upon our thin line of men.' At the other end of the
cantonment near the village, the redcoats were soon embroiled
in heavy fighting.

'Suddenly . . . close to Bimaroo village, arose a din as if
every fiend in hell had broken loose,' wrote Major Reginald
Mitford.

The undercurrent or base, was one ceaseless roll of musketry broken at frequent intervals by the roar of a heavy gun. Above this rose British cheers and Sikh war-cries answering the yells of the Moollahs and Ghazis, screams, shrieks, and noises of every hideous description. Add to this that the bullets were whistling about us, knocking up the stones, splintering the abbattis, and tearing through the empty tents, and you may form a very inadequate idea of the scene on which the peaceful stars looked down.

The rest of the garrison heard but could see nothing in the darkness until a cascade of star shells threw into sharp relief wave after wave of tribesmen moving swiftly through the fields and orchards a thousand yards away. The screams of 'Allah-il-Allah! Din-Din!' grew louder and then were lost in the continuous crackle of breech-loading rifles expertly handled by seasoned campaigners of British and Indian regiments.

Against field guns firing over open sights and the destructive power of massed rifle fire, the attack withered. Again and again the fanatical Ghazis stormed forward, striving to place their scaling ladders against the walls. A few reached the top rungs only to be impaled on the bayonets of the Gordons, and by 10.00 a.m. the frozen ground was piled high with corpses. 'Suddenly the din ceased and the silence which succeeded was intense by contrast,' recalled Mitford; '. . . from the valley below rose the long mournful wail of a jackal, answered further off by the rest of the pack. One of the native officers . . . laid his hand on my arm saying in an awestruck voice, "Sahib! The Devil has sent them to the banquet!"'

A renewal of the battle came an hour later with such ferocity and in such numbers that it seemed nothing could prevent the Afghans from breaking through the defence perimeter. It was then that Roberts exhibited the touch of genius which marked him out from his contemporaries. Finding that the enemy could not be flung back solely by defensive power, he resolved to attack them in flank.

Lieutenant-Colonel Williams with the 5th Punjab Cavalry was sent out under the covering fire of four field guns to attack the least protected section of the enemy's rear. This cavalry charge along a dip in the Bemaru Heights took Muhammad

Jan completely by surprise and even outstripped Roberts' expectations. From the moment their rear came under attack, the Afghan onslaught began to wither and by early afternoon Muhammad Jan's army was in full retreat, leaving a thousand dead on the battle ground.

When the mounted patrols of the Guides began a cautious probing of Kabul's labyrinth of alleys on Christmas Day 1879, not a single soldier of Muhammad Jan's army was to be seen – not that they had all disappeared: 'These men now hide their arms and appear in all the beautiful simplicity of peaceful citizens,' reported Hensman, 'but the subterfuge is too easily detected for them to escape punishment.'

That same day, the advance guard of Gough's relief force rode into the Sherpur cantonment to the ironic cheers of the garrison.

With the departure of the Afghan Army peace of a kind returned to Kabul, but the question of who might safely be installed as ruler without plunging the country into anarchy was still unresolved. The danger of an Afghan ruler turning his kingdom against British India's northern frontier with the help of a foreign power had persuaded both Lytton and Roberts of the desirability of reorganising Afghanistan into a number of independent provinces. It would make it easier to control the unruly tribes and would avoid the necessity for an army of occupation. So argued Lytton, and there was a sound basis to his reasoning in that the presence of British troops in Afghanistan was becoming unacceptable to a growing portion of the British electorate.

Gladstone and the opposition Liberal Party, in judging the public mood correctly, were quick to press party advantage. 'Remember the rights of the savage, as we call him,' thundered Gladstone in one of his rousing speeches to the God-fearing Victorians; '. . . remember the happiness of his humble home. . . . the sanctity of life in the hill villages of Afghanistan among the winter snows is as inviolate in the eyes of almighty God as can be your own. . . .'

The hero of the day, General Roberts, was not spared criticism and the hanging of the Afghans responsible for the massacre of Cavagnari's Mission came under attack from many Parliamentarians. Roberts was justifiably enraged and wrote to his wife:

> I believe it is a fact that when the news of the battle of Waterloo reached England, some man of the opposition rushed into his club and said, 'There's been a misfortune, Wellington has won a great victory at Waterloo'. . . . I'm quite satisfied that I have not done anything to be ashamed of. If the British public want to have a repetition of the disaster of 1841 to 1842 they had better send someone else to command in Kabul, for while I am here I intend to do all I can to preserve the army entrusted to my charge, and if any Afghans are proved guilty of treachery, or try to murder my soldiers or followers, I'm afraid I shall hang them, not withstanding all the rubbish the 'Spectator' and 'Statesman' write.

Whilst General Roberts fumed in Kabul, the Governor-General thought long and hard on the question of a replacement for Yakub Khan, who was now the recipient of a pension in India. One act to be avoided at all costs was the installation of a puppet unpopular with the Afghan people, and with this in mind Lord Lytton instructed Roberts to invite Abdur Rahman, a grandson of Dost Muhammad – arguably the greatest of recent Afghan leaders – to take up the throne.

Early in February 1880, Roberts and his assistants began the difficult and protracted task, and a month later the matter was on the way to being resolved with a letter from Abdur Rahman, stating that he was prepared to cross the Hindu Kush for discussions with Sir Frederick Roberts. '. . . night and day I have cherished the hope of revisiting my native land,' the letter read. 'I have entered into no secret or written engagement with the Russians. I am bound to them . . . simply by feelings of gratitude. I have eaten their salt and for twelve years was dependent on their hospitality.' But his long association with the Russians did not prejudice him in the eyes of the British and, since he was the only candidate strong enough to fulfil British expectations, he was invited to Kabul. Lepel Henry Griffin, of the Indian Civil Service, who was appointed to conduct the negotiations, left this report: 'Abdur-ur-Rahman is a man of about forty, of middle height, and rather stout. He has an exceedingly intelligent face, brown eyes, a pleasant smile, and a frank, courteous manner. . . . He appeared animated by a sincere desire to be on cordial terms with the British government.'

Meanwhile, in order to take part in the pacification of northern Afghanistan, General Sir Donald Stewart marched north from Kandahar. It was a journey beset with difficulties from the start, for the Hazaras harried his line of march, burning and looting Afghan villages and carrying off into slavery every family which did not possess the means of defending itself. On 19 April their numbers were swollen by a host of Ghazis, who attacked with suicidal ferocity at Ahmedkhel some twenty miles west of Ghazni. Stewart hastily formed a line whilst his artillery began to shell the tribesmen massed on the heights to his front. The gunfire brought on a furious rush of swordsmen against the British centre whilst the Afghan horsemen swept over the intervening ground in an attempt to encircle Stewart's flanks. 'Down they came,' wrote Lieutenant-Colonel E. F. Chapman, '. . . at least three thousand in number . . . quite regardless of our fire. . . . the whole hill seemed to be moving.'

On the British left flank a squadron of the famed Bengal Lancers was put to flight, creating havoc in the ranks of the 19th Punjabis. At the centre, some companies of the 59th did not even have time to fix bayonets before the Ghazis were upon them. For an uneasy period it seemed that the whole battalion might have to give way as the Horse Artillery, unable to stem the charge even though firing over open sights at thirty yards, limbered up and retired to a new position in the rear.

It was at this critical point in the battle that Stewart ordered up his Reserve and, with the Gurkhas and 3rd Sikhs holding firm, the danger was averted. The renewed fire from the breech-loading artillery, which had now unlimbered, began to take effect and the Afghans gradually lost heart. Some, shamming death or wounds, reached up to slash at the horses of the 2nd Punjab cavalry as they leaped over them, but after two hours of bitter fighting the battle ended in victory for Stewart's troops.

The successful outcome of a confrontation such as this

between tribesmen armed with swords and disciplined troops using modern weapons was never in doubt, but the European officers were quick to acknowledge the bravery of their poorly armed adversary. 'Anyone with the semblance of a heart under his khaki jacket', wrote Captain Elias, 'could not help feeling something akin to pity to see them advancing with their miserable weapons in the face of our guns and rifles, but their courage and their numbers made them formidable.'

On 21 April, Stewart's column reached Ghazni, which fell without a shot being fired. Two days later a concentration of tribesmen was broken up at Arzu, seven miles to the south-east, leaving 400 dead on the field for the loss of two sepoys killed and eight wounded.

Later that month, General Stewart left his force encamped at the Shutargardan Pass and rode to Kabul where, as senior to Roberts, he became Commander-in-Chief of the Kabul Field Force. With his arrival came news from England of the outcome of the general election. The Liberal Party was back in power. Mr Gladstone was Prime Minister and Lord Lytton had been replaced as Governor-General by the Marquess of Ripon. 'Notwithstanding the pleasure of meeting an old friend in my new Commander,' complained the former chief of the Kabul Field Force, 'I dreaded that a change of government might mean a reversal of the policy which I believed to be the best for the security of our position in India.'

Events were shortly to prove the validity of Roberts' opinion.

Chapter 8

Kabul to Kandahar

Sir Donald Stewart, who had taken political as well as military control in Kabul, was mindful of the effect events in Britain would have on Roberts, whose prospects for advancement had rested to some degree upon the previous government remaining in office. 'He is rather in a state of mind about his future because he will have no appointment when this force returns to India,' he wrote to his wife. 'There is no telling what may happen after Lord Lytton goes. It will be a great shame if they don't do something for Bobs.'

Happily, his fears were groundless, for in a move warmly applauded by the new Commander-in-Chief Roberts retained command of the two divisions at Kabul. 'He is very true to me,' confessed Stewart, 'and is of great use to me in many ways, and if there is to be fighting he will be my right hand.'

Indeed, there was a strong possibility of further conflict, for at the opposite end of the country Herat was held by the fanatically anti-British Ayub Khan, supported by a well-equipped army strong in artillery. Determined to make a bid for the throne of Kabul, he had marched on Herat in the spring of 1880 and persuaded the local chiefs to accept his leadership in an all-out war against the Feringhee. By mid-June he had gathered an army of 7500 trained Durrani tribesmen and ten pieces of cannon. Certain in the knowledge that his numbers would increase en route, Ayub Khan rode at the head of his disciplined fighting force heading not for Kabul, but for Kandahar, 350 miles to the east.

In Kabul, the temperature was rising as also was the hope

Kabul: Upper Bala Hissar from the west.

The interior of Chitral Fort, overlooking the Kunar river.

The Gordons and Gurkhas storming the Dargai ridge.

The Dorsets: hand-to-hand fighting in a nullar.

Colonel J. G. Kelly (centre, with beard) and
officers of the 32nd Punjab Pioneers.

'The Mahsud'.

The 44th Hill looking towards Jugdaluk.

Sherpur Cantonment in winter.

Last stand of the 55th Foot at Maiwand, August 1880.

Afghans firing from a Sangar, January 1880.

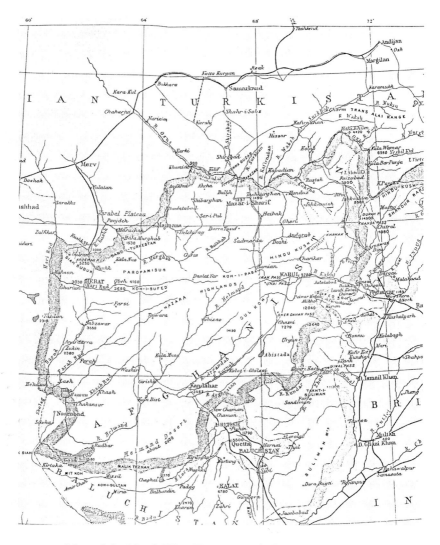

Map of the North-West Frontier including Afghanistan.

for better things to come. Stewart wrote again to his wife informing her that the British garrison there was preparing to leave for India early in August. 'I can hardly believe that we are to get out of this country without trouble. Abdur Rahman seems sensible. . . . It is a regular lottery though.'

Early in July the Political Officer at Kandahar telegraphed the news that Ayub Khan had declared himself Amir and was marching with 25,000 men and thirty guns towards the northern frontier of Sher Ali's princedom. As Ayub Khan's formidable army neared the Helmand River, the ruler of Britain's buffer state could be excused for displaying a marked lack of confidence in the ability of his own force to meet the threat, and he requested assistance, a plea to which Lord Ripon, the new Governor-General, readily acceded.

The mixed force of British and Indian troops sent out from Kandahar to restore the situation was of brigade strength and was accompanied by twelve guns. Marching in temperatures of up to 100° across an arid landscape of rock and sand, it reached the Helmand on 11 July as Sher Ali's troops mutinied and hurried away to join the ranks of Ayub Khan – a circumstance which left Brigadier-General George Burrowes and his heavily outnumbered brigade eighty miles from the nearest military base at Kandahar.

On 27 July, the day that Abdur Rahman accepted the throne, an advance patrol discovered that the rebel Afghan Army was across the Helmand River and firmly entrenched on high ground close to the village of Maiwand. The village was less than a dozen miles from Burrowes' own position and the British Commander barely had time to deploy his troops before a mass of cavalry emerged from a thick haze to threaten both his flanks. Two thousand Afghans from Ayub's regular cavalry swept from the high ground on his left, whilst 5000 screaming Durrani tribesmen hurled themselves fearlessly against the troops on his right flank.

Although outnumbered by more than seven to one, Burrowes stood firm on the open plain as Ayub Khan attacked with his disciplined regular troops. Outgunned and outflanked, Burrowes' soldiers were in no position to hold their ground against such odds and, after four hours of fierce fighting, they suddenly broke. A punishing bombardment from thirty Afghan cannon had panicked the inexperienced sepoys of the 30th Native Infantry and thrown the 1st Bombay Infantry into confusion as the two regiments became inextricably mixed. So tightly packed did the companies become that the men could neither use their bayonets nor fire a shot in their own defence as the Ghazis dragged one after another out of the square to be butchered in the open.

Fifty yards from where the square was being decimated, the 66th Foot halted another rush of Ghazis with a disciplined volley but the panic of the sepoys in the neighbouring square was contagious and they too were forced to retire to a new position behind a walled garden. Here, the hundred or so survivors met the tribesmen in a savage hand-to-hand scuffle of slashing knives and whirling rifle butts in a fog of black powder smoke. When ammunition ran low, the Afghans were seized by their beards and pulled on to outstretched bayonets, or strangled by soldiers who had no other weapon but their bare hands. British officers hurled stones, whilst Burrowes rode up and down the line picking off Afghans with his revolver until his horse was shot from under him. 'Oh, for one hour of Roberts!' a subaltern was heard to cry; '. . . he would get us out of this rat trap.'

An Afghan source recorded that the last ten soldiers, led by two officers, charged out of the garden and fought back to back until they were all shot down. So impressed was an Afghan colonel of artillery who had witnessed the event that he later caused a brick pillar to be erected in the walled garden to honour the British and Indian dead who had fought so gallantly.

On another part of the field, only the Horse Artillery and the Sappers were still engaged when General Burrowes finally ordered a general retirement on Kandahar. More than a thousand of his men had been killed and in the rear all was confusion as fleeing soldiers and camp followers fought with each other to plunder the military treasure and commissariat stores. The retreat quickly degenerated into a rout. Wild with thirst, a panic-stricken rabble streamed acrᴏss twenty-five miles of sun-baked earth closely pursued by Ayub Khan's regular troops and horse artillery.

At Kandahar, the first intimation of disaster came when a Jemahdar of the 3rd Scinde Horse rode into cantonments with the news of Burrowes' defeat. An alarmed garrison commander sent out an escort to bring in the survivors. Among the last to arrive was the General, who had given up a second horse to a wounded officer and now walked with his men. His voice had gone, noted a witness, and he was close to tears for the loss of his brigade. Of the 2734 officers and men who had gone into action with him, only 1595 were there to answer the roll-call on the following day.

It was night before the last of the stragglers from Maiwand limped into the citadel, and the garrison made preparations for a lengthy siege. Fortunately there were adequate stocks of food and ammunition and with thirteen guns and 5000 men to defend 6000 yards of curtain wall, the citadel was unlikely to be taken by storm. In a further safeguard against the possibility of an Afghan rising within the city, General Primrose expelled the entire native population, amounting to some 15,000 Pathans.

Meanwhile, 320 miles to the north, in Kabul, General Roberts was concerned that news of a major defeat of the British should not affect relations with Abdur Rahman. The possibility could not be ruled out that, encouraged by exaggerated rumours, the Amir might seek to emulate Ayub Khan. It seemed to Roberts that only a swift and decisive blow against Ayub Khan would restore British prestige in India, which might be achieved if the beleaguered garrison in Kandahar was relieved without further delay.

On 30 July Roberts, after dining with Stewart, telegraphed Simla seeking approval to lead a force against the army of Yakub Khan. 'I strongly recommend that a force be sent from Kabul to Kandahar,' he signalled. 'It is imperative that we should now show our strength throughout Afghanistan.' Four days later his request was sanctioned by the Governor-General, Lord Ripon, and Frederick Roberts, with feverish intensity, began to organise a relief column.

Since he had promised Simla that his force, which included

eighteen guns, would reach Kandahar within the month, heavy pieces of transport had to be sacrificed in the interests of mobility. Therefore only iron rations for the 9987 officers and men were to be taken, sheep and oxen for the day's consumption being purchased on the march. Wheeled artillery, of course, was entirely unsuited to a rapid passage over a mountainous terrain, and Roberts resolved this problem by the simple expedient of carrying screw guns on the backs of mules. 'We were not letting the grass grow under our feet,' wrote Howard Hensman, who accompanied the expedition, 'for we have only mule and pony carriage, and our progress is not delayed by camels or bullocks persistently casting their loads. . . . the troops are all very fit, and march splendidly.'

At Kandahar, the garrison had suffered continuous bombardment from Ayub Khan's artillery since the beginning of August. By the 13th, the Afghans had successfully enfiladed the north face of the citadel, thus denying the defenders freedom of movement, and gaining for themselves a position from which an assault could be made upon the city walls. The Afghan battery at Deh Kwaja was particularly effective and at dawn on the 16th Brigadier-General Brooke led a sortie against the battery position. When the assault force reached the village it found to its dismay that the defences were too strong and, in the bitter street-fighting which followed, the British suffered a severe mauling without so much as reaching the battery. At 7.30 a.m. the survivors were back in Kandahar, having left more than one hundred dead on the field, including General Brooke and six other officers.

Five days earlier, the Kabul–Kandahar Field Force had broken camp and was now marching with all possible haste across a trackless waste of sand and rock. Roberts' British troops had been hand-picked from the fittest of the Kabul garrison, among them two battalions of Highlanders and one of the 60th Rifles. He was particularly well served by cavalry, from the elite 9th Queen's Royal Lancers to three crack regiments of Indian cavalry. All were about to undertake one of the most gruelling marches in military history.

At first, the route through the Logar Valley was easy and supplies plentiful. The worst section was undoubtedly the

120 miles between Ghazni and Khelat-il-Ghilzai, where the thermometer reached 110° during the day and fell to freezing point at dawn. 'If shadows could have been made saleable,' wrote one long-suffering officer, 'they would have fetched any price, even the patch of shade under a horse's girth.' 'The worst torment that pursued us', recalled another, 'was unquenchable thirst. Tantalizing dreams of ruby-coloured claret cup, or amber cider, used to haunt my imagination till I felt I must drink something or perish.' Fortunately there were a few dehydrating stream beds to be found, but the water, scooped up in sandy lumps and strained into buckets, went chiefly to the cavalry horses, ammunition mules and camels. The men could only stand and watch whilst the animals were watered. The greatest tribulation undoubtedly came with sub-zero temperatures at night. The kilted Highlanders suffered in particular for the 650 Gordons possessed less than 100 greatcoats between them and these were allocated to the sentries on guard duties.

Ever present was the threat posed by parties of Afghans ready to plunder at the first opportunity. 'It was certain death', wrote Roberts, 'for anyone who strayed from the shelter of the column; numbers of Afghans hovered about on the look-out for plunder, or in the hope of being able to send a Kaffir, or an almost equally detested Hindu, to eternal perdition.'

In what must have seemed an interminable march, the hungry, exhausted troops hobbled forward on blistered feet, wrapped in a choking cloud of dust by day, snatching a brief rest in the paralysing cold at night; until finally on 23 August they reached Khelat-il-Ghilzai. Here, there was a garrison and, upon learning that there was no immediate danger of Kandahar falling, Roberts called a halt for twenty-four hours. It was a well-deserved rest. The column had covered a distance of 225 miles across mountain and desert since leaving Kabul and the strain was beginning to tell. But if the present pace of fifteen miles a day could be maintained, the column would be on schedule and Kandahar relieved in a week.

On the 25th, a seventeen-mile stretch was completed and the relief force halted at Jaldak, where camp was pitched on ground liberally dotted with the skeletons of camels which

had perished in General Stewart's advance. On 26 August
the column arrived at Tirandaz, less than fifty miles from
Kandahar, where a message awaited General Roberts from
General Primrose containing the welcome news that rumours
of the approach of a relief column had been sufficient for Ayub
Khan to raise the siege and retire to the hills outside the city.

The following morning the column's Commander, struck
down by a sudden and virulent fever, was obliged to take to a
doolie: 'a most ignominious mode of conveyance for a General
on service', remarked Roberts, 'but there was no help for it,
for I could not sit on a horse.'

Poor food had swollen the numbers of sick and a chance
encounter with a flock of 3000 sheep did much to avert a
crisis. Hugh Gough, whose cavalry patrol took charge of the
flock, recalled the incident in his memoirs: 'I shall not readily
forget the baaing and bleating that nearly maddened us, or
the hullabaloo of the owners who followed the sheep! We just
paid the price and regaled ourselves on mutton and melons!'

Roberts' sweat-caked troops marched into Kandahar at 8.30
on the morning of the 31st and found a demoralised garrison
which had not even bothered to hoist the British flag until
the relieving force was close at hand. In sharp contrast to
the garrison, the morale of the relieving troops was high.
A forced march of 313 miles in twenty-one days over a most
difficult terrain was a noteworthy achievement and for his
part Roberts never forgot the debt he owed to his men. When
recording his army life years later, he stated with conviction:
'never has a commander been better served . . . all were eager
to close with the enemy, no matter how great the odds against
them.'

Roberts' satisfaction with his own men was tempered
with disgust at what he considered to be a dereliction of
duty on the part of a garrison composed of 4000 professional soldiers protected by walls thirty feet high. 'I confess
to being greatly surprised, not to use a stronger expression,'
he wrote, 'at the demoralised condition of the greater part
of the garrison. . . . They seemed to consider themselves
hopelessly defeated.' When the General discovered just how
strong the defences were, his indignation knew no bounds:

'For British soldiers to have contemplated the possibility of Kandahar being taken by an Afghan army, showed what a miserable state of depression and demoralisation they were in.' The garrison Commander did not escape censure, for the subsequent report made by Roberts to the authorities in Simla was instrumental in thoroughly discrediting General Primrose, who was relieved of his command and eventually sent back to England.

General Roberts, having assumed command of the army in southern Afghanistan, lost no time in getting to grips with the enemy. A reconnaissance in force during the morning of 1 September established that Ayub Khan had occupied the high ground each side of two razor-backed hills and thrown up stout defensive works around the village of Pir Paimal north of the pass.

Roberts' tactics were those he had employed so often in the past with a fair measure of success. He would launch a feint attack against the Afghans' left flank with Primrose's troops supported by artillery, and at the same time mount a two-pronged drive against the village and Ayub Khan's right flank. The plan worked perfectly. In a short but bitter struggle the village was carried and the Afghan flank turned. By midday Roberts was threatening to overwhelm Ayub Khan's rear.

Less than an hour later, however, as Roberts refreshed himself with a customary glass of champagne, Pir Paimal was suddenly enveloped in a pall of dust, smoke and flying fragments of steel as Ayub Khan's artillery and three or four hundred riflemen poured a heavy fire into the village from the commanding heights.

Major George White, recognising the futility of delay, drew his sword. 'Highlanders! Let us close the business.' The skirl of the pipes was almost lost in the roar that rose from the ranks as bayonets were slammed tight in their fittings.

As the Scots began to climb the rocky slope they were joined by the 2nd Gurkhas in a combined assault against the escarpment. Bursting shells and a punishing rifle fire thinned their ranks, but as the attackers closed on their objective the shell fire suddenly stopped. The prospect of

facing Scottish bayonets and Gurkha kukries had persuaded
even the fanatical Ghazis to disperse. When the assault party
reached the escarpment, only a litter of abandoned weapons
and empty entrenchments were to be seen.

Employing their customary skill, the Afghan troops had vanished by discarding their uniform for the tattered garments
of peasant farmers. A mile away, Ayub Khan's enormous camp
was entirely deserted. Wrote one British officer: 'All the rude
equipage of a half barbarous army was left at our mercy
– the meat in the cooking pots, the bread half kneaded in
the earthenware vessels, the bazaar with its ghee-pots, dried
fruits, flour and corn.' Of the Afghan staff there was no sign.
In fact, Ayub Khan, having left the field earlier in the action,
was on his way to Herat with an escort of cavalry and mounted
gunners.

Frederick Roberts was now a sick man and on 8 September a medical board decided that he had reason enough to
return to England. He left Afghanistan by way of the Bolan
Pass and, as he overtook the units which had served him so
well on the march from Kabul to Kandahar, their regimental
bands struck up an emotional chord in 'Auld Lang Syne'. 'I
have never since heard that memory-stirring air without its
bringing before my mind's eye the last view I had of the
Kabul–Kandahar Field Force,' he wrote. '. . . I shall never
forget the feeling of sadness with which I said goodbye to the
men who had done so much for me. I looked upon them all,
Native as well as British, as my valued friends. . . .'

With the victory at Kandahar, the policy of fragmenting
Afghanistan was abandoned in favour of a complete withdrawal of all British garrisons to India. That such a move
could be safely carried out was due principally to fears of a
similar rising led by Abdur Rahman having proved groundless. Abdur Rahman was now firmly seated upon the throne,
having agreed not to enter into any form of treaty with other
countries without the approval of British India. Consequently,
every British occupying force in Afghanistan was back in India
before the end of the year, with one exception. The garrison at
Kandahar remained, to stir up a bitter controversy in England.

Gladstone's pledge of withdrawal had met with fierce

opposition from Lytton, who assured Parliament that, whilst Britain held Kandahar, 'You may look upon the permanent security of the North-West Frontier of India as a question practically closed.' It was all in vain. The spectre of Maiwand still haunted the Conservative Party and the Commons voted for withdrawal. By March 1881 Kandahar was back in Afghan hands. It was not the end of the fighting, however, for in the absence of the British Ayub Khan made another, and this time successful, attempt to take the city. The capture of Kandahar infuriated Abdur Rahman and in a fierce battle outside the city on 21 September Ayub Khan was again defeated. This time no refuge was to be found in Herat. In his absence the city had fallen to another of Abdur Rahman's armies and Ayub Khan was forced to seek asylum in Iran.

To British India, the second Afghan War, in addition to the grievous casualties sustained, was a severe drain on the Treasury, which had expended many lakhs of rupees to little purpose. Whilst the strategically important Kurram Valley and Khyber Pass were recognised by Abdur Rahman as being effectively under British control, they remained so only for as long as the Amir kept his word.

Not that the Russians profited from the situation, for although relations with British India remained cool, Abdur Rahman regarded the court of the Tsar with even greater suspicion. Recent Russian incursions along the northern border of Afghanistan, culminating in the annexation of Merv in 1884 and the occupation of the Panjdeh Oasis the following year, had alarmed not only the Amir but had brought Britain and Russia to the brink of war. In this heightened atmosphere of mistrust the importance of the North-West Frontier became increasingly apparent not only to the Indian Defence Committee but also to Afghanistan.

In 1893, Abdur Rahman, who over the years had watched the Indian government take control of the Khyber Pass, the Kurram Valley and much more along the vaguely defined Indo-Afghan border, approached the government with a suggestion that a high-ranking British official attend a conference in Kabul to discuss the question of establishing a recognised demarcation of the disputed border.

The man selected for this delicate task was Sir Mortimer Durand and he and his mission arrived in Kabul on 2 October. The discussions continued for several weeks until finally on 13 November a promise to increase the Amir's subsidy persuaded Abdul Rahman to fix his seal to a treaty delineating the boundary from Chitral to Peshawar and from there to the junction of Persia, Afghanistan and Baluchistan.

The new border became known as the Durand Line and was marked by a series of white boundary posts over a thousand-mile length, following the curve of hills but spaced so far apart that it was sometimes difficult for a traveller to know whether he was in British tribal territory or Afghanistan. The Durand Line was a major irritant to many of the clans but early in 1895 when news flashed from India that pandemonium had broken out in Chitral, even well-informed readers in Britain were obliged to lay aside their newspapers and consult an atlas.

Chapter 9

Chitral

The beginning of March 1895 brought serious trouble to an area of geographical and strategic importance on the northern frontier of India. Chitral, a country ringed by high snow-capped mountains on the north-west shoulder of India, became the focal point of attention for all patriotic Victorians when a garrison of 400 Kashmiris and Sikhs, with six British officers, were reported cut off from the outside world and facing odds of more than fifty to one from the white-robed Chitralis, led by Sher Afzul, and the Pathans of Umra Khan, the ruler of the neighbouring state of Jandul.

The death of the Mehtar three years earlier had been followed by the customary hereditary and internecine disputes until the eldest son, Nizam-ul-Mulk, won temporary control and was recognised as Mehtar by the British. In January 1895, however, he fell victim to his nineteen-year-old half-brother Amir-ul-Mulk, who, when refused immediate recognition by the British Agent in Chitral, turned to Umra Khan for assistance.

The situation soon became fragmented. The British, anxious to maintain a semblance of stability in their northern territory, reacted by sending a small force under the command of Surgeon-Major George Robertson to depose the self-proclaimed Mehtar in favour of his younger brother Shuja-ul-Mulk. Sher Afzul, a brother of the old Mehtar, demanded that Robertson evacuate the fort and return to Mastuj, whilst Umra Khan, who nurtured ambitions of adding

113

Chitral to his own domain, lost no time in mobilising his army to invade Chitral and join Sher Afzul.

On 3 March news was received that Sher Afzul was approaching with a large force and Robertson, conscious that to withdraw would be to invite disaster, concentrated his small body of troops in Chitral Fort. The building in which they had taken refuge was barely eighty yards square, possessing a fifty-foot tower at each corner buttressed by twenty-five-foot-high walls of stone embedded in mud mortar held together with a cradlework of wooden beams. Overlooked by high ground at its rear, the blockhouse was also exposed on every side to sniper fire from the high branches of pine trees, but at least a covered way down to the river's edge afforded some protection and ensured that an adequate supply of water was always available.

Although Surgeon-Major Robertson was in nominal charge of the post, actual command devolved on Captain Charles Vere Townshend of the Central India Horse, with Lieutenant Harley as his subaltern. The other British officers were Surgeon-Captain Whitchurch, Captain Campbell, who had been wounded in an earlier reconnaissance in which another officer had been killed, and Lieutenant Gurdon, the Assistant Political Officer. Taking shelter in the fort with them was the ten-year-old Shuja-ul-Mulk, together with his household, a few women and more than fifty Chitrali non-combatants.

Supplies were no cause for immediate anxiety as there was sufficient ammunition and it was estimated that food rationing would enable the garrison to hold out for three months, by which time it was hoped the siege would be lifted. Among a scanty supply of tinned beef were many tins of pea-flour, 'So every day from the beginning to the end of the siege,' wrote Robertson, 'we had pea soup for dinner.'

Initially the tribesmen were content to pour a dropping fire into the blockhouse from a village across the river, but on the night of 7 March the first of several attempts to cut the garrison's water supply was made when the timbers of a fifth tower guarding the covered way were set ablaze. The flames were quickly doused by a party with buckets and the attackers driven off by section volleys from the walls of the fort.

It was then that the authorities in Peshawar learned of the uprising. A few days later came equally alarming news from the isolated garrison at Mastuj, a square structure of mud and stone surrounded by saltpetre swamps some sixty miles from Chitral. A party carrying sixty boxes of Snider ammunition and engineering stores under the command of Lieutenants Edwardes and Fowler had set out for Chitral on 5 March not knowing that it was under siege.

The column had covered less than ten miles when it came under attack from a strong force of Chitralis, who by rolling huge boulders down the hillside forced the party to seek shelter in a village deserted by its inhabitants. Here at Reshun the two officers and their sixty sepoys maintained a stout defence for seven days until a truce was arranged by Muhammad Isa, a foster-brother of Sher Afzul. Then on the 13th, while watching a game of polo at the invitation of the Afghan chieftain, Edwardes and Fowler were seized and dragged behind a wall out of sight of their men. (They were later to be released unharmed after the Chitral relief column had crossed the Panjkora River.)

Meanwhile, word had reached Captain Ross at Mastuj that Edwardes was in trouble and he immediately organised a relief party with Lieutenant H. J. Jones and a detachment of Sikhs. Twenty miles of the journey was completed without incident, but in passing through the Koragh defile not far from Reshun the party was ambushed and forced to seek the shelter of a cave. In a desperate sortie the survivors attempted to cut their way out but only Lieutenant Jones and fourteen Sikhs, ten of whom were wounded, managed to reach the small village of Buni, where they resisted every attempt to drive them out before a relief column from Mastuj brought them safely away on 17 March.

Back in Chitral, conditions were becoming increasingly trying. The need for constant vigilance placed an intolerable burden on the British officers, whilst three days of heavy rain followed by a spell of arctic weather made life in the fort a miserable affair for the Indian troops. 'Rain falls in sheets,' complained Captain Townshend. 'From time to time a piece of the wall falls down. . . . Everything in the fort is soaked.

Mud, stinks, dirt, all the result of the incessant rain. . . .'
Provisions were getting low and the small luxuries with
which to while away the long periods of inactivity had long
since disappeared. The frustration felt by Charles Townshend
is clear from his diary entry of the 25th: 'Our tobacco is all
finished and cheroots only exist in the imagination. No whisky;
no liqueurs. Nothing!'

Whilst Robertson in his capacity as British Agent was
engaged in negotiating with the Chitralis under a flag of
truce, Townshend's chief concern lay in strengthening the
fort's defences. In this he was greatly assisted by the
Kashmiri sepoys, who proved able and willing workers
in making loopholes and hanging screens fashioned from
carpets and blankets, to hide the garrison personnel from
the ever-vigilant snipers in the tree tops.

Night attacks against the fort were attempted but without
success, due chiefly to the defenders' astute use of fireballs.
These were made from pinewood chippings mixed with straw,
the mixture being rolled into a canvas-covered sphere about
a foot in diameter and soaked in kerosene. The fireballs,
when thrown over the ramparts, illuminated a wide area
and were of great assistance to the defenders in picking off
their assailants.

On 15 March, under a flag of truce, a letter was delivered
from Sher Afzul. In it the writer assured Robertson of a safe
passage if he would return to Gilgit, and a subsequent message disclosed the fate of Captain Ross and the capture of
Lieutenants Edwardes and Fowler. The garrison was unmoved
and expressed its defiance by flying an odd-looking Union Jack
made up from scraps of cheap red-dyed cloth, white cotton
material from a pair of sepoy's trousers, and a blue turban. 'It
seemed almost improper, not to say illegal, to fight without the
Union Jack floating over our heads,' remarked Robertson. In
the early morning when the troops paraded, it was streaming
boldly from its mast. Continued the British Agent: 'a smile of
confidence, one might almost say the smile of adoration for a
fetish accompanied the action of saluting the fluttering rag.'

Heavy snow blanketed the area and the garrison began to
wonder whether a relief column would be able to negotiate

the passes. Robertson himself was affected by this period of inaction. 'Often no sound would break the heavy stillness,' he wrote; '. . . with the exception of the keen-eyed sentries crouching on the towers, all the garrison were asleep or resting. Sometimes this unnatural silence was so oppressive that an outbreak of rifle fire came as a relief. . . .' On the 18th the snow turned to rain and Robertson was again approached, this time by Umra Khan to say that the garrison could retire by way of Jandul to Peshawar. The invitation was declined.

The garrison, had they but known it, were the heroes of the hour. The name 'Chitral' was becoming familiar in almost every parlour circle and great was the relief felt by all Englishmen when it became known that a column was being mobilised at Peshawar to march from a southerly point to fall upon the rear of Umra Khan's Pathans.

By the third week of March, 15,000 troops of the 1st Army Corps and 28,000 pack animals had been assembled under the command of Major-General Sir Robert Low. Before his division was ready to march, however, the first positive step towards the relief of Chitral was taken when Colonel J. G. Kelly, who had been employed in the construction of roads along the Indus Valley, set out to cover the 220 miles from Gilgit with 400 Sikhs from the 32nd Punjab Pioneers, forty Kashmiri sappers and two seven-pounder mountain guns. The task confronting Kelly was formidable. Between Gilgit and Chitral were huge mountain ranges covered with deep snow over a route swarming with rebels flushed with the success of their uprising and determined to hold on to their gains. By dint of hard marching with a minimum of baggage, which did not include tents, Kelly's men covered more than half the distance by 4 April, which brought them to the ten-mile-long Shandur Pass.

Twelve thousand feet above sea level and deep in snow, the pass proved too difficult for the mules, which continually plunged and floundered, upsetting the guns and carriages. It was suggested that sleds might answer the problem of conveying the guns and with the help of the battery carpenters' tools two were made using felled poplars coated with the tin linings of old commissariat chests as runners.

Thirty men were assigned to each of the two sleds but, despite the most strenuous efforts, they quickly proved unmanageable in the deep snow. Just when it seemed that the guns would have to be abandoned, volunteers were found to carry the 200-pound loads slung from long poles, and pioneers, gunners and footsoldiers struggled forward in the teeth of a freezing wind which turned beads of perspiration into a thin coating of ice. Lieutenant William Benyon, commenting upon the struggle, confessed that his face 'felt as if it had been dipped in boiling water'. The rarefied air gave rise to breathing problems and for the first time in his life Beynon experienced bouts of mountain sickness: '. . . a curious and distinctly unpleasant sensation', he recorded, 'very much like having a rope tied tightly round one's chest and back.'

The struggle to move the guns continued for ten hours across twenty miles of deep soft snow, but no one dropped out and even those who sank down suffering from exhaustion, frostbite or snow blindness stumbled to their feet upon the return of the first ounce of strength. At length the pass was conquered and the advance continued until 9 April, when the column found its path blocked by upwards of 400 tribesmen who had taken up a strong position behind sangars built on the opposite bank of a fast-running stream. Colonel Kelly at once opened fire with his two mountain guns and in a brief skirmish lasting no more than an hour he drove the enemy from their sangars, clearing the way for the relief of Mastuj. Here, a small garrison had held the tribesmen at bay for eighteen days and had even been able to rescue Lieutenant Jones from his perilous situation at Buni.

Meanwhile, Major-General Sir Robert Low's division of three infantry brigades, two regiments of cavalry and four batteries of mountain artillery, having left Nowshera, was making slow progress across broken unmapped uplands never before penetrated in force. If the geography of the country was largely unknown, the strength of tribal opposition could only be guessed. 'We are still uncertain as to the attitude of the Swat tribesmen,' reported Lionel James, a Reuters correspondent with the relief force, 'but . . . the general opinion deduced from the interviews with these people is still that we shall not meet with much opposition.' It was a view not borne out by subsequent events.

Three passes gave access to the Swat Valley, the Malakand, Shahkot and Mora, each some seven miles apart and 3500 feet high with only rough tracks for pack animals. Low had decided to use the Malakand Pass and on 3 April after sending the cavalry to stir up a fine cloud of dust in a feint approach to the other two passes, he launched two brigades against the Malakand.

Unfortunately, the pass he had chosen narrowed sharply and the thousands of tribesmen who lined its heights and occupied the sangars on the forward slopes were determined to dispute every yard. As the Guides and 4th Sikhs scrambled for a footing in the loose scree, the 2nd King's Own Scottish Borderers and 1st Gordon Highlanders began to scale the thousand feet of rock which separated them from their adversaries on the Guides' flank. This frontal attack by the Scots was made in the face of an avalanche of small stones and rocks which swept down upon them in a terrifying deluge.

It had been estimated that the Guides would take three hours to reach the crest but even with the assistance of a covering fire from the mountain guns it was another two hours before these experienced troops drove the tribesmen from the last of the sangars. On their right, British and Indian infantry forced their way along a watercourse to turn the enemy's left and pursue the fleeing tribesmen as far as the Swat River, whilst the Scots went on to carry the crest of the pass at the point of the bayonet. 'It is difficult to praise too highly the dash and determination with which the pass was carried,' enthused Captain George Younghusband, in his capacity as acting war correspondent for *The Times*. 'Nor is it possible to forget the sterling bravery of the enemy, who for five hours withstood a most searching and splendidly directed shell fire from three batteries, and yet were still firm enough to stand up to a bayonet charge at the end of it.'

The cost to Sir Robert Low's column in this action was less than seventy killed and wounded, a comparatively light casualty list due in no small measure to the accurate fire of the artillery and, in the opinion of a private soldier of the Bedfords, to the Swat tribesmen's poor marksmanship. 'Their usual method', observed Private Pridmore, 'is to sight their weapons for a certain mark before-hand and they keep firing at this throughout the battle. If any of our men got within the line of fire they would probably be hit, but our method was first to send a few men forward to make a dust and induce the enemy to fire. Then we noticed where the bullets hit, kept just outside the mark and picked off our opponents.'

Upon resuming his march, Low met with few obstacles until reaching the Panjkora River some twenty-five miles further on. The river was in flood and was crossed only after a rough footbridge was constructed from logs lashed together with telegraph wire and floated into position. During the night of 12/13 April, a freak torrent swept the bridge away, leaving the Guides stranded on the opposite bank and cut off from all support. A replacement bridge was quickly put under construction and, showing remarkable coolness, their commanding officer, Colonel Fred Battye, left two companies of Guides to guard the crossing, and with the five remaining companies took to the hills, driving off the Afghan sharpshooters and burning a number of hostile villages. It was in retiring to the river the following morning that his position became critical, for swarms of Umra Khan's men had hastened down the valley to get within rifle shot of the Guides. Battye, refusing to bend under pressure, calmly heliographed for instructions from the General on the opposite bank.

By now, 5000 of the enemy were massing on Battye's flank, making retirement down the mountainside a hazardous undertaking and requiring the utmost steadiness if it were to be accomplished without incurring severe casualties. Watched by anxious eyes from the opposite bank, the Guides began to fall back by companies, each in turn pausing to pour a withering fire into the charging mass of tribesmen from behind a scattering of boulders. As the Guides fought their way back to the bridgehead closely followed by a streaming mass of banners marking the path of the Afghans, a sudden shift by the enemy threatened to cut their line of retreat. Seeing the danger, the two companies of Afridis which had remained behind advanced to check the flanking movement, whilst from the east bank the rifles of the 1st Devons began to crackle in a rapid supporting fire.

The bravery of the enemy in crossing that bullet-swept ground made an indelible impression upon Captain Younghusband. 'Standard bearers with reckless gallantry could be seen rushing to certain destruction,' he wrote; '. . . sometimes men, devoid of all fear and having used up the whole of their ammunition, rushed forward with large rocks and hurled them at the soldiers. . . . They were like hounds on their prey.'

Colonel Battye had handled a difficult operation with consummate skill but, just when the safety of his Guides was assured, the gallant Colonel fell at the head of the regiment he had served with distinction for twenty-five years. If proof were needed of his popular standing, it lay in the manner with which the Afridis rallied to the spot where he had fallen. Unhappily his wound was mortal and Battye died as they carried him back through a field of green barley.

During the hours of darkness, a company of Sikhs and a Maxim-gun team were floated across the river on rafts to strengthen the Guides, but it took star shells bursting overhead in a fiery display of pyrotechnics to overawe the superstitious tribesmen and hold them back until it was too late for them to intervene.

News of this action and of the rapid advance of Low's column soon reached the ears of Umra Khan. Now that his own territory was threatened he abandoned all thoughts of violating another's and immediately set out to bring the advance of Sir Robert Low to a halt, much to the relief of the Chitral garrison, which was down to its last few rounds of ball ammunition.

Far to the north, Kelly's small band was engaged in a fierce little action. Having relieved the fort at Mastuj, Kelly had discovered that the way ahead was barred by a mass of Chitralis at Nisa Gol. There, the road following the line of the river was bordered on one side by rock walls which soared almost vertically, whilst on the other side a steep slope loosely covered with shale lay between the river and the mountains

contiguous with the valley to the north. Added to these natural obstacles there were dozens of sangars or small redoubts
constructed from timber and rocks behind which the Chitrali
chief, Muhammad Isa, had assembled nearly 1500 men armed
with relatively modern weapons.

Kelly began his attack on 13 April with a bombardment
from two mountain guns at a range of 500 yards. The shells,
bursting over and around the sangars, forced the Chitralis
into the open, where they suffered more casualties from the
rifle fire of Kelly's main force as his Hunza and Punyal levies
scaled the hill. So great was the steepness of the terrain that
at times ropes and ladders had to be lowered down the side of
the ravine to the nullar below. Nevertheless, showing great
determination against an enemy using Martini-Henry and
Snider rifles, Kelly's troops carried one position after another
to threaten the Chitralis' rear.

Lieutenant Beynon thought it all too easy:

That sangar was a death trap to its garrison since their only line
of escape was across some open shaley slopes within 400 yards of
our firing line and the Levies were now working along the hill,
and would catch them in the sangar if they didn't clear out. The
result was like rabbit shooting. You'd see a man jump from the
sangar and bolt across the shale slope, slipping and scrambling
as he went, then there would be a volley and you'd see the dust
fly all round him – perhaps he'd drop, perhaps he wouldn't; then
there would come another volley and you'd see him chuck forward
amid a laugh from the sepoys, and he'd roll over and over till he'd
fetch up against a rock and lie still. Sometimes two or three would
bolt at once; one or two would drop at each volley, and go rolling,
limp and shapeless, down the slope, until they were all down and
there would be a wait for the next lot. . . .

The forcing of the ravine at Nisa Gol dented the morale
of the tribesmen, who had believed it to be impregnable, and
the Chitrali River was reached on the 17th without further
opposition. But the stream was not easy to cross since it was
breast-high and fast-flowing. The sepoys managed it by link-
ing hands in a human chain but it was a different story for the
Pioneers, many of whom were carrying large loads. 'One man

I thought was bound to be drowned,' related Beynon. 'He had somehow tied his load onto his head and being washed off his feet, his head was kept down below the water, whilst his legs remained waving frantically in the air. The load, being light, floated and in this manner he was washed down-stream, till two levies reached him and swinging him right side up, brought him spluttering ashore.'

That afternoon, Kelly decided that rather than risk his small force in the defiles where Ross had fallen, he would take to the hills. The mountain scenery, had they but time to appreciate it, was spectacular and, after some nerve-racking marches along narrow, winding tracks beside seemingly bottomless ravines, the column dipped down into the village of Barnas.

Kelly's troops were now less than thirty miles from Chitral, where the garrison continued to maintain a stubborn defence under the most dire circumstances. The makeshift hospital was crowded with patients in various degrees of misery and Surgeon-Captain Whitchurch, without adequate medical supplies, could do little to minimise their suffering. He readily agreed to act as Townshend's subaltern, and at night, despite his own poor health, took a turn on the walls and shared the military duties with the regimental officers.

As the days grew warmer, the smell in the hospital, in the stables and from the latrines became almost intolerable. 'TThe stenches in this awful fort are simply appalling,' confided Townshend to his diary. 'How the men in the stable picket do not all get ill coming off duty, I can't imagine. I feel sick every time I go to the stables to inspect. . . .' The morale of the Kashmiris, never very high, fell dramatically as the temperature soared, but their British officers strove to present a cheerful face and continued to direct operations with resourcefulness despite the strain of thirty days' siege.

At the end of March a horse was killed to supplement the rapidly diminishing food stocks, and Robertson was the first to sample an improvised soup prepared by the Chitrali cook. 'One sniff of that dreadful fluid sufficed,' he wrote. 'How it had been concocted was unknown and never enquired into but its odour was appalling.' Nevertheless horseflesh was welcomed as a necessary supplement to the diet and on those occasions,

Robertson recollected, 'The topic of conversation converged around a subject of never dying interest and always began after the first pangs of hunger had been assuaged effectually. Someone would say, "What excellent dinners they give you at the Savoy!" Then everyone would brighten up, and ate Savoy dinners or suppers over again in imagination.'

The next few days were fairly quiet but on 7 April a heavy outbreak of firing from the trees presaged an assault against the covered way to the river. Although the attack was beaten back by the Sikhs, the enemy succeeded in setting the south-east corner of the gun-tower ablaze. 'Running and shouting as I ran . . .', related Major Robertson,

> every unarmed man except the Chitralis who were safe in their rooms, were quickly collected in the lower storey of the gun-tower and on the promenade roof which led to it. Marvellously quickly each fell into his place, as though he had been carefully drilled for such an emergency. Lines of men were organized . . . and passed buckets, pails, or pots of water from hand to hand . . . or carried up earth in their coats.

For a time it seemed that the fire had taken too strong a hold. Choking clouds of smoke and falling beams, to say nothing of the occasional bullet, made things difficult for the fire-fighters, but gradually the blaze was brought under control and finally extinguished, fortunately without serious damage to the fort's defences.

Around midday on 17 April, the sound of picks betrayed the fact that a shaft was being dug from a summer house forty yards from the walls of the fort and had now reached to within twelve feet. It was clear that some sort of action would have to be taken, and quickly. Townshend discussed the problem with Robertson and both agreed that there was no time to construct a counter-mine. Lieutenant Harley, with forty Sikhs and sixty Kashmiris, was detailed to attack the summer house at the point of the bayonet and deal with the miners.

At 4.00 p.m. the gate was thrown open and the powder party dashed for the mine-shaft whilst the stormers engaged the thirty Pathans holding the summer house. The Sikhs had no intention of taking prisoners and the thirty-five Chitralis caught inside the tunnel were summarily despatched with the bayonet, allowing Lieutenant Harley to stack the kegs of powder and light the forty-foot length of fuse. There were a few seconds of uncertainty but, just as Harley was about to return, a blast of hot air knocked him flat on his back and with a tremendous upsurge of earth and stones the mine erupted.

The sortie had been spectacularly successful and at the expense of only eight killed and thirteen wounded. It had probably saved the fort from total destruction and the garrison's morale was restored. 'What a cheery dinner we had that night,' recalled George Robertson. 'Even the famished smokers suffered less than usual. Our tobacco had long been exhausted while cloves, chopped straw and the bark of the plane tree proved wretched substitutes for the gentle narcotic. . . . we talked more and more of the Savoy and other tantalising thoughts.'

The garrison was in high spirits and indeed Robertson expressed his opinion that their ordeal was almost over, a view confirmed on the 18th by news that Sher Afzul had fled and Kelly had defeated Muhammad Isa at Nisa Gol. The garrison did not relax its vigil, however, and as George Robertson related, 'Nobody wanted to sleep. One or two made the attempt, but soon gave it up and fell to talking again. The reins of our tongues were loosened.'

Two days later, the sound of bugles was heard and a rising cloud of dust a mile or so away signalled the approach of Kelly's little column. After forty-seven days of hardship, Robertson and his fellow officers could have been forgiven had they shed a few tears of joy, but with typical Victorian reserve there was no greater show of emotion than a quiet handshake and the ready appreciation of being in the fresh air after the poisonous atmosphere of the fort. 'Poor chaps,' wrote Beynon. 'They were walking skeletons, bloodless, and as quiet as the ghosts they resembled, most of them reduced to jerseys and garments of any description, but still plucky and of good heart.'

On that same day, 19 April, Major-General Sir Bindon Blood – a descendant of the notorious Captain Blood – with an escort of Lancers, rode into the village of Miankilai in search of Umra Khan. A villager who knew where the Sirdar was agreed to take a polite message from Blood pointing out that in an hour or so the British Army would arrive and the Sirdar would very soon have to choose between surrender or crossing the border into Afghanistan. 'In Afghanistan,' Blood pointed out, 'he would be looted and would probably be dead in three months.' If he surrendered he would be treated like a gentleman.

In an hour, the villager returned with an answer to the effect that, although Umra Khan knew he would be safe if he surrendered to Bindon Blood, he was surrounded by Ghazis and other cut-throats who would not allow him to do what he wished to do. 'He finished', wrote General Blood, 'by observing that I also had my usual cut-throats with me! – meaning the Guides – who were quite pleased when they were told what he called them.'

Just one week later, the advance guard of Sir Robert Low's column, led by Major Owen and accompanied by Captain George Younghusband, arrived at Munda fort, the deserted headquarters of Umra Khan. 'The enemy had left little behind them,' reported Reuters correspondent Lionel James, 'but one curious find awaited the search party of the 11th Bengal Lancers. A letter was found from a Scottish firm in Bombay offering to provide Umra Khan with every modern pattern of war machine . . . from a 35 pdr quick firing gun to revolvers at Rs.34 each.' The firm in question, he added, had found it expedient to transfer itself to Cairo.

The end of the campaign brought a deserved knighthood to Surgeon-Major Robertson and a Victoria Cross to Surgeon-Captain Whitchurch in recognition of his risking his life to bring in a mortally wounded officer at the beginning of the siege. Lieutenants Gurdon and Harley were each awarded the DSO. Surprisingly, Colonel Kelly, although awarded a CB, as was Townshend, never received the newspaper coverage that his epic march deserved; possibly this was because the

Reuters correspondent was with General Low and the British regiments.

None of this seems to have been of any great concern to Lieutenant Beynon and the others of Kelly's small party. 'There are only one or two of us left now in Gilgit, who took part in the march,' wrote that young man, 'but, black or white, it is a bond between us which will, I hope, last our lifetime.'

Of the Afghan leaders, Umra Khan fled to Afghanistan, only to be imprisoned by the Amir, whilst his confederate Sher Afzul was sent back to India under escort where, remarked Lionel James, 'his presence will now swell our list of paid dependants'.

Captain Younghusband, who was with the party escorting Sher Afzul to the railhead at Nowshera, adds an interesting and humorous footnote:

> Sher Afzul wore a high astrakan head-dress, a thick double breasted Russian great-coat with brass buttons and a pair of high Russian boots; a suitable costume for the highlands of Central Asia and in the depths of winter, but a little inappropriate as we dropped down towards the plains of India in the hot weather. I could see the perspiration pouring down Sher Afzul's face and thinking perhaps that he had no other kit, proposed to get him a cooler outfit at the next halting place. This offer he rather abruptly refused and as it was no business of mine, if it pleased him to be boiled alive, I let the matter drop.

The secret of the greatcoat was revealed later. Concealed in the coat and about his person, Sher Afzul had a large number of valuable stones, and in a belt around his waist gold coins and jewels valued at £20,000, a considerable fortune in those days. 'Needless to say', Younghusband continued, 'his fears were groundless. He had never met British officers and soldiers before, and thought they were the same class of scallywags and looters he was accustomed to.'

Now that the country was again in a peaceful state, the ten-year-old Shuja-ul-Mulk, known to the British soldiers as 'Sugar and Milk', was confirmed as Mehtar of Chitral and reigned for forty years over his people without further disturbance of any kind.

The vexed question of whether a Russian threat justified the presence of a British garrison in Chitral was widely debated in Parliament and it was left to Lord Salisbury, now Prime Minister following the demise of the Liberal government, to decide that it did.

Garrisons of regular army troops were also stationed on the Malakand Pass and a new political agency for Dir, Swat and Chitral was established under the leadership of a Major Harold Deane, whose skilful negotiations had been instrumental in obtaining the release of Lieutenants Edwardes and Fowler. Negotiations were also opened with the tribal maliks, who in return for special payments agreed to carry the mail, keep telegraph communications open and refrain from attacking the British post on the Malakand road.

The tribes of the Swat Valley appeared to be satisfied with their lot but in crossing the Malakand the Chitral relief column had given the mullahs the excuse they had been looking for and within twenty-one months of the Malakand Agency becoming established everything was once again thrown into the melting-pot.

Chapter 10

The Mad Mullah

A year after Waziristan became part of British India follow-ing the signing of the Durand Agreement in 1878, a garrison of regular troops was stationed in the southern part of the country to guard the strategically important Malakand Pass. The tribal chiefs, who were in receipt of special subsidies from the Indian government, seemed to have been appreciative of the advantages afforded by the British administration even to the extent of maintaining the telegraph line and effecting repairs on the road to Chitral.

For two years the rule of law prevailed until the murder of a Hindu clerk in June 1896 incurred a collective fine of Rs. 2000. The fine remained unpaid a year later when the Political Agent, backed by a strong escort of Sikhs, visited the north Waziristan village of Maizar five miles from the Afghan border.

The villagers exhibited every sign of goodwill, even to providing a midday meal, but as the sun climbed in the sky with the troops relaxing beneath the shade of a banyan grove, it was noticed that many of the villagers had drifted away. Suddenly, before Colonel Bunny or his officers could be aware that anything was amiss, a heavy fire was directed at them from every house. Colonel Bunny and two other officers were killed in the first volley and only the cool behaviour of Subahdar Sunder Singh enabled the Sikh riflemen to with-draw in good order to the camp at Datta Khel.

The authorities took no further action, preferring to treat the incident as simply one more example of tribal treachery.

That it might have been an indication of something more serious was not appreciated until much later.

It was the hot weather season, when even carrion crows sat in dejected isolation among the withered branches, and in the searing heat most Europeans sought the cooler temperatures of the hill stations. On the Malakand ridge overlooking the Swat Valley, a British garrison grumbled at the extra security recently introduced following reports of tribal gatherings in the hills. There was certainly reason for concern, for ever since the Maizar affair the mullahs had spared no effort in spreading rumour and preaching jihad against the hated infidel, from southern Waziristan to the Khyber.

Among the most active was a Swati religious leader known as Sadullah to the Pathans and to the British as the Mad Mullah. He possessed a striking black beard, burning eyes and, it was said by the superstitious villagers, the ability to work miracles. Throughout the weeks of July the bazaars resounded to the frenzied rhetoric of the Mullah. The British would be swept away and by the time of the new moon no one would remain. When that moment came, a vast army would descend from the mountains to destroy the infidel.

It was not only the religious leaders who were spreading inflammatory tales along the length of the frontier. The Amir of Afghanistan was taking an active part in the business of stirring up religious hatred. Abdur Rahman had become increasingly bitter over the setting up of the Durand Line and the announced intention to bring the frontier tribes under British control. Early in the summer of 1897 he addressed a meeting of mullahs from the Frontier and many parts of Afghanistan urging upon them their duty to preach holy war against the infidel. The mullahs needed little encouragement and the message carried back to their villages bore the added weight of the Amir's promise of military support.

The Political Agent for the Malakand area, Major Deane, knew of the troubles in Swat and was aware of the tribesmen's belief in the magical powers of the Mad Mullah, but since frontier gossip was rarely reliable he saw little prospect of any action that might enliven the dull routine of the Chakdara station. Winston Churchill, who was there at the time, took a similar view: '... everybody doubted if there would be a rising, nor did anyone imagine that even should one occur, it would lead to more than a skirmish,' he wrote. 'The natives were friendly and respectful! The valley smiled in fertile prosperity.'

On the evening of 26 July, the young officers of the Malakand garrison were sitting in their mess in polo kit having just returned from the customary game at Khar, where they had been in competition with the officers of Chakdara watched by an unusually large crowd of Afghans. At 9.45 p.m. a signal was received from the Chakdara post with a warning that the tribesmen were advancing in strength along the valley. It was the last telegraph before the line was cut. Fifteen minutes later, a sowar galloped in with a terse message: 'That the Fakir had passed Khar and was advancing on the Malakand, and that neither Levies nor people would act against him, and that the hills to the east of the camp were covered with Pathans.' At 10.00 a.m. the bugle sounded 'Assembly'. The garrison was about to come under attack from no fewer than 10,000 tribesmen, who had swarmed up through the polo ground under cover of darkness, skirting the bazaar area, the camp and the perimeter earthworks. The great Frontier War had begun.

At first all was confusion, as might be expected in a surprise night attack, but fortunately the officer in charge, Lieutenant-Colonel McRae, did not panic. He quickly despatched the quarter guard to a position where their flanks were protected by high rocks, with orders to hold the enemy while reinforcements were brought up.

The Sikhs he sent were under the command of a Major Taylor. They were among the elite of the Indian Army and the small party began to pour volley after volley into the mass of tribesmen before them. The Pathans were checked for a moment and then numbers of them began to climb a hill to the left of Taylor's position where they began to hurl down stones and rocks at the Sikhs, which forced them to retire. It was then that Taylor received a mortal wound. McRae, himself suffering from a neck wound, called out to his by now seriously depleted squad to bear in mind the good name of 'Rattray's Sikhs' and fight to the last man. For a time things looked grave, but after twenty minutes of desperate fighting, reinforcements came charging down the road from the camp and the situation was transformed.

Meanwhile, over to the right of McRae's position, the noise of battle increased. Great numbers of tribesmen had swept away the guard picket and overrun the camp. Desperate hand-to-hand encounters erupted over the whole area, around the huts and buildings, through the bazaar, into the commissariat lines and on to the football pitch, whilst a continuous crackle of musketry swept the camp from the surrounding heights.

By 3.30 a.m., however, the crisis was over. The tribesmen had suffered such punishing casualties that for the time being they had lost the will to fight, and when dawn came they withdrew, leaving their dead entangled in the wire, among the ravines and draped across the low stone walls and sand-bagged entrenchments.

By the afternoon of the 27th, the reinforcements requested by Brigadier-General Meiklejohn, the Malakand Commander, began to arrive. First came the Guides cavalry, followed a few hours later by the infantry. Then came the welcome news that the 11th Bengal Lancers, the 38th Dogras and the 35th Sikhs had left Mardan and were expected in three days.

That evening, the sepoys standing to in their weapon pits or behind the stone walls of sangars could plainly see thousands of white patches moving steadily down the hillside beneath an umbrella of fluttering banners. Grim-faced, the soldiers of the Indian regiments crouched patiently at their posts waiting for the attack they felt sure must soon be launched against them.

It came just as the light was fading, with line upon line of screaming swordsmen charging towards the camp perimeter. Rising above the cries of the tribesmen came the brisk crackle of Martini-Henry rifles as disciplined firepower blunted the attack and scythed through the ranks of the oncoming Ghazis. Heavy losses counted little with the Afghans, who fought with fanatical bravery, but, at daybreak, the weary garrison was still standing firm.

The little fort in a loop of the Swat River had also come

under attack. There, the Sikhs led by a lieutenant whose name had been given to the regiment by its founder, H. B. Rattray, worked their Martini-Henry rifles and two Maxims to such good effect that the enemy dead lay in heaps against the north and east walls of Chakdara. The Afghans had no ladders long enough for escalade purposes but over the next three days the small garrison was kept constantly on the alert against determined attacks by tribesmen whose religious fervour blinded them to the destruction being wrought by the garrison's modern weapons. Although never doubting for a moment the ability of his men to defend their posts, Lieutenant Rattray was acutely aware that, with each passing day, food and ammunition stocks were shrinking. Reinforcements were sorely needed.

At the Malakand, in spite of a harassing fire directed on the camp from the long-barrelled jezails of the tribesmen, the sepoys had been able to strengthen the defence works. This was a necessary task, since the eve of Friday 30 July was a Moslem holy day and a massed assault from every quarter could be expected. Earlier it had been the loose white and grey apparel of the local tribesmen which had predominated, but now the black flowing gowns of the Buner tribes were to be seen in their thousands along the ridge of the Malakand Heights.

Soon after sundown, a furious beating of drums heralded the start of yet another attack by tribesmen brought to a fever pitch of excitement by the exhortations of their mullahs. 'Was not the moon full, and had not the great Fakir declared that this should be the moment of victory?' For five hours the Pathans pressed home their attacks with undiminished frenzy and were punished severely. A Guides officer, Lieutenant Elliott-Lockhart, captured the animated scene for his readers when he recorded a typical attack: 'bands of Ghazis worked up by their religious enthusiasm into a frenzy of fanatical excitement, would charge our breastworks again and again, leaving their dead in scores after each repulse, whilst others would encourage their efforts by shouting, with much beating of tom-toms and other musical instruments.' At one point in the attack a mullah was heard promising that the infidels' bullets would turn to water.

In the small hours of the 31st, an attack was mounted on each flank and pressed home with such savage intensity that the Pathans succeeded in penetrating the breastworks. But this was as far as they got, and McRae's Sikhs did not allow a single tribesman to escape. After this latest assault had been thrown back the garrison was given the welcome news that they were no longer alone. Colonel Reid was at Dargai on the other side of the heights with the 35th Sikhs, the 38th Dogras and a detachment of Guides.

Meanwhile, ten miles away at Chakdara, the two companies of the 45th Sikhs were becoming battle weary. Since 26 July, the garrison, whose only heavy weapon was a single nine-pounder gun, had been under constant attack from 10,000 Pathans. Although their defence held firm, the defenders of Chakdara were without water and facing a desperate situation. Early that afternoon a Sikh signaller, showing great daring under persistent sniper fire, slipped out through a porthole of the signal tower to set up a heliograph. Just two words were flashed to the Malakand: 'Help us'.

That garrison, itself in dire straits, could do little for the moment, but early on the morning of the 30th, Colonel Reid's Sikhs marched into Dargai, having lost nineteen of their number from heatstroke. Even as they arrived, a much larger relief column was being formed. For at Simla the Governor-General, Lord Elgin, had at last acknowledged the gravity of the situation in the Lower Swat. Three brigades were to be designated the Malakand Field Force under the command of Sir Bindon Blood for an immediate march through the mountains and sparsely populated highlands.

They arrived in the Malakand at noon on 1 August and the Irish Major-General lost no time in assessing the situation. 'When I rode in I saw a string of litters bringing in the casualties and everyone looked rather melancholy. . . . I assumed command at once, clearing everybody out of the office, and had the orders out in less than an hour, for a sortie at daylight next morning.' The key to the enemy's position was a hill to the right of the camp which commanded a spur running down to the valley. Blood's plan of operation was to take this hill with 300 of his infantry and two mountain guns, whilst attacking the Afghans' centre with his main force.

At 4.30 the next morning, his troops got under arms and in the dawn light Colonel Goldney moved off towards his objective, the peak on his right. The attack was a brilliant success. Even as the Pathans were rubbing the sleep from their eyes, Goldney's men were among them with the bayonet, and the position was taken without sustaining a single casualty. 'By Jove, Sir!' gasped a breathless subaltern who had been sent back for orders, 'we have had a merry time.'

Blood's main force had been deployed to take the enemy in flank and, despite a heavy fire at close range, these troops now began to close on their objective. Winston Churchill in his capacity as correspondent, described the scene: 'without wasting time in firing, they advanced with the bayonet. The enemy, thoroughly panic stricken, began to fly, literally by the thousands, along the heights to the right.... The way was open. The passage was forced. Chakdara was saved.'

The Malakand and Chakdara garrisons were relieved barely forty-eight hours after the first order had been given to advance, and by the last week in August the only task remaining for the Malakand Field Force was the penetration of the boulder-strewn wilderness of Upper Swat. Not since Alexander the Great had any white man set foot in that mountainous region and, after being held up for more than a week by torrential rain, Sir Bindon Blood set out on 16 August with three brigades supported by cavalry and artillery.

The assault on the 'Gate of Swat' – a natural obstacle considered impregnable by the tribesmen – was preceded by an artillery bombardment of the tribesmen's sangars. The explosions from the heavy shells of the 10th Field Battery so unnerved the Swatis that many began to stream away before Blood's infantry had left their jumping-off point. Others, confused by the gun team's use of smokeless powder, ran blindly for the reverse slope behind the sangars.

The flank attack was led by Colonel Meiklejohn, but before

his sweating troops could reach the ridge, the tribesmen, realising that their line of retreat was threatened, abandoned plans for a counter-attack and fled to the hills. The next day Blood took possession of the valley of the Upper Swat and the Swatis were forced to capitulate.

Blood waited just long enough for the political negotiations to be finalised before returning to the Malakand. Once there, he set about organising a punitive force to march against the Bunerwals, but, before he could complete the arrangements, news came of a serious rising west of the Malakand.

On 7 August, twelve days after the tribesmen's attack on the Malakand and Chakdara garrisons, a further and not unexpected outbreak occurred fifteen miles north of Peshawar at Shunkargarh. During the afternoon 5000 Mohmands had descended into the Gandab Valley, burned the village and attacked the nearby border police post at Shabkadr. Fifty police held the fort and resolutely defended it for twelve hours until the approach of a column of Punjabis and a detachment of Somerset Light Infantry from Peshawar forced the Mohmands to retire.

Over the next two weeks little happened to disturb the peace. The Political Officers went about their business and the Peshawar Vale Hunt rode the countryside in pursuit of jackals. Such was the illusion of calm that, in reassuring an anxious government, the Commissioner of the district signalled: 'Everything quiet. Reliable sources indicate that Afridis are unaffected.' Within hours of the telegraph's despatch, there came news of an Afridi lashkar 10,000-strong which had left Tirah on 16 August led by 1500 mullahs. Its objective was believed to be the Khyber forts from Landi Kotal to Moude.

The Orakzais and Afridi clans who populated this region of the Khyber had long profited from generous payments in return for assurances of freedom of movement along the Khyber route, and the loss of the three forts came as a great shock to the Indian Army. Each of the forts had been garrisoned by an irregular corps of tribesmen raised by Sir Robert Warburton after the second Afghan War whilst he was acting as Political Officer for the Khyber ɛ ·ea. The corps,

known as the Khyber Rifles, was officered by Afridis, whose
reliability was such that the government of India had not
hesitated to employ it during the Black Mountain expedition
of 1888.

Ali Masjid, the fort in the centre of the Khyber, was the
first to fall when the Afridis betrayed the trust Warburton
had placed in them by abandoning their post without firing
a shot. Fort Moude at the eastern end of the pass held out
for just a few hours longer before its garrison retired on a
rescue column sent out from Jamrud.

The fort at the western end was an immensely strong
structure with two-storey loopholed walls and a garrison of 370
men of the Khyber Rifles. An account of its fall is dramatically
described by Sir Richard Udney, the Commissioner of the
Peshawar Division, in his report to the government of India:

The Landi Kotal garrison consisted of five native officers and 370
men of the Khyber Rifles, including 25 recruits, Munshis, etc, who
were unarmed. Of these, 120 belonged to miscellaneous classes,
principally – Peshawaris 40, Shilmani Mohmands 25, Adam Khel
Afridis 28, from Kohat Pass and neighbourhood. Of the remaining
250 men, 70 were Lowargai Shinwaris in whose limits Landi Kotal
stands, whilst the other 180 were pretty evenly divided between
three tribes, namely Zakha Khel Afridis, Malikdin Khel Afridis
and Mullagoris.

These 250 men formed the main strength of the garrison and
seemed to have behaved very well on the 24th when they inflicted
severe loss on the enemy by volley firing; but on the morning of the
25th, after the Shinwari Subadar Jawas Khan had been wounded,
the Shinwari sepoys made a sudden bolt of it by jumping down
off the northern wall of the post towards their own villages, and
the rest of the garrison were so disgusted at their desertion that
they fired after them as they fled, killing three or four of them.

The Commissioner continued:

A little later some Shinwari tribesmen and Zakha Khels of
the Bazar Valley managed to scale the wall of the post at its
north-east corner near the officers' bungalow, but were promptly
met by a party under Subadar Mursil and driven back over the

wall after a smart little fight in which Mursil was shot through the head and killed on the spot. On his death the defence fell to pieces: the sepoys on the walls began to exchange greetings with their fellow tribesmen outside the post, the gate was treacherously opened from inside and the Ghazis of all tribes swarmed in. The Mullagori sepoys and probably the Shinwaris too then made their escape over the wall with their rifles, as the Shinwaris had done before, whilst the Zakha Khel and the Malikdin Khel sepoys ran under the flags of their own clansmen in the lashkar, and joined in the general loot of the post.

The 28 Adam Khel sepoys also joined the Ghazis, and like the Zakha Khel and Malikdin Khel sepoys, returned with the lashkar when the sack of the post had been completed. Of the 40 Peshawaris, six are known to have been carried off prisoners, but the rest seemed to have been allowed to escape, of course without their rifles, although only a few have yet arrived at Jamrud.

After the looting of the post, the lashkar withdrew to China in the Bazar Valley, and, in spite of the remonstrances of their mullahs, the men are 'said' to be fast dispersing in order to carry home their dead and wounded.

It remains to be seen how many of the Mullagori and Shilmani sepoys will turn up with their rifles, but it is not improbable that a good many of them will rejoin sooner or later, and it is even possible that some of the Zakha Khel and Malikdin Khel sepoys, though not likely to rejoin in person, may send in their rifles when the excitement has subsided.

The fall of the Khyber forts, especially Landi Kotal with its great stock of ammunition, had left Peshawar dangerously exposed and the fact that only Fort Jamrud stood before the city and the advance of the rebel forces was sufficient to stir the Punjab and Indian governments into a realisation that it would take an army corps to deal effectively with the uprising. By the early autumn of 1897 the Pathan insurrection had spread south of the Kabul River, but despite growing concern over events elsewhere it was felt that an expedition against the Mohmands must be given top priority.

In spite of the tribes' habitual raiding of the Peshawar Valley, the Mohmand tribal territory had yet to be visited by the British, but now, with two brigades already across the frontier it was considered an appropriate time to teach them a lesson. There were very nearly 12,000 British and Indian troops in the Peshawar area, more than enough to form what became known as the Mohmand Field Force, led by General Elles. The usual difficulties of procuring transport having been overcome, the punitive column headed northward with orders to burn the Mohmand villages in concert with General Blood's Malakand Field Force in the east. On 8 September, Sir Bindon Blood vacated the Panjkora Valley and began to advance westward towards Nawagai, whilst General Elles marched from Shabkadr six days later.

Lieutenant Churchill, who was attached to General Elles' staff, brings out vividly the discomforts of hot-weather campaigning in his narrative of the Malakand Field Force.

> Slowly the hours pass away. The heat is intense. The air glitters over the scorched plain, as over the funnel of an engine. The wind blows with a fierce warmth, and instead of bringing relief, raises only whirling dust devils, which scatter the shelters and half choke their occupants. The water is tepid and fails to quench the thirst. At last the shadows begin to lengthen, as the sun sinks towards the western mountains. Everyone revives. . . . The feelings of savage hatred against the orb of day, fade from our minds, and we strive to forget that he will be ready at five o'clock next morning, to begin our torment over again.

By the 11th, the 3rd Brigade pushing forward to link up with Elles had reached Nawagai, where the General immediately established a staging post from which to launch punitive thrusts southward towards the Bedmanai Pass. This was captured on the 24th without serious loss but in repelling two night attacks on the camp at Nawagai the 1st Queen's sustained a few casualties, including Brigadier Woodhouse, who was hit whilst walking back from a conference with Blood.

Blood, meanwhile, had sent a second brigade commanded by Brigadier-General Jeffries into the Watelai Valley on a punitive strike against the widely scattered villages. The brigade ran into strong opposition and a company of the 35th Sikhs found itself isolated and under attack from a large party of Pathans. With the Sikhs was the correspondent of the *Daily Telegraph*, and the young Winston Churchill thrilled his readers with this account of the action:

> As the soldiers rose from the shelter of the rocks behind which they had been firing, an officer turned quickly round, his face covered with blood. He put his hands to his head and fell on the ground. Two of the men ran to help him away. One fell shot through the leg. A sepoy who was still firing sprang into the air and, falling, began to bleed terribly. Another fell close to him. Everyone began to pull those men along, dragging them roughly over the rocky ground in spite of their groans. Another officer was immediately shot. Several Sikhs ran forward to his help. Thirty yards away was the crest of the spur. From this a score of tribesmen were firing with deadly effect. Over it ran a crowd of swordsmen, throwing pieces of rock and yelling. The two officers who were left used their revolvers. The men fired wildly. One officer and two wounded sepoys were dropped on the ground. The officer lay on his back. A tall man in dirty white linen pounced on him with a sword. It was a horrible sight. The retreat continued. . . . the bullets struck dust spurts all round. Most of the wounded were however carried off.
>
> At length the bottom of the hill was reached. Then somebody sounded the charge. Bayonets were fixed. . . . the officers ran forward and waved their swords. Everyone began to shout. Then the forward movement began – slowly at first, but gaining momentum rapidly. As the enemy fled back . . . many dropped under the fire of the Sikhs.

Another party led by General Jeffries in person was obliged to remain during the night in the burning village of Shar Tangi, the supporting mountain battery having been immobilised by a heavy loss in gunners and mules. The next morning the 1st Buffs came to the rescue, but, as Churchill observed, 'It was an anxious night; perhaps the fitting close to an exciting day.'

With the end of the fighting around Nawagai, negotiations were opened with the Mohmand maliks at a jirga on 11 October. On three sides of a square sat the tribal elders, with Sir Bindon Blood, his staff and an escort of Guides on the fourth side. After the customary courtesies had been exchanged, the tribal leaders expressed their regret for the revolt, which they said had sprung from the tribesmen's fears of annexation, and promised security for the rifles yet to be surrendered. They swore to abide by the terms of the treaty and keep the peace. The meeting lasted a little less than fifteen minutes.

Blood had returned Rs 4000 which he had previously confiscated as a guarantee of the tribesmen's good faith, and as he rode away from the assembly, accompanied by several headmen, firing broke out behind him. Before the General could ask what was happening, the oldest chief turned in his saddle and said, 'Oh, Sahib! It is nothing. It's only our rascals having the usual fight over the money!'

On 12 October 1897, the column left for India, watched by the tribesmen from the hills. Whatever satisfaction they felt at the departure of the infidel quickly evaporated, however, when they looked back at their valley. 'Not a tower, not a fort was to be seen,' wrote Churchill. 'The villages were destroyed. The crops had been trampled down. They had lost heavily in killed and wounded and the winter was at hand. No defiant shots pursued the retiring column. The ferocious Mahmunds were weary of war.'

It was the end of the Mohmand campaign but, whilst Blood's column was leaving the area of Upper Swat, Sir William Lockhart with two divisions was heading for a region of the Afridis where no European had ever set foot.

Chapter 11

The Tirah Campaign

The two divisions which left Kohat on 11 October were better equipped than any that had taken the field since the days of the Mutiny. In command was General Sir William Lockhart – a Mutiny veteran – who although a strict disciplinarian of the Victorian school was an experienced soldier and had enjoyed a measure of success in punitive operations against the Orakzais.

Although Indian and Gurkha troops formed a major part of the Tirah Expeditionary Force, as it was called, there were four British battalions armed with the new bolt-action Lee-Metford rifle. Accompanying them were two squadrons of cavalry, four mountain batteries, a machine-gun detachment, Pioneers and a field hospital so well equipped that the medical personnel even possessed an X-ray camera.

There was just one major obstacle to be overcome. The territory over which it would be operating was totally unknown. 'Purdah nashin', the Afridis called the region, or 'concealed behind the curtain' – the curtain being the lofty range of mountains which surrounded the country on every side. The 900 square miles of the Tirah Maidan, a wide fertile valley enclosed on its southern side by the Samana Ridge and on its northern side by the imposing Safed Koh range of hills, had for generations been jealously guarded by the Afridis. The Indian government, until now, had respected the tribesmen's wishes and even the Black Mountain expedition of 1891 had not proceeded beyond the Samana Range.

The General's plan of campaign, on paper at least, seemed

straightforward. His column would enter the Tirah before the first fall of snow and, after crossing the Samana Range, would subjugate the tribes in a series of northerly and easterly marches. The campaign was expected to be brought to a successful conclusion with the recapture of the Khyber Pass before the end of December.

On 18 October, Lockhart's operation began with a minor mishap when the King's Own Scottish Borderers and the 1/3rd Gurkha battalion, after taking the Dargai Heights at little cost to themselves, were obliged to withdraw due to inadequate stocks of food and ammunition. No supply arrangements had been made, which meant that two days were to elapse before a sufficient number of pack mules could be assembled to carry out the urgent task of bringing up enough stores to enable the position to be consolidated. By then, the heights had been re-occupied by an Afridi lashkar and the frustrated Scots together with their Gurkha comrades gazed up from their camp on the plain to see the heights blossoming with the green banners of Islam.

Shortly after 10.00 a.m. on the 20th, the nine-pounder mountain batteries began a bombardment of the Dargai Heights from a range of 1800 yards. The enemy's position was soon obscured by drifting clouds of white smoke laced with the bright orange flashes of bursting shells. The spread of shrapnel, however, had little effect on the tribesmen, who were sheltering beneath rocky overhangs which gave good cover against anything but a direct hit.

Whilst the bark of Lockhart's screw guns echoed around the hills and kept the heads of the Afridis down, Colonel Eaton-Travers led his Gurkha scouts across an exposed neck of rock to a position in dead ground which afforded adequate cover from small-arms fire. The rest of the battalion was not so fortunate. The tribesmen soon became aware of what was in progress and, in spite of the shelling, an intense and accurate rifle fire caught the main Gurkha force on the open glacis. Many of the tribesmen were armed with breech-loading Sniders and Martini-Henrys and such was the curtain of fire they were able to put down that hardly a shot failed to find a human target.

Colonel Travers waited impatiently for the others to join him on a goat track where lay the odd boulder to give his men cover, but the finest marksmen on the Frontier, many of whom had several rifles, made sure that no one could do so. After a pause to recover, several companies of the Dorset and Devonshire regiments were ordered to make the attempt but they too suffered losses and as the morning wore on it seemed impossible that troops would ever cross that bullet-swept ridge in sufficient numbers to carry the heights.

It was now long past noon and so worried was he by the slaughter of his men that General Kempster asked General Yeatman-Biggs whether he considered it essential to recapture the heights. Yeatman-Biggs, whose task it was to seize the Kotal, knew that his troops could not be committed to a passage through the gorge until the tribesmen had been driven from the heights, and he was in no doubt that a second attempt must be made. Lieutenant-Colonel Mathias of the Gordons received the order without turning a hair. 'Highlanders!' he called to the assembled battalion. 'The General says that the position must be taken at all costs. The Gordons will take it.'

Mathias realised that only a concerted rush by a mass of men would stand any chance of crossing the open ground, and he immediately ordered officers and pipers to the front. As the pipes set up the stirring notes of 'Cock of the North', 600 cheering Highlanders scrambled out of cover and on to the exposed neck of rock whilst the artillery redoubled its shelling of the ridge.

The Afghan marksmen, although subdued, had lost none of their accuracy and the charge of the Scots left a litter of kilted figures sprawled in its wake. Piper Findlater was among the first to be hit but, although shot through both legs, he found support against a boulder and enough breath to continue his playing as the Highlanders rushed past.

If the knowledge that they were taking severe casualties did nothing to stem the ardour of the Scots, neither did the steepness of the slope; 'stiff climb, eh, Mackie?' puffed Colonel Mathias to his colour-sergeant. 'Not quite—so young—as I was—you know.'

'Never mind, sir,' answered the sergeant, and giving his

commanding officer an encouraging slap on the back which almost knocked the remaining wind out of him, added, 'Ye're gaun verra strong for an auld man!'

At the expense of thirty-five killed, the battalion crossed the neck just as their Colonel expected. They were quickly followed by Gurkhas, Sikhs and the men of the Dorset and Devonshires.

Now began the difficult climb upwards among the rocks and crevices leading to the summit. The narrow goat path was some 300 feet long and, as the foremost Highlanders reached the crest, bayonets gleaming in the sun, the Afridis began to melt away. When eventually the Union Jack streamed in the breeze above the Dargai, not a green banner was to be seen.

It was now late afternoon and, since it was clearly impossible to continue the advance in the fast-fading light, the troops were ordered to bivouac where they stood. Again, incompetent staff work was to blame and the soldiers were obliged to bed down as best they could without the comfort of greatcoats or blankets. There was very little food beyond that contained in their haversacks and, since fuel and water were impossible to obtain, most spent a trying and comfortless night in temperatures which fell to zero.

Six miles away, many hundreds of pack animals stood patiently all through the hours of darkness. They had not been fed or watered for forty-eight hours and all carried loads which no one had seen fit to remove. When the column of march was resumed the next day, hundreds of animals died or were destroyed on the difficult ascent through the Khanki Valley to the base camp beyond. For most of that week, although patrols were sent out to reconnoitre, the entire expedition was halted whilst 3000 camels were assembled to move the 600 tons of stores necessary to the next stage in the operation – the passage through the 6700-feet-high Sampagha and Arhanga Passes.

Shortly after daybreak on 29 October, orders were given to break camp, and with a regiment guarding each of their flanks, the main body of troops, supported by artillery, launched a drive against the difficult Sampagha Pass. By 10.00 a.m. the gorge had been taken in the face of only

token resistance. The Arghanga was in British hands before
the Afridis had time to recover from their earlier defeat, and
as October came to an end the troops began to wonder what
had happened to the fighting spirit of the tribes.

The Tirah Expeditionary Force was now close to the beautiful and fertile Tirah Maidan, the first non-Afridis ever to see
it. 'We have all been very much struck by the appearance of
this valley,' wrote Colonel Hutchinson of the Mastura Valley.
'It is wide, flat, well-watered land even here at its head, fairly
timbered with apricot and walnut trees about the villages,
which are very numerous and well built. . . . A great deal
is under cultivation, the fields are carefully terraced, and
signs of plenty and comfort are abundant. . . . the Autumn
tints remind one of England.'

Tidy-looking two-storey houses of stone and mud baked hard
from the sun dotted the now deserted valley. The villagers
together with their sheep and goats had vanished into the
hills, leaving stocks of Indian corn, beans, barley, potatoes,
onions and walnuts for the troops to plunder. Writing for
The Times, Colonel Hutchinson could truthfully inform his
readers: 'We have the valley to ourselves. It has been the
proud boast of the Afridis from time immemorial that no
enemy of whatever race or creed has ever attempted to cross
the mountain barriers which shut them in. . . . Well, we have
changed all that.'

His statement proved to be a little premature, for on 21
November, when Lockhart summoned the maliks to a jirga in
order to dictate the terms of their surrender, they remained
silent and unseen. Not so their band of warriors. Supply
columns were ambushed and telegraph lines cut. Foraging and
map-survey parties came under fire from cliff overhangs and
the dry beds of water courses. Sniping activities after sunset
were particularly effective. 'It is extremely unpleasant, this
whizz and spatter of bullets while you are at dinner or trying
to enjoy a pipe round a camp fire before turning in,' confessed
Hutchinson. 'If you have got to be shot leading your men into
action, that is all right, and a proper and honourable way of
being shot. . . . But to be potted in the dark is autre chose!'

The British troops were powerless to defend themselves in

the face of this latest harassment. Many of the rifles which fell into the hands of the Afridi were Lee-Metfords, which used smokeless powder; consequently the men in the camp could have little notion of where the shots came from or even from what quarter a skilful marksman fired his rifle.

In retaliation, Lockhart began to burn the tribal homesteads right across the valley. Fortified farms and even entire villages were dynamited and razed to the ground. Orchards were destroyed after the troops had denuded them of fruit, fields of grain were trampled, and wells filled with sand and rocks. Looting by the punitive parties on these occasions was widespread and unchecked, but, in keeping with the Victorian sense of respect for all forms of religion, the mosques were left undamaged. 'Whether this measure will have the effect of making them yield their submission, or whether it will exasperate them into making a big attack on our camp,' the Colonel mused, 'time alone can show!'

Whatever the consequence, the measures taken by Lockhart certainly impressed the Reuters correspondent. Wrote Lionel James: 'One of the most magnificent sights one could wish to see was the destruction of the valley by fire and sword as the evening waned into night. The camp was ringed by a wall of fire – byres, outhouses, homesteads, and fortresses one mass of rolling flame, until the very camp was almost as light as day.'

The British General's ruthless tactics produced the desired result. The winter snows were fast approaching and, since survival in the hills was next to impossible, the tribal leaders were forced to seek terms from the British. The first to arrive were the maliks of the Orakzais tribe. 'They were nearly all venerable old greybeards,' observed Hutchinson; '. . . there was certainly nothing either warlike or truculent in their bearing or demeanour.'

Squatting on their heels, the tribal elders listened impassively as Lockhart told them that all arms stolen from the British must be returned; that 300 of their own breech-loading rifles would be forfeited together with all subsidies and allowances, and a fine of Rs 50,000 would have to be paid in cash. 'It was not to be gathered from their countenances, or from anything they said,' wrote Hutchinson, 'whether they thought them severe or lenient.' The only consolation the Orakzais were able to draw at the end of the meeting was that their country was not to be permanently occupied.

Winston Churchill, who at the end of the Swat campaign had watched one clan hand in their rifles, commented bitterly, 'Perhaps these fire-arms had cost more in blood and treasure than any others ever made. . . . These tribes have nothing to surrender but their arms. To extort these few had taken a month, had cost many lives, and thousands of pounds. It had been as bad a bargain as was ever made.'

It was three weeks from the submission of the Orakzais before the Khumber Khels, Aka Khels, Malikdin Khels and Kamrai Khels came down to parley, during which time they continued to exact a considerable number of casualties among the occupying forces. Experts in guerrilla tactics, many of the tribesmen had put to good use experience gained during service with the Indian Army.

Unlike the Orakzais, the Afridis refused to accept unconditional surrender. 'With the exception of your field guns, which we have not,' an elder told a senior officer on Lockhart's staff, 'man to man we are as good as any of you.' Hutchinson would not have disagreed. 'They have absolutely nothing to learn from us, these Afridis,' he informed the readers of *The Times*. 'Contrariwise, their dashing and bold attack, the skill with which they take advantage of ground, the patience with which they watch for a favourable moment, and their perfect marksmanship – all these qualities have again and again won our admiration.' This expression of esteem or admiration was not reciprocated by the Afridis. Their hatred of the British was now more intense than ever.

It was December and time for the British to leave if they were to avoid the rigours of a Tirah winter. Lockhart's plan was to withdraw through the forty-mile-long Bara Valley and reopen the Khyber, which lay to the north of the Bazar Valley.

The columns began their march on the 9th in the teeth of a bitterly cold mix of sleet, snow flurries and thick mist. Crossing and recrossing the infuriatingly meandering River

Bara proved to be the stiffest test the 2nd Division had yet faced. 'The spray from the water, splashed up by wading, froze as it fell,' commented the observer from *The Times*, 'while moustaches became mere blocks of ice, and the horses' tails as they swished them about in the stream were covered immediately with long spiky icicles.'

On dry ground conditions were little better. The cultivated areas along the river bank had deteriorated into patches of icy bog in which the pack animals floundered up to their girths. Much of the column's tent equipment had been lost and the troops were obliged to bivouac around camp fires which constantly spluttered out in the driving rain, on ground stamped to frozen slush from the passage of earlier detachments. As if that were not enough to try their patience, the sleeping figures were often subjected to a sporadic sniping from Afridis ensconced on the upper slopes of the valley. Encouraged by their mullahs, the tribesmen on occasion swarmed down from the hills to attack not only isolated groups of soldiers at night, but also the column's rearguard during the day. These sudden rushes so unnerved the camp followers that many were only prevented at bayonet point from dropping their burden of wounded and decamping.

On the 13th, the enemy appeared in great strength just as the 4th Brigade was engaged in clearing the previous night's camp. Before the baggage could be moved, a heavy fire was opened by the Afridis, killing ten of the pack animals but fortunately none of the men. The native drivers, frightened by the constant singing of bullets passing above them, pushed wildly forward and swept like a human tidal wave between the baggage lines of the 3rd and 4th Brigades. There were many casualties and, since the doolie-bearers had fled with the camp followers, it was left to the troops to carry their own wounded. A halt was made at a point where the track led up out of the river bed and, as the enemy swarmed across the stream in pursuit, only a timely intervention by the mountain-gun battery and pickets from the Peshawar Column saved the day.

The five days and nights it had taken the 2nd Division to fight its way out of the Bara Valley trap cost Lockhart

164 casualties, but he could now turn his attention to the Khyber Pass. Here, Lockhart was on more familiar ground and by making good tactical use of the still habitable forts that had been recaptured by his troops, he soon had the Afridis reeling. Now began the slow but methodical advance of the British towards Landi Kotal, burning villages and seizing the tribal flocks of sheep and goats that had previously been beyond their reach in the Tirah Hills.

As the snows began to melt in the spring sunshine of 1898, even the most recalcitrant of the Frontier tribes had had enough. Faced with the prospect of starvation for their families and the knowledge that continued resistance would only prolong their own misery, the Afridi tribes finally abandoned the fight for their homeland. It had taken Lockhart more than five months, but for the first time in the history of frontier warfare an enemy who had perfected the art of guerrilla fighting had been decisively beaten.

The great uprising was over.

Chapter 12

The Pestilential Priest

The victory of the Indian Army in the two Tirahs culminating
in the peace durbar of 1898 left British India with expensive
military commitments. Ten thousand troops were garrisoned
in forward positions beyond the administrative border without adequate means of communication and in some danger
of becoming isolated or even overwhelmed.

A political solution was urgently required but it was
not until a remarkable junior statesman arrived upon the
scene that it was forthcoming. Thirty-nine-year-old George
Nathaniel Curzon had long sought a position of influence in
India. Almost the first task he had set himself upon being
elected Member of Parliament for Southport in 1886 was
the study of Asian affairs, particularly that of India. In five
years he rose to become Under-Secretary at the India Office,
and four years later Under-Secretary at the Foreign Office,
visiting Bokhara, Samarkand, Tashkent, Chitral and Kabul.

The Pathan uprising of 1897 paved the way to the office
he craved, for such was his knowledge of Frontier problems
that Lord Salisbury had no hesitation in appointing him to
the post of Governor-General or, as it was becoming more
widely known, Viceroy of India, in January 1899.

One of the first matters to which Curzon gave his attention
was the removal of the Frontier from the jurisdiction of the
Punjab and elevating it to the status of a new Indian province
directly responsible to the government of India. There was
good reason for his action. For too long the Frontier and
its turbulent tribes with their alien way of life had been

subordinate to a Governor whose chief concern was for the Punjab. It should be added that creating a separate Frontier province was not a new idea. Twenty years earlier, Lytton had recommended that Roberts be given the administration of a tribal territory stretching from Hazara to the Indian Ocean.

Even so, Curzon's action in raising the Frontier to the status of a separate province ran counter to the wishes of many British India officials who could not understand why such a savage frontier should be given equal standing with the Punjab and other recognised provinces. None was more vehement in his opposition than Sir Mackworth Young, Lieutenant-Governor of the Punjab. But, despite fierce opposition, Curzon's eloquent and logical arguments won the day and on 9 November 1901 all tribal territory up to the Durand Line was separated from the Punjab to form the North-West Frontier Province.

The man appointed as Chief Commissioner of this new province was a rising junior official who had enjoyed a successful career as Political Officer in the Malakand Agency since 1895. Churchill remembered the man from his days with the Malakand Field Force. 'We had with us', he recalled, 'a very brilliant political officer, a Major Deane, who was most disliked because he always stopped military operations. . . . Apparently all these savage chiefs were his old friends and almost his blood relations. Nothing disturbed their friendship. In between fights, they talked as man to man and as pal to pal.' The tall blue-eyed Sir Harold Deane could boast of a degree of trust and respect quite unique for a Feringhee among the tribes of the Frontier, which was as well if he were to convince the Pathans that the government of India had their best interests at heart.

With the establishment of the new Frontier Province, Curzon introduced a close border policy. No longer would troops of the Indian Army be stationed along a winding 200-mile strip of tribal territory from the Malakand Pass to Waziristan. The practice now was for the Frontier tribes to be responsible for the defence of their own territory, which necessitated a huge increase in the numbers of local militia under the control of British officers. The Khyber Rifles were a good example. This force had existed before the 1897 revolt, but many other paramilitary bodies came into being such as the fast-moving Tochi Scouts, the South Waziristan Scouts, the Samana Rifles and the Kurram Militia. The regular army was not forgotten and a complete restructuring was undertaken, designed to improve morale and efficiency.

Curzon achieved this measure of reform largely through the efforts of a man regarded by many as the greatest soldier in the Empire. General Horatio Herbert Kitchener of Sudan fame had just brought the South African War to a successful conclusion, but the task which confronted him on his arrival in India as Commander-in-Chief was formidable. Lord Kitchener not only had to install a fighting spirit in the sepoys, few of whom had ever heard a shot fired in anger, but also to raise the morale of the disgruntled British troops.

Kitchener's conviction that all units should be given the opportunity for training on terrain most likely to involve them in active operations resulted in the introduction of the Kitchener Test as a necessary part of training. Every infantry battalion was required to take part in a fifteen-mile route march followed by an advance in skirmishing order to a specified objective. Food for the day consisted of four army biscuits, a tin of compressed soup and three blocks of chocolate.

Although a severe test of stamina, the idea was popular with the troops and Frank Richards records that of the 900 men in his battalion only five dropped out – 'All on the return journey and all staunch teetotallers.' The Welch Fusilier Corporal believed that had they been fonder of beer than they were of tea, the five would have completed the course with the others, despite carrying a load of some 150 pounds.

The bulk of the army was, as Kitchener expressed it, 'scattered all higgledy-piggledy over the country, without any system or reason whatever'. By reducing garrisons to a minimum and reorganising the four existing divisions into a corps, the strength was stretched to nine divisions, three of which were permanently stationed on the Frontier.

In Kabul, events were shaping to a pattern not at all to Curzon's liking. In 1901, after a reign of twenty years, Abdur

Rahman had been succeeded by his eldest son Habibullah
Khan to enjoy a sovereignty which for once was not marred
by factional disturbances. Frank Richards, who was present
in the guard of honour when the new Amir visited India in
January 1907 (after Curzon's departure), described him as
being about five feet six inches in height and inclined to be
a little portly. Dressed for the occasion in a black European
suit, and wearing a red fez, his black whiskers and slightly
hooked nose reminded the Welch Fusilier of a 'well-to-do
Jewish pawnbroker'. Habibullah lacked the single-minded
purposefulness of his father and was powerless to rid his court
of a strong anti-British faction led by his brother Nasrullah.

With increasing pressure from Russia for a political agency
in Kabul, it seemed to Curzon that Afghanistan's usefulness
as a barrier against Russian or Persian designs upon India was
in jeopardy. Fate came to his assistance, for Russia became
embroiled in a conflict with Japan and, discomfited by defeats
on land and sea, turned her attention to a matter of greater
significance than a mountainous area in Central Asia – the
growing might of a militant Germany.

In 1907 this fear was real enough to persuade Russia of
the advantage to be had in having Britain as an ally rather
than an adversary, and representatives from both countries
put their signatures to a convention in St Petersburg by which
Persia was divided into spheres of influence and Russia agreed
to recognise Afghanistan as a British sphere if Britain agreed
not to occupy any part of that country. With the signatures of
the Russian Foreign Minister and the British Ambassador, the
spectre of a confrontation with Cossacks in the Khyber and
other passes vanished, and the 'Great Game' was over.

But this time, however, Curzon himself had faded from
the scene, a victim of a damaging quarrel with Kitchener.
The Viceroy had never been popular in military circles, even
among the rank and file, who considered that he was 'giving
the natives too much rope'. Corporal Richards was of the
opinion that the ordinary soldier's resentment grew from a
remark passed by Lady Curzon when she said that 'the two
ugliest things in India were the water buffalo and the British
private soldier'. Although Curzon's term as Viceroy had ended

in squalid intrigue, he could claim with some justification that during his six years of office he had accomplished more than any of his predecessors.

Whilst it was true that the administered districts were relatively peaceful, relations with the trans-border tribes were as volatile as ever. The Mahsuds of Waziristan had remained peaceful enough during the 1897 rising, but under the spell of a mullah whose magical powers, they believed, would make them impervious to the bullets of the English troops, they could be numbered among the most dangerous tribes of the frontier.

The Mullah Powindah, 'a first-class scoundrel' in the opinion of Lord Curzon, seldom missed an opportunity to confound and embarrass the government. Descending from the jagged piles of rock which formed their stronghold, the Mahsuds attacked border posts, farms and traders' caravans. Using modern breech-loading rifles, they went about their business so swiftly that they were often several miles away before the Militia could arrive upon the scene.

The first real punitive step taken against the Mahsuds had come late in 1900 when a fine of one lakh of rupees was imposed on the tribe to be paid within two weeks. It was ignored, a studied insult that the government could not allow to go unpunished. A punitive expedition was ordered and for four months regular Indian Army troops struck against tribal villages in various parts of Mahsud territory. The losses sustained by the Mahsuds in both men and cattle forced them to submit and in March 1902 the fine was paid in full.

For the next two years the Mullah Powindah – dubbed by Kitchener the Pestilential Priest – kept a low profile and the Mahsuds seemed to have settled into a peaceful coexistence with the neighbouring tribes. In the early autumn of 1904, however, the Political Agent for the district was murdered and the authorities had no hesitation in denouncing the incident as a political assassination ordered by the Mullah. A few months later, the Commandant of the South Waziristan Militia at Wana was fatally wounded by a Mahsud sepoy then on duty in the fort's keep. The sepoy was hanged but at his court martial it transpired that he was part of an elaborate plot by the Mullah to seize the magazine and treasure and to murder all the British officers.

An Indian battalion was moved to Wana in order to take reprisals, but the border raiding and killing continued even after the Mullah Powindah's death in 1913. One Afridi tribe which proved particularly troublesome was the Zakka Khel. This was a clan which had never forgotten the humiliation of their defeat in 1897 and they were determined to seek revenge. By raiding across the border from the Bazar Valley, they hoped to force the British into retaliatory action and by so doing drive other Afridi clans into joining them in a holy war against the infidel invader.

That their border raids enjoyed a large measure of success was due in no small way to the gross inefficiency of the border police and tribal militias. At least a quarter of their personnel were past retirement age and their Snider rifles were no match for the raiders' Martini-Henrys and Lee-Metfords. The time when a tribesman depended solely upon his long-barrelled jezail and Khyber knife was long past. Since the 1897 uprising there had been a marked improvement in the quality and quantity of breech-loading rifles available to the Pathans. Among Pathans generally the possession of a modern gun was a mark of prestige, and rifle thieves were constantly on the prowl around British cantonments. 'The best and most coveted rifles were those stolen from the army,' wrote Colonel Pettigrew, '. . . and they would fetch a price many, many times their value. . . . so rifle stealing was indulged not only in the frontier districts but all over India. But wherever they were stolen . . . rifles would all find their way north to the Frontier; that is why in India to lose a rifle was a terrible disgrace for any regiment, and a court martial for the offender.'

Corporal Frank Richards, in his biography *Old Soldier Sahib*, describes an incident in which a party of Pathans arrive in cantonments with a performing bear and several monkeys. At dawn the next day it was discovered that nine rifles were missing from the guard tent, but despite the most rigorous search the thieves were never apprehended and the rifles were presumed to have been safely carried back across the Frontier.

Rifles stolen from the army were faithfully copied in the Adam Khel factory near the Kohat Pass, south of Peshawar. But the supply coming from this source was a mere trickle compared to that available from the Persian Gulf in the gun-running trade. By 1905 shipments from Muscat carried by dhow across the Gulf and then by caravan through southern Persia became a flood. The British were powerless to interfere for the dhows sailing from Muscat flew the French tricolour. The smugglers were thus immune from search and seizure by the Royal Navy, and the caravans were always free to take the westerly route through Persia in order to avoid military patrols in southern Baluchistan.

The Zakka Khel, well-armed and confident, continued to exploit weaknesses in border security until eventually an audacious raid on Peshawar in January 1908 exhausted the patience of the Chief Commissioner Sir Harold Deane. The following month an expedition was sanctioned and the 1st Peshawar Brigade led by Major-General Sir James Willcocks pulverised the Bazar Valley with their new ten-pounder field guns so thoroughly that the Zakka Khel suffered more casualties in two weeks than this Afridi clan had during the entire Tirah campaign. By the end of February, Willcocks had so demoralised the clans by the rapid deployment of his troops that the headmen were forced to submit unconditionally. Although the swift and successful campaign of Sir James Willcocks had demonstrated to neighbouring tribes the futility of a concerted uprising, it was still found necessary to march north where trouble with the Mohmands threatened Shabkadr Fort. Willcocks met that threat with the same swift despatch and then marched to the western end of the Khyber to nip a threat by tribesmen from across the Durand Line. After this, the General returned to complete the pacification of the Mohmands and by the end of May 1908 he could justifiably claim to have contained a situation which might easily have developed into a major uprising.

For three troubled years from 1915 Habibullah had resisted a growing clamour for Afghanistan to unite with Turkey in a holy war against the allies in the belief that, by freeing Indian troops to fight in France and Mesopotamia, his claim for independence would be more readily appreciated. In fact his refusal to be dragged into the Great War was of considerable value to Britain, a circumstance recognised by King George V, when he wrote to Habibullah: 'I have been much gratified to learn . . . how scrupulously and honourably you have maintained the attitude of strict neutrality which you have guaranteed. You will thus still further strengthen the friendship I so greatly value. . . .'

Thus encouraged, Habibullah approached the new Viceroy, Lord Chelmsford, requesting recognition of the 'absolute liberty and freedom of administration and perpetual independence of the Sublime Government of Afghanistan'. Chelmsford was not unsympathetic but, before a reply to the Amir's letter could be drafted, an unknown assassin crept into Habibullah's tent at night and blew off the top of his head with a rifle shot. In the camp at the time of the murder was Habibullah's brother Nasrullah, who immediately assumed the title of Amir. It was a short-lived bid for power for the murdered man's son, Amanullah, who as Governor had ready access to the arsenal and treasury in Kabul, quickly summoned the tribal chiefs and had himself proclaimed Amir on 28 February 1919.

The new Amir, twenty-seven years old and in the opinion of General Molesworth 'a man of strange character, conceited, arrogant, and with a somewhat empty precocious mind', was immediately beset by problems. The troops suspected him of complicity in the murder of his father and Amanullah was forced to raise their pay and distract attention from himself with a major undertaking. The recovery of Peshawar was the hazardous enterprise he was seriously considering.

Concurrent with the upsurge of nationalism in Afghanistan, there occurred a state of unrest in India which was potentially even more dangerous to the Raj. The most vehement expression of protest centred upon the Punjab, and when on 11 April 1919 Gurkha troops acting upon the orders of General Dyer opened fire on a public assembly at Amritsar killing 379 civilians and wounding some 1200 more, Amanullah acted. In his durbar at Kabul two days later, he called for a jihad against Britain. 'Gird up your loins,' he exhorted the tribal chiefs, 'the time has come.' Few of Dyer's victims had been

Moslem, but the incident had provided Amanullah with the excuse he needed and he immediately announced his intention of moving up troops to the Frontier.

In Kabul the news was greeted with elation. A strong guard had to be put on the house of the British Agent to protect it from rock-throwing students and proclamations calling for a holy war were posted in mosques across the country. The new Afghan Commander-in-Chief, Saleh Muhammad, moved with commendable speed, and on 4 May 150 of his troops crossed to the British side of the Frontier and occupied the village of Bagh. This village, situated on high ground at the western end of the Khyber, was the source of the water supply to Landi Kotal, then garrisoned by 500 sepoys of the Khyber Rifles. With the pumping station out of commission due to the murder of its staff, the garrison was entirely dependent for its water supply on two reserve tanks.

By this time the whole country was in ferment. Thousands of tribesmen poured into Jalalabad and on 6 May the Indian government announced general mobilisation. The third Afghan War had begun.

In Peshawar tension mounted as mobs of Afridis rioted in the bazaars, whilst in the hills around the Khyber Pass Afghan lashkars, anticipating a move to relieve Landi Kotal, were poised to strike. The Indian Army, thanks to earlier disbandment and the granting of block leave, was in no position to meet such a threat, whilst the few British regiments then available were mostly territorials who were over-age for active service and had been sent to India in order to release regular troops for France. After four years of service on the North-West Frontier, these citizen soldiers wished only to return to civilian life. Frontier duty had no appeal for them.

At dawn on 7 May, in conditions of great secrecy, one battalion from the Somerset Light Infantry was sent through the Khyber Pass to reinforce the garrison at Landi Kotal. The troops were hurried through in a convoy of 30-hundred weight lorries covered with tarpaulins to conceal their loads from the tribesmen, who assumed it to be stores for the fort. The hooded lorries also deceived the military police, for three of the ammunition trucks which accompanied the convoy were later found to be carrying nothing but cases of beer.

That same day, Peshawar was surrounded by troops and, after a threat by Chief Commissioner Roos-Keppel to cut off the city's water supply, the principal agitators were surrendered to the police. The following morning peaceful trading was once again the norm in the city's bazaars.

At Landi Kotal, an assortment of British, Gurkha and Sikh troops had successfully reinforced that garrison, bringing it up to brigade strength. At dawn on 9 May they began to move across the mile of barren ground which separated the fort from the Afghan position at Bagh. Its capture proved far from easy, for the troops could only progress on a narrow front over difficult sloping around which made covering fire almost impossible. It was not until 11 May that Brigadier-General Crocker was able to overcome Afghan resistance among the rock-strewn hills with sufficient assurance to pave the way for an assault on Bagh.

Saleh Muhammad had deployed his forces along the crest of a rocky promontory, giving his men a clear field of fire against their attackers, who were obliged to advance in short rushes from one position to the next with seldom the chance to return fire. Crocker's men desperately clawed their way up the steep shale-covered slopes in the face of a machine-gun fire so effective that it was impossible to carry the wounded to the field hospital in the rear. It came as no surprise when after an hour the attack ground to a halt, for even the mules lost their footing so frequently that the gunners found it easier to remove their loads and manhandle the guns and ammunition to a position where they could strike back at the enemy.

For a while the attack was confined to an exchange of small-arms fire whilst the artillerymen prepared their charges, and then a concentrated barrage from four howitzers and sixteen machine guns enabled the advance to be resumed. When the North Staffordshires finally reached the summit, an accurate and telling covering fire helped them to neutralise the Afghan sangars with grenades. By early afternoon the troops were bivouacked in the village and General Crocker's concern that his line of retreat to Landi Kotal could be jeopardised if Bagh were not taken was eased.

Crocker's next objective was the village of Dakka, some five miles across the border towards Jalalabad in the north-east. This time, in a bid to soften up the opposition, a squadron of BE2Cs was sent to bomb the Afghan position. 'They were so under-engined and decrepit', wrote Molesworth, 'that they could not make height to cross the main Khyber massif and had to fly up the valleys. Consequently the pilots experienced the novel conditions of being fired down on, by tribesmen on the hills above them.' The sortie may have been a severe test of nerves for the aircrews, but their aircraft made a vivid impression upon the credulous tribesmen. 'I have seen wonderful things,' wrote a mullah to a fellow rebel. 'The wicked British have got aeroplanes in the Peshawar district where they fly in the sky. God knows whether we can fight against them or not. The Mullah of Khema is sent on to you in order to relate the account to you personally. But the grace of God is greater than such deeds of devils.'

The bombing had been largely ineffectual and when the British and Indian troops took up their positions outside Dakka on 13 May it was only to find themselves overlooked for the second time, by an Afghan lashkar 3000-strong along a summit quickly dubbed Stonehenge Ridge from the circle of stone slabs which formed a Moslem shrine.

For the next two days, apart from cavalry reconnaissance patrols, little was done. 'All we heard in Landi Kotal were glowing reports of the bathing in the river,' complained Molesworth. This period of inactivity was causing the General some anxiety, and on 16 May, Colonel G. N. Molesworth's battalion of the Somerset Light Infantry and the 1/35th Sikhs were ordered to join the main force at Dakka.

Just before the column moved off, Colonel Molesworth was joined by a tall, ascetic-looking officer in a dilapidated forage cap and a very old water-proof. Under the impression that he was the Bishop of Lahore, who was at that time visiting British troops in the Khyber, Molesworth took his leave. 'Goodbye, Bishop. I hope we shall meet again soon.'

'We shall probably meet again,' came the reply, 'but I am not a bishop. I am Major-General Skeen, commanding the 3rd Brigade.'

Considerably abashed, Molesworth recalls that he 'saluted and rode quickly away.'

By this time Afghan regular troops were in full possession of the ridge and Saleh pressed home his advantage by bringing into action seven modern Krupp field pieces whose rate of fire effectively slowed the progress of two Sikh regiments climbing towards the summit 2000 feet above them. At 8.00 a.m. the crest was reached but to the consternation of the leading companies it was found to be almost a razor's edge only a few yards wide, falling away steeply and in some places precipitously. The ground was impossible even for mountain guns and when the supporting battery fell silent due to the difficulty of bringing up ammunition, the entire attack faltered.

Later that day, 17 May, reinforcements from the garrison at Landi Kotal and the arrival of much-needed ammunition ensured that Stonehenge Ridge fell into British hands. But it was taken at a heavy price for, in the slow sweaty crawl up the shale-covered slope, 179 British and Indian troops were killed or wounded, including 18 officers. Many of the rifles used by the tribesmen were Sniders with, as Molesworth observed, 'a clay filled expanding bullet which caused dreadful, and nearly always fatal, wounds'.

The British erected their tents in the camp they had made at Dakka and waited for orders. The delay proved to be far from comfortable. The temperature under canvas averaged 117° and thick clouds of dust and myriads of flies created an atmosphere in which the stench of death was a major factor. Animal carcasses decomposed rapidly in the intense heat and so swiftly had the campaign been organised that few troops had been inoculated against cholera. This, together with that scourge of Victorian armies, dysentery, was sweeping the camp with deadly effect. Rations, too, were far from adequate; 'some of the meat was "Bullied Mutton" from Australia,' noted Molesworth. 'The gentleman who produced it had, rashly, put his portrait on the tin and many people kept those labels hoping that, in the future, they might meet him.'

If discomforts such as these were not enough for the troops to contend with, Mohmand sniper fire tested their patience to the limit. The dust-caked and sweat-soaked British and Indian soldiers found it increasingly hazardous, even with armed escorts, to bathe in the Kabul River. 'I do not think any bather was ever hit,' Molesworth remarked, 'but when the snipers opened up, there was a wild scramble of wet and naked men, hastily gathering up clothes and running for cover.' Eventually, a thirteen-pounder gun was brought up and the tribesmen were driven from the north bank of the river and Afghan rifle fire became less of a nuisance.

On 24 May, the Royal Air Force was again called into action when an ancient Handley Page 0/400 lumbered a few hundred feet over Dakka on its way to bomb Kabul. The bombs that were dropped did little damage beyond bringing Amanullah's harem to the verge of hysterics, which brought an outraged protest from the Amir.

One of your aeroplanes flew over Kabul and bombarded our Royal Palace, thereby causing great excitement and panic among our loyal people. Many other favourite buildings in our official quarter and unprotected town were bombed. It is a matter for great regret that the throwing of bombs by zeppelins on London was denounced as a most savage act and the bombardment of places of worship and sacred spots was considered a most abominable operation, while now we see with our own eyes that such operations were a habit which is prevalent among all civilised people of the west.

Despite the prospect of marching thirty miles in temperatures of 100°, the troops were glad enough to leave behind the dust and flies of Dakka for the next stage of the advance to Jalalabad. Before the march could get under way, however, disturbing news arrived from the south. Waziristan had been vacated and, on the banks of the Kurram River, the British garrison at Thal was in serious danger from the guns of the one Afghan general with enough military knowledge to put his advantage to good effect.

Chapter 13

Abdul Ghaffar Khan

If the Afghan Army was open to criticism it lay in the inability of its officers to plan a strategic operation. Few commanders possessed an understanding of modern military tactics and only one the skill to put that knowledge to good effect.

Suspicion that he may have been party to the murder of Habibullah had banished Nadir Khan to the relative obscurity of the Khost district, but in April 1919 he had been reinstated by Amanullah and given the command of fourteen infantry battalions, two regiments of cavalry and forty-eight pieces of heavy artillery. On 24 May that army had reached a point on the Kaitu River only thirty miles west of the British railhead of Thal in the southern half of the Kurram Valley. News of Nadir Khan's rapid advance brought about large-scale desertions of the Wazir and Afridi elements in the North Waziristan Militia, a disaffection which soon spread to Wana in the south of the country, where renegades seized the armoury. These incidents confirmed a suspicion many frontier experts had held for years, namely that the local militias were incapable of withstanding the strain put upon them and had become more of a liability than an asset.

The situation was grave, for unless regular troops could be speedily transferred to the Kurram area, there was a danger that Nadir Khan might reach the Indus and precipitate an uprising as widespread as that of 1897. The eastern end of the Kurram Valley at Thal was guarded by a small fort of chopped straw and mud manned by Sikhs and Gurkhas under the command of Brigadier-General Eustace. His garrison numbered little more than 800 young and inexperienced Indian soldiers with four mountain guns and a pair of mortars, and as the Afghan General led his army of 3000 well-equipped troops through the valley, the ill-defended railhead had every appearance of being an easy target.

Whilst tribal levies gathered in the expectation of rich pickings, Nadir Khan deployed his artillery to the best advantage in the hills overlooking the fort and village. Within hours, 100mm shells from his Krupps howitzers were causing extensive damage to the Militia barracks. On 2 May, despite the occasional bombing mission by the Royal Air Force, Nadir Khan's gunners had perhaps their most successful day, blowing up the petrol dump, setting fire to the fodder stored in the rail yard and destroying the radio station. This was followed by an attack on the fort, which was only narrowly beaten off and so alarmed the Frontier Constabulary guarding the water tower that when darkness fell they decamped, leaving this vital structure to fall into the hands of the Afghans.

Three days later, a well-directed shot demolished part of the south wall of the fort, but although the defending troops repulsed the attack with machine-gun and rifle fire, their position was becoming increasingly desperate as supplies of food, water and ammunition began to run low.

At Peshawar, General Sir Arthur Barratt, conscious of the grave situation, switched the troops he held in reserve for an advance on Jalalabad to the more pressing demands of General Eustace. The Thal Relief Force was quickly organised and command given to Brigadier-General Rex Dyer, an officer burdened with the threat of an official enquiry hanging over his head relating to the controversial massacre at Amritsar. Nevertheless, by employing a convoy of sixty-two lorries and the resources of the North-Western Railway, Dyer brought his brigade to Kohat on 28 May. Pausing only to reinforce his artillery with four light field guns from the local garrison, he arrived at Togh, a railway village twenty-seven miles east of Thal, on the last day of May. By this time the relief column had grown from brigade strength to five battalions of infantry, a cavalry squadron, an armoured-car unit and twelve pieces of artillery.

At Togh, Dyer paraded his troops and in a stirring address emphasised the urgency of their task. Rex Dyer may have been guilty of a tragic mistake at Amritsar, but he possessed the qualities needed to inspire troops under his command, and in response to his impassioned appeal even the disgruntled London Territorials swore to march to the limits of their strength. It was not an idle boast, for despite having had little sleep since leaving Peshawar, the men in his command covered the last eighteen miles of rugged hills, over stones which had absorbed the heat of a blazing sun, in a matter of twelve hours. General Dyer was not the man to spare himself. Very much the soldier's General, he marched at the head of the column for most of the way, using a car only for selecting a suitable site for the night's bivouac.

In the morning, the hill tribes who were awaiting the outcome of the battle before joining Nadir Khan in a sweep to the Indus noticed a moving cloud of dust in the north-east. Dyer's men were nearing their objective.

When the relief force came within nine miles of Thal, the General received his first detailed assessment of the Afghan positions. To his north there was a scattering of Orakzais and men of the Khel tribes, in the east and south-east 4000 Afghans and Waziris had gathered under a tribal chief called Malik Babrak, whilst to the west in the hills south of the Kurram River was the regular Afghan Army.

Dyer decided to strike first at the lashkar led by Malik Babrak before dealing with the tribal levies to the north. Opening fire with his artillery at both positions to create the impression that he would be launching a two-pronged attack, Dyer in fact restricted his infantry operation to an assault against the Afghan lashkar.

His plan was a complete success. Malik Babrak had not expected an attack and, after sustaining a severe mauling from Dyer's artillery, his men were reluctant to face the bayonets of Dyer's infantry. Before the afternoon was over, the tribesmen had broken and their position on the high ground was taken at the expense of a few wounded. The enemy battery south of the Kurram River was quickly silenced and the way to Thal lay open and uncontested.

The next morning, 2 June, Dyer reached the railhead and made preparations to engage the main Afghan Army in the Khadimak Hills west of the town. His attack began soon after dawn and, whilst it was still developing, an envoy arrived from Nadir Khan bearing a flag of truce and a request from Amanullah for an armistice. The experienced Dyer, now that he had committed troops to action, refused to be drawn and told the envoy: 'My guns will give you an immediate reply, and a further reply will be sent by the Divisional Commander to whom this letter has been forwarded.'

By early evening, six of the Afghan guns had been put out of action and a sharp reconnaissance confirmed that Nadir Khan was withdrawing his forces. Soon the enemy could be seen in full retreat along the Kurram Valley pursued by armoured cars and a squadron of Lancers.

On 3 June, a small force pushed forward to seize the Afghan camp at Yusuf Khel, only to find it deserted. That same day, General Dyer received a telegraph instructing him to break off pursuit since an armistice had been signed.

Thus the siege of Thal was brought to a satisfactory end but, less happily, so also was General Dyer's career as a soldier. By his skilful handling of men and artillery he had saved Thal and possibly the whole of the Frontier but it did not spare him the indignity of being relieved of his command. The severity of his action at Amritsar, where in the space of ten minutes 379 Punjabis had been shot dead, had overtaken events. Disgraced and discredited, General Dyer died a few years later in England.

The peace initiative from the Amir came not a moment too soon for the government of India. Its army was woefully short of motor transport, its aircraft were so dilapidated that the main planes of some Great War Bristol fighters had patches over German bullet holes, and the medical services were on the point of breakdown.

The Peace Conference assembled at Rawalpindi on 27 July was notable for its degree of acrimony. The Afghan Army had been driven from the British side of the Durand Line, but its delegates were determined not to return to Afghanistan without first having obtained total independence for their country. Several times the talks almost foundered. All that Sir Hamilton Grant, the British delegate, would concede was a recognition that Afghanistan's foreign policy was a matter for the Afghans, and finally on 1 August Grant presented the Afghan delegates with an ultimatum. Either they make peace or the British would resume hostilities. Reluctantly the Afghans reaffirmed the Durand Line as being the political boundary, and on 8 August the Treaty of Rawalpindi was formally concluded.

Amanullah was delighted that he had won the right to conduct foreign affairs without interference, but Sir Hamilton Grant, perhaps believing that this developing nation would experience teething problems, added a note to his communication to Lord Chelmsford. 'Liberty is a new toy to the Afghan government. Later on if we handle them well, they will come to us to mend their new toy when it gets chipped or broken.' He had sadly misjudged the mood of the Afghans.

The withdrawal of the militias from Waziristan had been interpreted as a sign of weakness by the tribes, and when a rumour spread that the territory was to be ceded to the Amir, grievances stirred up by the late war multiplied. Smarting from their recent reverses, the Mahsuds and Wazirs soon discovered a common unity in disorder and tumult. Their numbers swollen by militia deserters, the tribesmen embarked upon a bitter campaign of murder and pillage across the length and breadth of the administered districts.

In mid-November, Major-General Skeen struck back in a swift and highly successful series of minor actions against the Tochi Wazirs. But it was a different story the following month when his Indian troops found themselves facing a well-armed and implacable foe in the Mahsuds. In eight consecutive days of hand-to-hand encounters at Ahnai Tangi during January 1920, Skeen's young and inexperienced soldiers suffered some 2000 killed and wounded. The tribesmen's losses were even greater: 4000 Mahsuds falling in the fighting. Such a drain on manpower could not be sustained even by fanatics who considered it a religious duty to kill Feringhees, and when later in the year their villages were destroyed by punitive columns an uneasy peace returned to Waziristan.

For the next few years the Frontier was relatively tranquil, until in February 1923 the Adam Kheyl raided a police armoury in Kohat and carried off forty-six 0.303-calibre rifles. The Frontier Constabulary, supported by the army, acted with commendable speed and forcibly occupied a village inhabited by the clan, barely five miles from the police post. After a thorough search, thirty-five rifles were discovered skilfully concealed in a cellar with other stolen property, and several of the villagers were arrested. The ringleaders were away in the hills, and great was their fury when they were told that their women had been molested and disgraced during the search. To avenge the insult it was decided to kidnap an Englishwoman.

The plan was put into effect on 14 April, when Azab Khan and his brother Shahzada broke into the house of a Major Ellis during his absence. Mrs Ellis' fierce struggles were ended with a fatal knife thrust and her seventeen-year-old daughter Mollie was abducted. The chosen place of imprisonment for the hostage was the Tirah Massif, where the Afridis had a summer settlement, but bribed by Political Officers the Orakzai tribe delayed the kidnappers long enough for an intrepid Englishwoman to make contact. Mrs Lilian Starr, a nursing sister at the Peshawar Mission hospital, whose husband had been murdered by the Afridis, agreed to accompany a party of loyal tribesmen across the border where, with the assistance of an Orakzai mullah, she was ultimately successful in effecting a rescue.

But minor forays and cross-border raids continued and the Indian government decided that if the rule of law was ever to be upheld in Waziristan the bases at Razmak and Wana must be expanded to the status of military towns, with garrisons of regular army troops to support the militia. It was to be hoped that these two forts on the northern and southern Mahsud boundaries and in the very heart of Waziristan would be a sufficient deterrent against further outbreaks of lawlessness. But there were those who argued that the permanent presence of regular soldiers would simply act as a provocation to the fiercely independent Mahsuds. Despite such misgivings, military roads were built between the forts and a pool of motor transport was created to provide rapid access to every likely trouble spot in the 2500 square miles of wilderness which encompassed the Mahsud territory.

Curiously enough, whilst sanctioning lavish sums to be spent on a policy designed to isolate potential trouble spots, the authorities chose not to encourage an ordered way of life, by refusing to meet the tribesmen's pressing need for water-storage tanks and farming implements. Dried fruit had long been a thriving industry in Afghanistan, but in the administered districts the fruit withered on the vine from the want of a suitable marketing policy. Thus, grievances multiplied and fuelled by the Afghan's aggressive nature, a wave of anarchy swept the Frontier Province to such a degree that a visiting journalist commented: 'This is not British India but the most lawless country on the face of the earth.' Events were soon to bear out the truth of his remarks.

At Landi Kotal one afternoon in April 1929, two officers of the Seaforth Highlanders had no sooner set foot outside the perimeter of the fort for a leisurely stroll than two sharp reports echoed around the rocks high above the valley and a bullet smashed into each man's skull.

In Peshawar, rumours spread of poisoned water being piped into the houses of Europeans and, although armed sepoys stood guard, race-goers could never be entirely sure that a bomb would not be thrown into the grandstand. During one brush with Afridis, a number of women were given shelter for the night in the Peshawar Club. The billiard room was hastily arranged to serve as a dormitory, which apparently offended the sense of propriety of at least one bucolic major. 'I say,' he spluttered to the club secretary, 'isn't it a bit thick to jam a colonel's wife among all these other women? Couldn't you give her the bridge room to herself?'

Lawlessness among the hillmen was by no means an unusual feature of Frontier life, but what disturbed the government was the willingness with which Amanullah seized every opportunity to disseminate anti-British propaganda among the tribes on both sides of the Durand Line.

At Jalalabad in 1923 he presided over an assembly of tribal chiefs among whom were many Pathans from the administered areas. The discussion turned inevitably to reminiscences of past jihads, and encouraged, if not inspired, by Amanullah's exhortations a rash of Frontier incidents afterwards broke out which tried British patience to the limit. The Viceroy's blunt warning to the Amir that he risked severing diplomatic relations if they continued had some effect, for the number of outrages noticeably diminished.

Amanullah's surrender to British pressure brought him trouble from an unexpected quarter when in March of the following year the Ghilzais of Khost rose in revolt. It was not in the interests of Britain to have Amanullah replaced by a rabble of unpredictable frontier Pathans, but it was the Russians who came to his aid in decisive fashion by providing another batch of military aircraft. The Russian pilots speedily brought the revolt to an end by scattering the laskhar in the Khost Valley with a few extremely effective air attacks.

But it was merely a postponement of the inevitable, for Amanullah had made too many enemies among the religious leaders with his forceful programme of change. To a people whose way of life for centuries had been governed by superstition and fanatical bigotry, his attempt to drag them into the twentieth century had proved so unpopular that it had weakened the whole fabric of Amanullah's realm.

In the late autumn of 1928 his attempts to modernise the country provoked another, and this time successful, revolt in the Khost Valley. Brushing aside the weak resistance of troops loyal to the Amir, the rebels reached the outskirts of Kabul on 12 January. Before the month was out, Amanullah was thrusting the crown into the reluctant hands of his brother Habibullah and seeking refuge in Kandahar.

The reign of Habibullah Khan lasted less than six months. By the end of October Nadir Khan had taken possession of the throne and assumed the title of Muhammad Nadir Shah. Simla welcomed the change, for the new ruler was known to be a good soldier, tempering firmness with old-world courtesy, and there was every reason to hope that he would bring a period of stability to that side of the Frontier.

The greatest source of mischief for the government of India, however, was to come not from Waziristan, but from a newly formed political organisation, paramilitary in style and led by a powerful personality who had been politically active since 1919.

Shortly after the Great War the Government of India Act had granted several important concessions to Gandhi's Indian National Congress whilst excluding the North-West Frontier. The reforms, which favoured greater local autonomy as a step towards self-rule, had not been extended to the Pathans. The tribesmen in the settled districts were not considered ready for democracy. Indeed, Sir George Roos-Keppel, the Chief Commissioner, was of the opinion that extending a secret ballot to include the Frontier would be akin to lighting matches in a powder magazine.

Nevertheless, Western education had come to the North-West Frontier. Two colleges, which were open to Pathans entering the civil service, became the aspiration of every ambitious young man who, having tasted the fruits of higher education, would never be satisfied with the parochial way of life of his father. Abdul Ghaffar Khan, a six-foot-four, bearded Pathan from a wealthy Yusufzai family, understood this very well. He was known to his colleagues by a Pathan sobriquet meaning Pride of the Pathans and to the authorities by the less flattering term, the Frontier Gandhi, from the questionable alliance of his Moslem organisation with the Hindu National Congress. This controversial association preached sedition along the length of the frontier from Bannu to the Malakand, and after his release from a three-year jail sentence imposed in 1920 Ghaffar Khan waited for an opportunity to exercise his violent opposition to a policy which he believed discriminated against the Pathans of the province.

With the backing of Congress in 1929, he formed the Khudei Khitmatgars – a body of young Pathans colloquially known as Red Shirts from the practice of dyeing their shirts with brick dust. Its members, ignored by the authorities, who chose to cast a blind eye in their direction, drilled regularly and carried out military training under the supervision of Afghan Regular Army instructors.

By April 1930, Ghaffar Khan's organisation in the Peshawar district had grown to such proportions that it could hold openly seditious rallies designed to incite the population against the civil government. Abdul Ghaffar Khan and a number of his lieutenants were arrested and for more than a month anarchy prevailed with Indian troops facing crowds of stone-throwing youths supported by groups of Red Shirts armed with knives and clubs. During the riots, armoured cars were attacked with fire bombs and at least one unfortunate despatch rider who had mistakenly followed the cars was set upon and killed by the mob.

After four weeks, during which time the sound of machine-gun fire was a daily occurrence, the military and civil authorities gained control and peace was restored. Outside the city and in Waziristan, trouble flared among the Afridis and a lashkar advancing on Peshawar in June was only dispersed by a strong force of cavalry supported by the Royal Air Force.

In August, the lashkar reformed and surged forward once more, this time penetrating the city suburbs and putting an army supply depot a few miles to the north-east of Peshawar under heavy attack. Armoured cars and strafing runs by the RAF finally dislodged them but the government was taking no chances and the entire Peshawar district was placed under martial law.

For the rest of the year the situation remained tense, with the Afridis demanding the release of Ghaffar Khan and his party officials. It was not until the spring of 1931, when grazing became scarce and considerable hardship was suffered by the tribesmen, that the maliks agreed to settle their differences with the British peaceably.

During these events, Nadir Shah had adopted a remarkably cool attitude towards the many Pathan delegations which visited Kabul from the tribal territories seeking financial help for their cause. The Afghan ruler received his guests politely enough, even to the extent of supplying their need for opium-laced coffee. Advice he gave freely, money for weapons not at all.

Abdul Ghaffar Khan was released from jail in March 1931, but his inflammatory speeches had not lost any of their venom, and, when he again began to promote civil disorder, his Red Shirt organisation was declared illegal and Ghaffar Khan was deported from the province with four of his lieutenants. But his campaign had not been in vain, for continual political pressure eventually brought the North-West Frontier Province the same rights and institutions as the rest of British India. In 1932 a Pathan was appointed as the province's first Chief Minister. A moderate man, Sahibzada Sir Abdul Qayyum nevertheless continually badgered the Crown for responsible government on the Frontier. To the official view that the Frontier was too small for any advance towards self-government, Abdul Qayyum replied that 'fleas were small too, but a nuisance in one's trousers'.

Afghanistan under the rule of Nadir Shah was at last beginning to emerge as a progressive nation. It had a modern army and an expanding air force. Communications had greatly improved with the construction of the Great North Road across the Hindu Kush, whilst in the fields of public health and education Nadir Shah's enlightened policies were rewarded by the growing reputation of his country as a stable twentieth-century state. But, unfortunately for Muhammad Nadir Shah, history was about to repeat itself.

His ready acceptance of British India's Frontier policy and a desire to cultivate friendly relations with a country which had once occupied his own provoked a violent reaction even on the British side of the Durand Line. Towards the end of 1932 a conspiracy to restore Amanullah to the throne had become so open that the Afghan King ordered the arrest and execution of the leader of the pro-Amanullah faction. A year later, on 8 November, Nadir Shah was himself assassinated by the schoolboy son of the man he had put to death, and Nadir's nineteen-year-old son Zadir succeeded to the throne.

For a few years relations with the Indian government remained cordial, but in the hills the tribes were far from peaceful. Whilst the Afridis had been less active in their predatory excursions, the Mohmands demonstrated their ability to create trouble by embarking upon a two-year rampage of robbery and murder which even the most experienced troops in the Indian Army found difficult to contain.

The government was slow to act but in February 1935 it despatched the Nowshera Brigade to bring to heel a powerful lashkar led by the Fakir of Alinger. For several weeks the brigade stalked the Fakir over a region of craggy rocks and steep wooded valleys before engaging the Mohmands in a few minor actions. Then, on the night of 5 April, the tribesmen attacked a position known as Kila Hari, held by a company of Sikh riflemen and a Gurkha machine-gun platoon, with a ferocity reminiscent of the engagement at Ambela in 1863.

The attack began at 7.00 p.m. when a party of Afghan swordsmen rushed out of the darkness from the dead ground below the post. Screaming and shouting they forced a way through the barbed-wire fence to reach the stone walls of the sangar, even seizing machine-guns by their over-heated barrels in an attempt to drag them from the grip of the sepoy gunners. The close-quarter fighting raged for some hours but every assault was repulsed by bearded giants from the Punjab and the kukri-wielding little men from Nepal. As this desperate hand-to-hand encounter spilled across the hillside, a rifle platoon on the summit, not having the protection of even a wire fence, came under attack from a mass of tribesmen determined to succeed where their brothers had failed. Rapid-round rifle fire and able work from the Lewis gunners repelled first one assault and then another, but it was the timely intervention of a mountain battery which prevented the platoon from being over-run. The screw guns were able to put down an accurate curtain of fire to break up the tribal concentration and at 5.00 a.m. the weary defenders were gratified to see torch signals in the hills summoning the Afghans back to their villages.

Six days later, a full-scale operation by a reinforced Nowshera Brigade routed the enemy lashkar west of the Malakand, and with this defeat the Fakir's influence over the tribesmen evaporated.

Waziristan, unlike the other territories, had been relatively tranquil. Family feuds broke out occasionally, but tribal looting on anything like the scale of the April violence was deterred by the presence of 30,000 Indian Army troops garrisoned in the three great forts of Wana, Razmak and Miram

Shah. John Masters, who as a junior officer undertook a spell of garrison duty in Razmak, described the barracks as:

> low and made of stone . . . inside a low stone wall three or four miles long that surrounded the whole fortress. Beyond the wall stood a row of electric lights on tall posts, and just beyond the lights, three double aprons of barbed wire. Beyond the wire the tilted plateau sloped away to jagged mountains, and across the plateau tribesmen strode slowly with the full, free lilt of their kind, leading their camels behind them. We watched them enviously from the safe imprisonment of the walls and the wire.

Living at such close quarters imposed an intolerable strain on officers and men alike. John Prendergast, a subaltern serving there at the time of John Masters, was almost driven frantic by the half-strangled braying of thousands of mules and by the Adjutant, who talked of nothing but hockey. Boredom was endemic. Garrison duty in Razmak was likened by many to serving time in a government prison. Much was done by the army chiefs to keep the men interested by furnishing such amenities as football and hockey pitches, squash and tennis courts and a tin-roofed cinema, which in the winter was so cold that Prendergast took to viewing programmes in knee-length boots of heavy felt, and a sheepskin coat worn with the fleece inside. That most sought-after social contact, the company of women, was strictly forbidden, for Razmak was a non-family station with the unenviable reputation of being the military world's largest monastery.

Occasionally there came a break in the dull routine of garrison duty with a ten-day exercise designed to show the flag or curb the activity of a clan suspected of threatening the peace. Forming part of a column was looked upon as an enjoyable experience. In the rarefied atmosphere, the morning sun picked out the hills speckled with dwarf ilex in rich warm colours and, despite the furnace heat reflected off bare rocks, John Prendergast discovered alpine plants rich in aromatic scent. Lieutenant Hugh Pettigrew remembered the 'incredible change of colour at sunset when the browns and khakis and greys of the day-time . . . suddenly became blues and mauves and purples. A new dawn would bring the same entrancing, misleading colours of the evening, gone again in a single moment as the hot sun came above the crests of the mountains.'

'At evening', wrote John Masters,

> the day's march done and the stone wall built, we sat sweat-stained around the cookers and smoked and drank strong tea. At nights as we made our rounds of duty, the stars gleamed on the bayonets of the silent sentries along the wall.
>
> At dawn we awoke to the shrill sweet call of the mountain artillery trumpets blowing a long reveille. The call seemed to last a golden age while I huddled deeper into my blanket and embraced my returning senses. Then fully awake and once more on the march, we rampaged up and down the mountains, playing at being scouts and soldiers. . . .

These cross-country exercises, however, had to be carried out with a great deal of caution. To advance along a narrow valley bed without first occupying the heights would be to risk turning the path into a death trap. It became established practice for the advance guard to send up pickets to man the heights, whilst the main column passed below. But sometimes events did not always go as planned. John Prendergast was skirting a valley near the Mahsud border with Waziristan when a brisk fire opened up on his platoon from the rocks high above. The valley was flanked by stunted ilex and, as the air shook to the rapid crack-thump of rifle fire, the young subaltern found himself standing alone on the track. Prendergast recalled that events happened too rapidly for him to feel frightened and when he finally reached the ridge, after deploying his company into open formation, the tribesmen had slipped away. A senior officer had been killed in the engagement and there were other casualties. In the subsequent enquiry it was established that the pickets had been stationary and had failed to notice the enemy, who had crept up under the shelter of rocks. A mobile patrol along the ridge might have seen the danger. 'So we learned our craft in the best of all training grounds,' wrote John Prendergast. '. . . One mistake and the Pathan raider was in.'

Chapter 14

The Fakir of Ipi

In the summer of 1936, a young Waziri student was arrested by the authorities and charged with the abduction of the daughter of a Hindu merchant living in Bannu. The tribesman had taken her across the boundary – whether by force or persuasion was not made clear – and through a Moslem marriage ceremony. It was an act which infuriated the Hindus, who sought the jurisdiction of the court on a charge of kidnapping. The court's decision in favour of the girl's parents attracted much publicity and inflamed religious prejudices which had smouldered in the Waziri settled districts for years.

Shortly after the return of the girl to her family, several hundred tribesmen from the Turi Khel clan, stirred up by agitators who claimed that the verdict was an affront to Moslem law, ran amok and had to be dispersed. Prominent among the leaders had been a forty-six-year-old hermit from the village of Ipi close to the road from Bannu and the Tochi Valley. Obsessed with a fanatical hatred of all infidels and possessing sufficient charisma to unite the clans in a tribal revolt, Mirza Ali Khan, or the Fakir of Ipi as he became known to the British, was able to fan the smouldering embers of the Islam Bibi incident into a conflagration which occupied the British military forces until the beginning of the Second World War.

The tribes, already chafing at what they considered to be growing government interference in tribal matters, needed little persuasion to assert their independence. Within a few months, the Fakir was at the head of a lashkar in the Khaisora

Valley and in a position to threaten communication lines with Razmak and the area around Bannu.

By the beginning of 1937 the Mahsuds and Wazirs under his direction had carried out thirty outrages across the Durand Line marked by a trail of gutted Hindu shops and houses, rustled cattle and more than a dozen corpses. British pickets were attacked and in one incident in April a convoy of fifty lorries on its way to Wana was ambushed in a narrow gorge known as the Shahur Tangi. The attack was well planned and for fifteen minutes a rapid and accurate rifle fire from well-concealed positions was brought down upon almost every vehicle in the convoy. Thirty-four soldiers were killed in the first few minutes, including seven British officers. When Lieutenant Pettigrew arrived the next day, an armoured car and several lorries still blocked the road, but there was no more fighting. 'The tribesmen had melted away in the night, no doubt pleased with their loot and glorying in the slaughter. They had certainly come out best,' conceded Hugh Pettigrew.

This Wazir victory was related with great satisfaction by one of the Fakir's followers. 'Haji Sahib [the Fakir of Ipi] told us that if we threw a stone into the air it would turn into a hailstorm killing British and Hindus; and slivers of wood from an olive tree would turn into rifles. Once we started the hailstorm the enemy would not be able to escape, not even in England. We killed many Feringhis and made many women widows.'

In May, the government struck back. Two brigades composed largely of Sikhs and Gurkhas formed the spearhead of an attack against the village of Arsal Kot, known to be a stronghold of the Fakir of Ipi. Serving with the Gurkhas was the author John Masters, whose baptism of fire occurred one night as he lay pressed to the earth on a stony hillside. The sudden smack–thump of a bullet close to his head set off a fit of uncontrolled trembling and he wondered for a moment 'whether it would be his neck, stomach, legs, or eyes, and what it would feel like'. Close by, a Scottish curse rent the air accompanied by a long, low whistling sound. 'Hamish, are you hit?' called the commanding officer anxiously. 'No, sir,' came the reply. 'I just let the air out of my Lilo!' In the subdued laughter which followed, the tension relaxed and young John Masters forgot his fear.

Intelligence sources reported that the Fakir had his headquarters in a cave some twelve miles east of Wana, and after a day of confused fighting, Masters and his Gurkhas reached the spot to find cooking fires still smouldering, but of their quarry there was no sign. He had been warned by sympathetic villagers and had slipped away only minutes beforehand. A decision was made to blow up the soot-blackened entrance to the caves and John Masters recalled the unfortunate plight of the young subaltern and two Sappers who were obliged to vacate the cave hurriedly, 'cursing and slapping at their bodies. From the waist down all three were literally and absolutely covered with fleas.'

Supporting the Gurkhas in this drive against the Fakir of Ipi were the Tochi Scouts, and on the following day John Prendergast was ordered to take three platoons to the village of Gariom, where several loop-holed towers were to be blown up as a punishment for harbouring the Fakir. As he neared the village, a sharp burst of rifle fire from a clump of dwarf ilex which overlooked the path effectively pinned down his platoon along a dip in the ground. The sharp whip–crack of bullets close to Prendergast's head set his eardrums singing. It came as a shock to the young subaltern as he pressed his body into the ground to know that fear could be so intense. 'Was this me?' he mused, 'trying to dissolve my whole quaking body into the very soil. . . . I'm supposed to be a leader. Then the thought came back, well, lead then.'

Feeling that his legs were made of rubber, Lieutenant Prendergast rose and was immediately covered in dust from bullets which struck the ground around his feet. A few choice words were sufficient to get the other platoons to fix bayonets, and with a loud shout of 'Halla! Halla! [attack!]' he tore across the open ground towards the crest of the hill. Zig-zagging wildly, Prendergast led his Pathans over the 300 yards of scrub at the expense of a few casualties. The tribesmen had second thoughts about staying to face the outstretched bayonets, however, and when the leading platoon reached the trees their opponents had vanished to a man.

Taking the hill had opened the way to Gariom and at the close of the action John Prendergast learned that he was to be recommended for the Military Cross. 'To me', he wrote, 'this was tremendous – the first piece of appreciation after some years of puppyish pressing forward, trying to succeed, trying to please.'

It was in small actions such as these that the Pathans excelled, despite a shortage of modern weapons. Their professional opponents, although possessing such sophisticated hardware as armoured cars, aircraft and long-range artillery, laboured under a handicap not of their choosing, namely a frustrating set of rules laid down for operations in the field and aimed at limiting casualties. Political Officers restricted the movement of troops to certain 'proscribed areas' in which they were not allowed to fire at any group of less than ten men unless the men were armed and not using a path or track. Outside these areas the patrol was powerless to act until they came under fire.

In the mountainous country west of Razmak, the Pathans, after firing upon a patrol, would simply flit across the Durand Line into Afghanistan where the British were not allowed to operate. 'We felt', commented John Masters, 'as if we were using a crowbar to swat wasps.'

The elusive tribesmen took every care to avoid potentially costly confrontations, preferring hit-and-run tactics against isolated posts, poisoning wells and rigging booby traps from stolen hand-grenades. Hugh Pettigrew helped to prise one such bomb from a track regularly used by patrols. 'It was the usual thing,' he wrote. 'An old cylindrical cigarette tin, the kind that held fifty with a sealed top, filled with gelignite and fitted with a crude plunger and cap.'

Protecting the lines of communication was a wearisome and often dangerous business. The convoys ran every other day and it was the army's duty to search out all the sites favourable to an ambush. Lieutenant John Masters often found himself engaged in RP (road protection patrols), 'and every day it became more difficult to obey the cardinal

Frontier principle of never doing the same thing in the same way twice running,' he wrote. 'We had to fight against fatigue and carelessness, because someone was watching. Someone was always watching – someone with an inborn tactical sense, someone who missed nothing.'

A soldier rash enough to disregard that rule seldom lived to repeat his error for the Pathan never took prisoners other than Moslem. Any of the wounded unfortunate enough to fall into his hands, especially Sikhs or British soldiers, were lucky only to be castrated and beheaded. It was not unknown for a wounded man to be pegged to the ground and his jaws forced open with a piece of wood to prevent him from swallowing. A woman of the clan would then squat over his open mouth until he drowned in her urine.

John Masters, in his book *Bugles and a Tiger*, relates an incident where a British officer of an Indian battalion was severely wounded on another part of the Frontier. Twice his battalion tried to rescue him, but had to give up when they lost more men than even the disgrace of leaving him in enemy hands warranted. The next day they recovered what was left of him. 'He had been castrated and flayed, probably whilst still alive,' wrote Masters, 'and his skin lay pegged out on the rocks not far from the camp.'

The British troops, incensed at such barbarity, retaliated in the only way open to them. Tribesmen taken into custody on suspicion of being brigands and subsequently released for lack of evidence would sometimes meet with a fatal accident. The rifle of one youth sent back for questioning by Lieutenant Masters was found to have traces of burned powder in the chamber. Under the pretence of further examination, the battalion armourer took the weapon in a vice and secretly bent the barrel a fraction of an inch. The young Pathan noticed nothing unusual when his rifle was returned to him but the misalignment was enough to cause a malfunction and perhaps inflict a serious injury upon him when next it was fired.

The frustration of the troops at not being allowed to strike back openly at their foe led to other forms of retaliatory action such as the dropping of 'doctored' clips of cartridges. The low-explosive cordite had been replaced with high explosive, thus when the tribesman – usually short of ammunition – picked up his find and used it, he ran a grave risk of severe facial burns if not worse.

The Royal Air Force also suffered from an imposed 'Alice in Wonderland' situation, for whilst it was permissible for the artillery to shell villages without warning, the same was not true of bombing missions. These could only be carried out if they had first been sanctioned by the Political Officer, and even then only after due warning had been given to the tribesmen of the impending attack.

Not only was the use of aircraft 'cribbed, cabin'd and confined' by rigid instructions as to when and against what they should be used, but since the tactics of air-to-ground attack were in their infancy, the aircraft's effectiveness left much to be desired. A tribal enemy in the hills was usually few in number and since his clothing was often indistinguishable from the colours of the hillside, the pilot had to rely upon the ground troops to tell him roughly where the enemy was hiding.

The villagers invariably profited from their nefarious excursions, knowing that they had little to fear from retaliatory air strikes. 'We plundered everything from the convoy,' recalled a tribesman in Waziristan.

After that a notice was sent to us. Leaflets were dropped from aeroplanes telling us that after three days we were going to be bombed. We were told that we should vacate our village and all houses within a radius of three miles. We were told that the bombing was in retaliation for the raid on the convoy. They bombed us for many days but then we made peace with them. The Political Agent told us to stop fighting the British but we wanted them out of our area.

Since the twenty-pound bombs dropped by the Audaxes, Hawker Harts and Wapitis rarely did much damage, it was sometimes necessary to occupy a village to enable the army engineers to blow up the watch towers with explosives. This operation was not without its lighter side, as John Prendergast relates:

On one occasion the tower of the headman, a man of some influence who had failed to keep the peace, was included in the programme unknown to him. The engineer officer, fearing that the mob would become restless if he blew up the headman's property, called him forward and suggested that he might like to press the plunger to detonate the next tower. The headman, delighted at the signal honour, pressed it and blew up his own house. Far from showing indignation at their chief's discomfort so obviously written on his face, the crowded bystanders laughed till they rolled down the hillside. It was the joke of the year. . . .

For the next two years, despite the restrictions imposed upon it, the army did its best to curtail the movements of a skilful foe operating in a wilderness of hills and mountains, baked in summer by temperatures of up to 130°, and buried under a mantle of snow in the arctic winter. Even in cantonments there was little comfort to be had in this hostile environment. Second only to the heat was the petty irritation caused by dust clouds which formed at ground level. Dust penetrated everything. Writing of the base at Jandola, Pettigrew had this to say: 'Furniture was covered with a deep layer; even the dining table could not be kept clean for more than a few minutes. So we drank it in our soup, the grit grating between our teeth; it turned our pillows to emery paper, it filled our noses and eyes, our whole miserable lives, until the wind rose and blew it away.'

In July 1938, the Fakir of Ipi was run to ground for the second time. Again it was a cave which sheltered him but the terrain proved to be so difficult that even the Gurkhas could not get within striking distance and once more the turbulent priest evaded capture. After this, the Fakir transferred his theatre of operations to the area west of Razmak and closer to the Afghan border. Government forces were getting too close too often.

It was now the turn of the tribes to take the offensive and on 23 July a 200-strong lashkar launched a daring night attack against the town of Bannu and so terrified the Hindu traders that a third of the population fled east across the Indus. British artillery and armoured cars soon drove the Afghans out of the town, but £30,000 worth of damage was done to the shopping areas and British prestige on the Frontier suffered a blow from which it never quite recovered.

In the dying months of 1938, the technical superiority of British weaponry began to make itself felt. The Wazirs and Mahsuds were sustaining debilitating losses and clan after clan began to accept peace terms, albeit reluctantly. By the beginning of 1939 fighting on the Frontier had all but petered out, although the Fakir of Ipi was to remain a thorn in the side of not only the British, but also Pakistan, until his death in 1960.

The Waziristan campaign, in common with many others on the North-West Frontier, had proved to be an expensive undertaking. Costing some £50 million, there was little to show on the credit side other than the provision of a useful battle area for the training of troops fresh from England. An officer destined for field rank admitted benefiting from the experience. 'The campaign had taught me much that was to be of value in the coming world war,' wrote John Masters. 'I also learned to respect the enemy – any enemy. Whoever he was, he was only a man doing something that he believed right.'

All through the Second World War, whilst British and Indian troops put their Frontier experiences to good effect in the Western Desert, Italy and Burma, the hill tribes remained passive. The greatest threat to India came not from the fear of an invasion through the Khyber or Bolan Passes, but from the Japanese in the north-east. In later years it became a bar-room jest to ask, 'Were you in the war or did you stay up on the Frontier?'

Within a year of the ending of hostilities the Labour government announced that India was to gain her independence. The news brought little satisfaction to the Moslem population. They wanted no part of Hindu rule. The population of the Indian sub-continent at that time could be divided into 800 million Hindus and 100 million Moslems, which meant that Frontier affairs would almost certainly be administered by the Congress Party and not the Moslem League.

Until now, tribal leaders had been content to accept

Congress funding and political backing against their traditional enemy, the British, but with the ending of the Raj
there came a massive increase in support for Muhammad
Ali Jinnah and the Moslem League. So much so that
Congress decided that only a visit from an eminent person
of Jawaharlal Nehru's standing could arrest the demand for
an independent state. In fact, Nehru's visits to Razmak and
Landi Kotal resulted in a near riot and he was fortunate to
escape with a grazed forehead and a damaged car. Support
for the Congress Party among Moslems on the Khyber was
non-existent.

Another distinguished visitor to experience the fury of
the mob was Lord Mountbatten. In April 1947 he arrived at
Peshawar with Lady Mountbatten to be confronted by a huge
crowd of Afridis howling for an independent state of Pakistan.
The Viceroy and his lady, showing commendable courage, left
their car and approached the crowd, many of whom were arm-
ing themselves with stones. Fortunately for him, Mountbatten
was not wearing the robes of office associated with the hated
infidel rule, but the jungle-green uniform appropriate to his
position as Supreme Allied Commander in South-East Asia.
Green was the colour of Islam and many in the crowd had
fought in Burma. Gradually the shouted insults were drowned
in a rising chorus of 'Salaam alaikum!' and 'Mountbatten
zindabad!' In this raucous demonstration Mountbatten recognised the necessity for testing a measure of public opinion.

In July, a referendum was held among the Pathans.
In each polling booth two boxes were placed, one red and
the other green. It was afterwards established that the
pro-Pakistan party had told the illiterate tribesmen that
if they were true believers they must vote green and if
infidels red. Since the North-West Frontier Province was
fanatically Moslem, it surprised no one that 289,244 votes
were cast for Pakistan, and only 2074 for the Congress Party
and India. Following this overwhelming majority in favour of
partition, Mountbatten agreed that the sub-continent would
be divided into two unequal portions, the Moslem part being
Pakistan, which would include the North-West Frontier and
Baluchistan, together with part of the old Punjab.

Partition was not achieved without a mass migration of refugees and wholesale massacres of a horrendous nature, but on 14 August 1947 Jinnah was sworn in as Pakistan's first Governor-General, and on that day, at sunset, the Union Jack was lowered for the last time in Karachi and all over India. On the North-West Frontier, because of its geographical position, the British flag remained flying a few minutes longer at the highest point on the fort at Landi Kotal before it was removed, leaving the bare wooden pole to be lost in the gathering darkness.

In September, the Pakistan government decided to withdraw all military personnel from tribal territory to cantonments along the administrative border. The South Waziristan Scouts took over Wana, but the great base at Razmak was abandoned and as late as 1961 the fort was found in a sorry state of neglect with weeds growing and the barracks doors swinging idly in the dry wind. Little remained but a few faded regimental insignia emblazoned on the walls to remind the traveller of a century of British rule.

The departure of the British, although the last British officer did not leave Waziristan until 1950, did nothing to diminish the tribes' appetite for armed conflict. Two months after documents had been signed drawing up the partition of India, a motorised lashkar took the road east out of Peshawar heading for the Vale of Kashmir. This area had from time immemorial been looked upon as Moslem, but after the Sikh Wars it had been ceded to the Hindu Rajah of Jammu as a reward for loyalty. After partition, the Hindu government of Kashmir began a systematic persecution of its Moslem subjects, who very quickly turned to their co-religionists, the Frontier tribes, for support.

The response was immediate and but for the burning and looting of a Catholic Mission and some Hindu bazaars, which delayed the tribesmen for forty-eight hours, the whole of Kashmir might have fallen to the Moslems. As it was, the delay was sufficient to allow a detachment of Sikhs to occupy Srinagar's airstrip, from where Indian armoured units spread out across the Vale.

The Afghan lashkar was driven back but sporadic fighting

continued, and for the next eighteen years the issue of Kashmir poisoned relations between India and Pakistan until in 1966 the United Nations ruled that most of the country should remain under Indian control.

Long before this issue was resolved, Abdul Ghaffar of Red Shirt fame had been vigorously campaigning for a Pathan homeland on both sides of the dividing line which would have sovereign status as Pushtunistan. By that time a man in his sixties, he tirelessly stomped through every town and village in the province, but in 1948 he was again arrested and sentenced to six years' imprisonment by the new government of Muhammad Ali Jinnah.

The Red Shirt Organisation's avowed intention of wresting the tribal territories from the jurisdiction of Pakistan did not cease with the incarceration of Abdul Ghaffar Khan. The work to which he had devoted the better part of his life was carried on by his disciples, prominent among them being the Fakir of Ipi. From the security of his Waziristan caves the Fakir plotted an endless series of forays against frontier villages together with murderously successful ambushes of Pakistan frontier patrols. On his death in 1960, an illustrious English newspaper printed a eulogy describing him as 'a man of principle and saintliness', which contrasted sharply with the opinion of a Pakistan official, who referred to the Fakir of Ipi as 'a vicious old man, twisted with hate and selfishness'.

Afghanistan had long expressed interest in the concept of 'Pushtunistan' and when in 1953 Prince Muhammad Daoud, who was personally attached to the idea, came to power in a bloodless coup, an influential politician in the person of Nikita Khrushchev, no less, was won over in support.

Four years later, fresh from his term of imprisonment, Abdul Ghaffar Khan again championed the issue. A tall gaunt man, he quickly established himself as a tireless organiser. Under a new name, the National Awani Party (NAP), his band of Red Shirts took on an increasingly seditious role positively encouraged by Daoud. At a school in Kabul, teenaged Pathans received not only a basic education, but were also taught the techniques of sabotage and terrorism. As activists they soon became embroiled in cross-border raids, the destruction of railway tracks and bridges, and generally creating havoc along the whole of the trans-Indus border. As a result of their campaign, relations between Pakistan and Afghanistan became strained to such an extent that in September 1961 diplomatic ties were broken off and the border closed.

This created serious problems for Premier Daoud's government since a sizeable proportion of its income was derived from fruit farming and virtually all Afghanistan's export of nuts, raisins, grapes, melons, oranges and even cotton had to pass through Pakistani territory. The difficulties in which Daoud's government found themselves presented the Soviet Union with an opportunity to exploit Afghanistan's need for an alternative market, and for the next two years until relations were restored with Pakistan the Kremlin mounted fifteen flights a day to import Afghanistan's large fruit harvest. Daoud's urgent requirements for economic aid met with little response from the West, and the Soviet Union in meeting that need was able to achieve a measure of control over the economy that Afghanistan's Premier was slow to perceive. Daoud Khan resigned in March 1963 but, attracted by Afghanistan's untapped resources of natural gas, Soviet investment continued to grow until by the end of 1968 the Afghan economy was virtually dependent on the Soviet Union.

The late sixties and early seventies saw a marked improvement in health and education under the able leadership of Babrak Karmal. No longer was the local mosque with its literal interpretation of the Koran in a form virtually unchanged since the tenth century the only source of schooling, and through a policy of equal rights for national minorities a growing number of Tajiks and Kirghiz students were finding places at Kabul University.

This period also witnessed the visitation upon Afghanistan of a great many hashish-smoking hippies, an example of Western decadence which the young Afghan student could not fail to contrast with his own government's policy of a way forward through development and social change. Who could blame him if he was then reinforced in his Marxist belief?

In July 1973, King Zahir Shah, who had ruled for forty years in relative obscurity, was unwise enough to entrust the running of the country to his brother-in-law whilst he sought eye treatment in Italy. The sixty-three-year-old Muhammad Daoud seized this opportunity to return to a position of power and in a coup masterminded by sympathisers in the armed forces proclaimed himself President of the new Republic of Afghanistan. Daoud's two main rivals, Babrak Karmal and Nur Muhammad Taraki, had been out-manoeuvred, but when he attempted to stem Afghanistan's drift into the Soviet camp by trying to forge close ties with Iran and Saudi Arabia, Daoud's days as President were effectively numbered.

Meanwhile, any expectation of Abdul Ghaffar Khan that Pakistan would give way on the question of Pushtunistan under pressure from the regime in Afghanistan quickly faded. It was left to his son, Abdul Wali Khan, and the NAP to force the issue through a series of mini-riots and inflammatory speeches in Rawalpindi. All through 1973 and 1974 terrorist activity and demonstrations by vociferous crowds of Pathans continued, culminating in an attempt upon the life of Pakistan's Prime Minister, Ali Bhutto.

In February of the following year, a leading opponent of the NAP' was blown through the roof whilst addressing a student gathering in the auditorium of Peshawar University. That act of terror exhausted Bhutto's patience. The NAP was declared an illegal organisation and its leaders were arrested. Abdul Ghaffar Khan and his son were tried and sentenced to long terms of imprisonment. Bereft of its leaders, the NAP collapsed and the Pushtunistan movement came to an inglorious end.

Chapter 15

Soviet Invasion

The enforced termination of King Zahir Shah's reign had bene-fited Afghanistan to some extent in that it brought greatly increased economic and military aid from the Soviet Union. Under the leadership of Muhammad Daoud, who was never more than an expedient communist, the country's policies had been largely nationalistic but, with the upsurge in Soviet influence, Russian advisers and Moscow-trained Afghans were able to penetrate the armed forces and administrative infra-structures to the extent that in 1977 a new constitution was introduced based upon a one-party state.

Daoud, whilst quick to stifle any opposition from the fundamentalist groups then emerging, sought to initiate a policy of neutrality by looking for improved relations with Pakistan and seeking closer ties and economic aid from such countries as Iran, Saudi Arabia and Egypt.

Daoud's belated attempt to reduce Afghanistan's depend-ence on the Soviet Union, however, only succeeded in antago-nising Communist Party members and, when he began to purge Marxists from key military posts, they retaliated by assassinating his closest associate Ahmad Ali Khorram, the Minister for Planning. A further killing in mid-April 1978 gave Daoud an excuse to arrest the leading activists in the People's Democratic Party of Afghanistan, including Nur Muhammad Taraki, Babrak Karmal and Hafizullah Amin.

Muhammad Daoud was now regarded by Moscow as being no longer worthy of their trust and on 27 April the PDPA took control in a coup which became known as the Saur Revolution, masterminded possibly by those Daoud had thrown into jail and almost certainly by the KGB. Tanks were used to secure the airport and Defence Ministry, and at midday the Presidential Palace came under air attack. The 1800-strong Republican Guard loyal to Daoud refused to surrender and, in the fighting which followed, the President, his brother and several government officials were killed as were most of the loyalist soldiers who fought in their defence.

Within weeks of the coup, Afghanistan, guided by the policies of the Revolutionary Council under the presidency of sixty-one-year-old Nur Muhammad Taraki, with Amin and Karmal as deputy prime ministers, had moved closer to the Soviet bloc.

Six weeks into the new regime the first purges were carried out, and civil servants were instructed to join the Party if they valued their employment. Key positions in the Ministries were filled by trusted Party nominees, and tribal and religious leaders were summoned to Kabul in an attempt to contain a growing rural feeling of discontent.

At the beginning of July, the rival Parchami group in the PDPA suffered a severe blow when Babrak Karmal was manoeuvred out of his position as Deputy Prime Minister and sent to Prague as Ambassador by another faction in the PDPA, the Khalquis of Nur Muhammad Taraki. This was followed in the late summer by the unprecedented step of changing the national flag. Traditionally it had always been Islamic green, and the red star and wheatsheaf emblem adopted by the Taraki regime, together with a policy of equality for women, was completely at variance with the teachings of Islam.

The Islamic faith stood as a formidable obstacle to the spread of communist ideology and those conservative mullahs who dared to vent their feelings were prosecuted with a ruthless intensity. Passive resistance was not a policy which appealed to the fundamentalists, however.

Mike Martin, a journalist then in Peshawar, asked a mullah why he had been thrown into jail by the Taraki regime. 'I was in Mezar-i-Sharif in the bazaar,' replied the Imam. 'I was with two hundred imams at a meeting. Into the bazaar came some communists. They were giving propaganda to the people which said that Islam was bad. So we stoned them to death.'

When the villagers and tribesmen of the hills realised that protest was futile and that the Khalqui party in Kabul was determined to enforce policies which would inevitably undermine their centuries-old social and religious customs, contempt for the communist non-believers erupted into violence.

In the Panjsher, a self-proclaimed Islamic government was set up with its own judiciary and tax collectors, and on 15 March defecting troops joined the citizens of Herat in clashes with government forces. In a bloody insurrection, hundreds of Party workers and their families were hunted down and brutally murdered, including more than a score of Russian advisers who were cut to pieces and their remains paraded around the city. For five days Herat was held by the rebels until bombing raids and a counter-attack with tanks restored control to the communists after some 5000 citizens had been killed or injured.

Such had been the scale of the revolt that an investigative team was sent from Moscow headed by a general who had played a prominent part in the Russian invasion of Czechoslovakia. General Alexi Yepishev's tour of inspection and his findings were quickly followed by a considerable build-up of Soviet military strength in a package which included T–62 tanks, MiG fighters and helicopter gunships. One opportunist politician to profit from events in Herat was Hafizullah Amin, and on 27 March it was announced that he had been appointed to the post of Prime Minister.

Although government authority had been restored in Herat, attacks upon Afghan army posts and convoys continued all through the summer months of 1979. During this time the number of Russian advisers in Afghanistan had grown to something approaching 5000, but one Afghan who had been in the army before the invasion had nothing but contempt for them. 'They were animals,' he told Peregrine Hodson of the *Sunday Times*. 'They never washed before meals and they used to urinate next to us while we were eating. When the invasion happened there were thousands of them, but none of them knew why they had come. They were told they would be fighting Chinese and Americans – they were surprised when all they found were Afghans.'

Hafizullah Amin, a fervent admirer of Joseph Stalin, having assumed considerable power by March, met a growing problem of resettling large numbers of destitute nomads by a ruthless programme of 'ordered change' directed against the recalcitrant peasants in Paktia and Kuner provinces. In carrying out his policy, the atrocities committed by the Afghan Army were as savage as any in Afghanistan's violent history. On 20 April 1979 the Pushtun village of Kerala in the Kunar Valley was razed to the ground and every male over the age of twelve was shot – a massacre of more than a thousand of its inhabitants.

Brutality such as this and further outbreaks of violence in the rural areas so alarmed the land-owning Panjshers and farmers that the stream of refugees to Pakistan increased to a flood. Curiously enough, this influx of 400,000 Afghans gave rise to little friction between the indigenous population and the newcomers, although the Afghans were astonished by the comparative wealth exhibited by the Pakistanis. 'There are many unbelievers in Pakistan,' one told the correspondent of the *Sunday Times*. 'Perhaps they speak the words of the nemaz with their lips, but in their hearts they can only think of money.'

It has long been accepted practice among the Islamic peoples to offer hospitality to fellow Moslems in need, and more concern was expressed in Moscow over the influx of refugees than was the case in Pakistan. Indeed, such was Brezhnev's unease that Taraki was invited to the Soviet capital where his Russian hosts voiced the opinion that if Amin's brutalities were not brought to a halt, they could redound to the disadvantage of the PDPA. It was a point of view that reflected Taraki's own belief and it was perhaps with Amin's replacement in mind that in September the Chairman of the Revolutionary Council agreed to meet the Russian Ambassador in Kabul. Unfortunately for Taraki, Amin was warned of a possible trap and it was Taraki who was eliminated – strangled, it was said, by Amin's henchmen.

New and even more severe measures were taken against rebel factions, but as the number of executions mounted so too did resistance to government measures. By the end of the year, so unpopular had Amin's regime become that the likelihood of his government being overthrown could not be discounted. A spirited revolt by elite units of the Afghan Army had in fact taken place in August 1979. The rebellion led by junior officers from the Bala Hissar was quickly put down with the aid of helicopter gunships and tanks, but whatever satisfaction the regime might have drawn from this success was soon dispelled with the outbreak of a new spate of guerrilla operations in the Kunar Valley. There, a 2000-strong brigade of government troops went over to the mujahiddin with all of its heavy weapons. An increased reliance on Soviet advisers and instructors had demoralised the Afghan Army, whose officers had never forgiven Amin for the downfall of their supporter, Nur Muhammad Taraki. Many thousands of regular troops defected to the rebels, who were operating close to Kabul, and for a time it seemed likely that the government would fall. But three months after the mysterious disappearance of Taraki, Amin himself was dead.

On 4 December, the anniversary of the Afghan–Soviet Treaty was marked by a rally to raise popular support for Amin's government, but by now it had become obvious to Moscow that without Soviet assistance the Khalqui government could not long survive. Military aid was stepped up and Russian civilians as well as army personnel began to participate in all administrative and security operations.

Finally, in the last days of 1979, rather than see its influence of the past two decades come to nothing, Moscow made the fateful decision to fly airborne forces into the Bagram airbase twenty-five miles north of Kabul. A brigade of elite troops struck northward to clear the Kunduz–Kabul road of Afghan rebels and, in a logistically brilliant operation, Soviet Army divisions were moved up to the border. A week later, a shuttle service of Antonov transport aircraft brought a huge build-up of Russian troops, and on 27 December 1979 80,000 troops including motorised divisions poured across the Oxus to begin the invasion of Afghanistan.

The Soviet armed forces had not been engaged in combat duties since the end of the Second World War and the Afghan government's request for assistance provided a unique opportunity to test men and equipment under battle conditions. As one Soviet commentator succinctly pointed out, 'Commanders with grey on their temples found themselves under fire for the first time in the foothills of Afghanistan.'

Within a matter of days Afghanistan's principal cities of Herat, Kandahar and Kabul had been secured, together with every airport and military base.

It was during the attack on the Presidential Palace that Amin was killed. Whether he was assassinated by the KGB or met his end by accident when Russian troops stormed the Darulaman Palace must remain a matter for conjecture, but in the political language of the Kremlin Hafizullah Amin became an unperson and the former deputy Prime Minister, Babrak Karmal, was recognised by the Soviets as the new leader in Afghanistan. But, as the British had discovered 140 years before, an attempt to install a puppet ruler in Kabul was the one act guaranteed to unite the different clans in a national revolt.

New measures designed to win popular support were introduced by the Karmal regime but an attempt to gain the backing of the Islamic clergy was dismissed with contempt by the majority of the religious elders. To them, Babrak Karmal was 'just another communist'.

In April 1980, an alliance of various Islamic parties was formed and fierce fighting between the mujahiddin and government troops broke out in the Kunar province. The Afghan Army of Babrak Karmal reacted adversely to Soviet intervention and completely disintegrated. From a strength of 90,000 at the time of the Russian invasion, it collapsed to less than 30,000, of which only a small proportion could be relied upon to resist the attacks of the mujahiddin. 'Almost all the conscripts in the State Army ... support the mujahiddin,' Peregrine Hodson was told. 'When they are sent against us they fire high in the air over our heads. Once they have received a rifle and a new pair of boots many of them join the mujahiddin. That is why the Shuravi [Russians] put mine fields round the military camps; not only to stop us getting in, but to prevent the soldiers getting out.'

The Russian troops, many of whom genuinely believed that they were coming to the aid of a popular government threatened by American-backed bandits, found themselves caught up in a conflict they did not understand and which placed some of them in the dilemma of having to do battle with their co-religionists.

In the spring of 1980 the Russians embarked on their first major offensive in the Kunar Valley with an armoured task force which resulted in the virtual obliteration of the town of Azmar and the deaths of up to 1500 people. It was to be the beginning of a classic spiral of ruthless oppression followed by more resistance and a rapid depopulation of the valley. Thousands of refugees from almost every part of Afghanistan began the long trek across desert and through difficult mountain passes to seek asylum in Iran or Pakistan.

Nigel Ryan and his colleagues met just such a party in the fading light as they travelled up the valley towards their ultimate goal of Pakistan. 'They passed like phantoms in the underworld,' he wrote. 'Whole families pausing in the narrow path to let us by, women silent, the men solemnly greeting us; many had all their worldly goods with them; donkeys half buried under loads of mattresses, veiled women with cooking pots on their heads, or the outlines on their backs of sleeping children wrapped in blankets.'

One middle-aged Pathan on his way to Pakistan showed Mike Martin his battle wounds. The journalist, suitably impressed, asked him what it was that made him risk his life against the superior firepower of the Russians. The Afghan hesitated. 'Because the Russians come to destroy Islam . . . because they bomb my village . . . because they kill my family . . . because they kill my sheep. . . .' There followed a few moments of silence, then he continued, with a smile, 'And because, my friend, I like to fight!'

Early in September Soviet and Afghan forces turned their attention to the Panjsher, a huge valley fifty miles north of Kabul, in the first of six major assaults over a period of two years. At first, the unsophisticated tactics of the mujahiddin led to large-scale casualties until the guerrillas learned to retire before the Russian advance and reoccupy the area after the Soviet troops had pulled back. Under the inspired leadership of twenty-seven-year-old Ahmed Shah Massud, who had taught himself guerrilla warfare from reading the works of Che Guevara and Ho Chi Minh, the mujahiddin brought the Russian offensive to a halt.

Ryan, who met the mujahiddin commander, was immediately impressed with:

> the quiet confidence that he radiated, seemingly untinged with personal vanity or with religious fanaticism. . . . There was a speed and concentration about his movements as if he needed to dispatch his business before his enemies could catch up with him. He never announced his whereabouts in advance or if he did he changed them; seldom stopping more than an hour in one place; and only the tiny elite that guarded, cosseted and worshipped him knew where he slept, which was rarely more than two nights in the same house.

A striking, energetic, youthful figure, there could be no doubt that he was justifiably the most effective military leader in the Panjsher.

Repeated attacks, with the Russians employing specialist units, failed to take the Panjsher and when in December 1982 Massud negotiated a temporary truce, the valley was still firmly in control of the rebels, whilst 300 miles to the south Commander Esmatullah held large areas of Kandahar province with a force of 5000 mujahiddin deployed around the city in four zonal commands.

Before the year was out the Soviets began to experience difficulties from within the ranks of their Reserve divisions. Unrest among troops from the Central Soviet Republics, many of whom shared a common culture and ethnic relationship with the Afghans, obliged the Kremlin to replace the Tadjiks and Uzbeks with European Russians before the reservists fell victim to the persuasions of their mujahiddin cousins. Unhappily for the Soviet High Command, the replacement troops achieved no greater measure of success, for the mujahiddin were easily able to avoid the ponderous mechanised thrusts of twenty-year-old Soviet armour, and Russian losses mounted. Reliable reports from correspondents such as Mike Martin and Peregrine Hodson backed up by photographic evidence of burned-out transport, captured tanks and downed helicopter gunships confirmed the fact. On the western slopes of the Tagob Valley, Martin counted thirty-five burned-out military vehicles, including a few tanks.

In their spring offensive of 1981 the Russians had fought for three weeks in an attempt to gain control of the road which ran through the valley. That offensive had failed and, in the tribal areas where the rugged terrain gave the guerrillas a decided advantage, the Soviets were forced to adopt new tactics. In a policy aimed at starving the population into surrender by destroying its crops and livestock, MiG jet strikes reduced villages to heaps of smoking ruins. But, as Mike Martin discovered in a landscape pockmarked by craters, farming activity continued and the all-important grape crop did not go unattended. The attitude of the survivors reminded him of 'that British capacity for ignoring brutal reality and carrying on as normal'.

Near Lowgar, Peregrine Hodson passed through an area where before the war 3000 families had lived. Now, it was as if an earthquake had devastated the land. 'Not a building remained intact. Beyond the piles of rubble tangles of weed grew among fields of cannabis.' The *Sunday Times* correspondent asked what would happen to the harvest. In that part of Afghanistan, he was told, only old men bothered themselves about it. 'They forget the war and they are happy. Mujahedin are not allowed to smoke it; our commanders say it makes our spirits weak. . . . But sometimes a few of us smoke in secret,' Hodson's guide added with a smile.

In crossing the Panjsher Valley, Nigel Ryan and his party were fortunate to escape injury when they came under attack from jets flying from the Bagram airbase. Sheltering beneath the walls of a terraced field, Ryan confessed,

we pressed our faces in the mud as firmly as if we had been modelling for our death masks. There was a deafening crash as rubble soared into the air, followed by a second explosion and a crimson flash twenty feet or so above the first. The Russians were apparently using cluster bombs that explode above ground . . . and scatter thousands of plastic needles that cannot be detected in the body by X-ray. Until then we had felt safe in the belief that only a direct hit could kill. Now we were not so sure.

Ryan wondered what the war meant to the young Russian pilots. 'Did they really believe the authorised version that they were mopping up bandits? Or was it all simply a video game played from their cockpits with computers and knobs, with map references for enemy and electronic dots for targets, to be completed in the few minutes before the canteen shut at Bagram airbase five minutes' flying time away?'

On the edge of the valley Mike Martin saw the graveyards of those killed in the bombing. 'A large stone marked each grave and little flags of white and green fluttered above.' Standing in the field of stones he was conscious of the one-sided nature of the conflict. It was a feeling not shared by the Afghan farmer standing next to him. 'Islam can defeat anything,' the Afghan muttered and Martin sensed that the aside 'came not from bravado but of faith'.

More than a year later, that philosophy was still much in evidence when Peregrine Hodson was told, 'The struggle in Afghanistan was a battle between a dying political system and a living religion. The Russians were mad to think they could conquer a people who were under the protection of God; it was like a fly attacking an elephant.'

Nevertheless, in May 1982 the Soviets launched 11,000 men in the biggest offensive operation of the war to date. For a whole week the tribesmen of the Panjsher were subjected to daily bombing and rocket attacks by Su–25s and MiG–21s before paratroopers and airborne commandos occupied each end of the valley. It proved a costly exercise for the Russians which merely drove Mahsud's mujahiddin to the high ground before resuming their pattern of deadly ambushes.

A letter home, found on the corpse of a Russian soldier, expressed the disillusionment felt by the average Soviet con-script. 'Sometimes they descend on us – we a. ? hard pushed things get so bad. From our company four have already been killed and our zampolit Batuyev was blown up by a mine and they hardly found anything left of him. . . . there's practically nothing f—ing left of the third company, they're all either in coffins or the hospital.'

By 1983 Afghan resistance to the 105,000-strong army of occupation had grown strong enough for the mujahiddin to control 80 per cent of the country and, although the cities and major highways were held by the Russians, the only way they could ensure that they remained open was to establish a string of posts manned by a small garrison at all times. These could easily be overrun and each attack by the mujahiddin against the posts or on passing convoys was met by a nervous outbreak of gunfire in every direction.

Morale among the poorly fed Soviet troops fell sharply and the Afghans who had previously refused to take Russian prisoners began to help deserters who had accepted Islam to fight alongside the mujahiddin. Peregrine Hodson asked one twenty-year-old Georgian if it were not ironic that he should now be dodging Russian bombs. 'It's mad,' he was told. 'If bombs kill me I'm dead. Russian bombs, [sic] Afghan bomb, American bomb. It's all the same I'm dead. . . .' His head fell and then with an expression of false jollity he added, 'Everyone is happy. I live. You live. They live. Everyone is happy. . . .'

The situation was far from rosy for the Soviet troops in the base camps. In cantonments, discipline frequently collapsed, with brawling between the different ethnic groups a frequent occurrence. There was also widespread resentment by the Moslem rank and file at the racist attitude adopted by many of the officers. 'Sometimes we felt the officers treated us no differently from the way they treated the enemy,' a Tajik prisoner confessed to an American journalist. 'When things got too rough, we'd smoke hashish. We couldn't get vodka; that all went to the officers. We'd buy the hashish from the villagers, trade it for ammunition.'

There was also the problem of sickness in the camps. 'The thermometer crept over 60°,' related a Russian soldier on Radio Free Europe. 'We quickly became weak and dried out in the heat. At the time the sickbays were not in a position to accept people with heatstroke. I know of nine cases that proved fatal.'

In Kabul it was unwise to shop alone in the market areas. A number of Russians, soldiers and civilians, fell victim to a knife quietly thrust into their back as they examined some trinket laid out for display in the bazaar.

The use of unguided rockets in attacks upon the city by the mujahiddin undoubtedly damaged morale and the vulnerability of Kabul to this type of weapon prompted the Russians to create so-called 'Free Fire Zones' in which on the slightest suspicion of insurgent activity an observer was able to call down the awesome firepower of the helicopter gunships, without fear of retaliation.

Sheltering in a copse near the Kabul River, Nigel Ryan heard the rotor blades of an MI–24, the world's most lethal helicopter gunship. Peering out from a gap in the branches, he watched the lone helicopter 'hovering in the air, its stillness somehow more frightening for being against nature. A jet of smoke shot from it, followed by a noise like the trumpeting of a bull elephant. . . . It was an unearthly sound and it instilled the fear of God in us.' Ryan afterwards learned that the noise was that of its heavy machine-gun, capable of annihilating all life within its range within a matter of minutes.

In furtherance of their policy of creating Free Fire Zones, the Soviets destroyed every village for a distance of twenty miles around the capital. Buildings were razed to the ground and the inhabitants driven to seek shelter in the city itself, where in the poorer and more densely populated parts it was not uncommon to find fifteen people sharing one room. Ironically the increase in the number of refugees from the rural areas worked to the advantage of the mujahiddin by providing safe havens for those engaged in sabotage activities. Electricity pylons were prime targets and such was the disruption caused by resistance attacks on power lines and diesel-fuel, kerosene and petrol dumps that electricity supplies to Kabul in 1984 were only a fraction of pre-war levels.

In 1983 the supply of arms to the mujahiddin was greatly increased. Funds channelled through the CIA were used to

buy weapons from China and Egypt and then shipped by
circuitous routes to the port of Karachi. Much of what was
supplied dated from the end of the Second World War. 'Is is still
good?' a mujahiddin commander was asked. 'Only God knows,'
came the reply. 'We don't find out until tonight!' Whilst travelling with a group of Hezbe-Islami, Hodson noticed a young
boy stripping down a Lee-Enfield rifle with an expression of
total concentration. Proudly he showed the gun mechanism
to the *Sunday Times* correspondent. It was more than fifty
years old.

From the shipments of those early years, the weaponry has
become increasingly sophisticated. In the summer of 1986
President Reagan authorised the release of ground-to-air
missiles to the mujahiddin and by November they had received
the first shipment of the heat-seeking missile known as
Stinger. The British Blowpipe is now being used to good effect
as also, by a stroke of irony, is the Russian designed Sam–7
supplied from China. These deadly shoulder-held weapons
have completely changed the course of the war, for once they
had become proficient in their use, the mujahiddin were bringing down on average one plane a day. Now, a sequence of heat-
decoy flares trace a pattern in the sky as Russian pilots fly
over rebel-held areas at heights which must all but preclude
accurate bombing. 'Western aid', a mujahiddin spokesman emphasised, 'has changed us from the hunted to the hunters.'

Early in 1986 reports from Kabul news agency suggested
that Babrak Karmal 'did not appear in the best of health'.
The Afghan leader had for some time been out of favour
with Moscow, where there were signs that Mikhail Gorbachev
was less than satisfied with the slow growth of support for
the Afghan government. It came as no surprise to political
observers when on 4 May 1986 Kabul Radio announced that
for reasons of health the Chairman had resigned in favour
of thirty-eight-year-old Muhammad Najibullah, the erstwhile
Chief of the Secret Police. Showing a commendable degree
of pragmatism, the new leader lost no time in furthering
relations with the mullahs by attending prayers at the
mosque immediately upon his return from Mazar, where

he had assured the local clergy that his government was pro-Islamic.

On 28 July 1986 the Soviet leader announced a limited withdrawal from Afghanistan, a move which, whilst welcomed at the peace talks in Geneva, between Pakistan and Afghanistan, was received with a certain amount of cynicism by the Pentagon.

These peace talks convened by the UN in February 1988 were designed to pave the way for a peaceful withdrawal by the Soviet troops subject only to Pakistan effectively halting the supply of weapons going through its borders to the mujahiddin. Nevertheless, hopes were raised and when a year later the Kremlin confirmed that it would pull troops out of Afghanistan even if a peace deal could not be reached in Geneva, a timetable was set for phased withdrawal which began on 15 May 1988, when 1200 Soviet troops climbed into tanks and armoured personnel carriers to begin a long dusty drive north from Jalalabad to Kabul.

The Russian Army of occupation, unlike the British-led Indian Army of the Victorian age, did not face the same daunting problem of logistics, but economic exhaustion, an ever-lengthening casualty list and the recognition of the impossibility of curbing widespread guerrilla activity in a mountainous terrain with its frontiers open for a ready supply of sophisticated weaponry persuaded Gorbachev to end his partnership with Dr Najibullah, who seems determined to cling to office to the bitter end. The Afghan Premier's bold assertion of independent existence cannot be lightly dismissed, however, for the Kabul regime still possesses most of the major centres of population, and the longer it retains them the greater must be its claim to legitimacy.

In ten years of fighting the mujahiddin have never won a setpiece battle, which is precisely the situation which confronts them at Jalalabad and Kabul. Should they be successful in overthrowing Najibullah, for no group is prepared to offer his Party any concessions, it will only be at the expense of a prolonged civil war with its inevitable prospect of devastation and starvation. Given its history of interfactional and tribal rivalries, a precise pattern of peaceful recovery for

Afghanistan is impossible to envisage. The mujahiddin, who come from many ethnic groups and rarely communicate, will be locked in a power struggle to dominate the Provisional Government. It is difficult to believe that a broad-based agenda acceptable to all Afghans can be formulated at a shura (the traditional Afghan Parliament). The fundamentalists are pressing for the creation of an Islamic state similar to that of Iran, whilst others less authoritarian look to Pakistan as a model. One group even favours a merger with Pakistan to form a new country – not the Pushtunistan favoured by Abdul Ghaffar, but Islamistan.

Whatever the outcome, one truth has been established which transcends all ideological differences: the unquenchable spirit of the Pathan in his determination to ensure the freedom to conduct his affairs in the time-honoured tradition of his forefathers.

Josiah Harlan, writing in 1842, had this to say concerning the British occupation of Afghanistan:

> To conquer a dominion by controlling the political parties of a state is a feasible policy, or to reform by gradual means without annihilating the institutions of a subjugated country may be the effect of time and perseverance, but to subdue and crush the masses of a nation by military force, when all are unanimous in the determination to be free, is to attempt the imprisonment of a whole people: all such projects must be temporary and transient, and terminate in a catastrophe that force has ever to dread from the vigorous, ardent, concentrated vengeance of a nation outraged, oppressed, and insulted, and desperate with the blind fury of a determined and unanimous will.

A statement as true for Muhammad Najibullah and Mikhail Gorbachev today as it was for the British a century and a half ago.

Glossary

Abattis Defence work of felled trees with sharpened branches pointing outwards
Begeer Afghan equivalent of 'seize'
Chuprassi Indian messenger or door-keeper
Crore 10,000,000 units
Doolie Covered litter or stretcher
Durbar Royal court or levee
Forlorn hope Band of volunteers for a hazardous mission
Ghazi Fighter for the Faith who has killed an infidel
Ghilzais One of two main tribes of eastern Afghanistan
Heliograph Signalling apparatus using the sun's rays reflected from a mirror
Infidel An unbeliever
Jemahdar Sepoy rank equivalent to lieutenant
Jezail Tribesman's long-barrelled matchlock
Jihad A holy war
Jirga Assembly of tribal elders
Kotal A mountain pass
Lashkar Tribal army
Lakh 100,000 units
Mullah Religious teacher or Holy man
Malik A headman
Nemaz A Moslem prayer
Nullar A stream or ditch
Poshteen Sheepskin jacket worn with the fleece inside
PDPA Peoples Democratic Party of Afghanistan
Sangar Breastwork built of loose stones
Screw gun So called because the muzzle and breech screwed together
Sepoy Indian infantryman
Sirdar A commander
Sowar Indian cavalry trooper
Subahdar Sepoy rank of company officer
Tulwar A sabre
Wazir Chief Minister or Adviser
Zampolit Deputy Chief of Ideology

Select Bibliography

J. Adye, *Recollections of a Military Life*, London, 1895.

J. Atkinson, *The Expedition into Afghanistan*, London, 1842.

W. Beynon, *With Kelly to Chitral*, London, 1896.

Sir Bindon Blood, *Four Score Years and Ten*, London, 1933.

Sir Winston Churchill, *Story of the Malakand Field Force*, London, 1898.

V. Eyre, *The Military Operations at Kabul*, London, 1843.

G. W. Forrest, *Life of Field-Marshal Sir Neville Chamberlain*, Edinburgh, 1909.

J. Greenwood, *Narrative of a Campaign in Afghanistan*, London, 1844.

J. Harlan, *A Memoir of India and Afghanistan*, Philadelphia, 1842.

H. Havelock, *Narrative of the War in Afghanistan*, London, 1840.

H. Hensman, *The Afghanistan War of 1879–80*, London, 1881.

P. Hodson, *Under a Sickle Moon*, London, 1986.

H. Hutchinson, *The Campaign in Tirah*, London, 1898.

L. James, *With the Chitral Relief Force*, Calcutta, 1895.

J. Marshman, *Memoirs of Major-General Havelock*, London, 1860.

M. Martin, *Afghanistan – Inside a Rebel Stronghold*, Poole, 1984.

J. Masters, *Bugles and a Tiger*, London, 1956.

R. Mitford, *To Caubul With the Cavalry*, London, 1881.

G. N. Molesworth, *Afghanistan 1919*, London, 1962.

H. Pettigrew, *Frontier Scouts*, Selsey, 1965.

J. Prendergast, *Prender's Progress*, London, 1979.

F. Richards, *Old Soldier Sahib*, London, 1936.

Lord (F.) Roberts, *Forty-One Years in India*, London, 1898.

G. Robertson, *Chitral*, London, 1898.

N. Ryan, *A Hitch or Two in Afghanistan*, London, 1983.

Florentia, Lady Sale, *Journal of the Disasters in Afghanistan*, London, 1843.

D. Stewart, *An Account of his Life*, London, 1903.

C. Townshend, *Townshend of Chitral and Kut*, London, 1928.

J. Vaughan, *Service in the Indian Army*, London, 1904.

H. C. Wylly, *The Military Memoirs of Lt. Gen. Sir Joseph Thackwell*, London, 1908.

G. Younghusband, *The Relief of Chitral*, London, 1895.

Index

209

Picture Acknowledgements

British Library: page 4; *Illustrated London News*: pages 2 and 3; India Office Library: page 1 above, page 5 above; National Army Museum: page 1 below, 5 below, 6, 7, 8, above and below